Statement from our
Surgeon General,
Dr David Satcher

Surgeon General David Satcher is planning to release a major report on sexuality in America. Two years in the making, the report will address many topics that make Americans squeamish.

"Our nation is suffering in so many ways because of the failure to address human sexuality," said Dr Satcher. "I'm hoping our report will contribute to moving our nation forward," he said.

Dr Satcher commented that, often the gulf between science—what we know—and policy—what we can do—is so large as to be dangerous, and potentially, fatal. "I can think of no other area where the gap between what we know and what we do is so lethal as in human sexuality," he said.

~ Reuter's Health Report, June 5, 2001

WHAT WOMEN (AND MEN!) ACROSS THE COUNTRY ARE SAYING ABOUT THIS GROUNDBREAKING BOOK

"I have always had a problem having an orgasm. A close friend told me about the strategies in SHE'S GOTTA HAVE IT, and I am still in shock. I not only have orgasms, I'm having multiple orgasms."

~ Shirley Gantner

"I got Betty Kamen's book and read it with my wife and she loved it. It made me look like a hero and what we learned increased the frequency of our sex life. Now she never says no."

~ Robert Benedict

"I understand how important healthy sexual response is to a woman's overall health. Now that I am single again, I can still enjoy the healthful benefits my body can produce naturally for itself, thanks to this book."

~ Bernice Rudolph

"I have used the strategies outlined in SHE'S GOTTA HAVE IT about ten times now, and each time I have sex it keeps getting better and better. I am lubricated almost immediately and I have no problems achieving orgasm."

~ Sandra Colton

"After using the information in SHE'S GOTTA HAVE IT, I found the effect radiating, rippling, lasting! Most exciting."

~ Asia Spears

"I'm thrilled that there is this book that truly helped me to enhance and expand my sexual experience. For me, in a perimenopausal transition in my life, having this information really delights me, and makes the future of sensual play and lovemaking very desirable again!"

~ Terry Powers

"I got a jar of the cream described in this book about two weeks ago to use with my girlfriend, and her response was great! One time was not enough for her. This is WOW!"

~ George McMahan

SHE'S GOTTA HAVE IT!

Sexuality

Euphoria

Orgasm

**Discover Natural Ways To
Enhance Libido
Increase Sexual Euphoria
Have Satisfying Sex
Every Time...At Any Age**

Betty Kamen, PhD

N_E

Nutrition Encounter, Novato, California
www.bettykamen.com

All of the facts in this book have been very carefully researched and have been drawn from the
scientific literature. In no way, however, are any of
the suggestions meant to take the place of advice
given by physicians. Please consult a medical or
health professional should the need for one be
indicated.

In some cases, the names associated with the anecdotal stories have been changed to preserve pri-
vacy. The original testimonies are on file.

2001

Nutrition Encounter
PO Box 5847
Novato, CA 94948-5847
(415) 883-5154

Website: www.bettykamen.com

Email: betty@well.com

Printed in the United States of America
First Printing 2001

ISBN 0-944501-14-1

DEDICATED

to

The Women Who Shaped My Life And My Sexuality

ANNA DICOV MOSKOWITZ
Grandma

CLARA MOSS BANOFF
Mom

TRUDY POGRELL HARRIS
Sister

KATHI KAMEN GOLDMARK
Daughter

ABOUT BETTY KAMEN

Years ago, on her popular radio program in New York City, Betty Kamen alerted her listeners to dozens of newly available supplements and treatments. Her program quickly developed into a center for disseminating innovative research and discoveries, featuring interviews with prominent alternative health care pioneers from around the world. Betty has written many cutting-edge health books, including the bestselling *Hormone Replacement Therapy, Yes or No? How to Make an Informed Decision* and *New Facts About Fiber.*

She received her MA in psychology in 1949, an MA in nutrition education in 1979, and her PhD in nutrition education in 1982. Betty taught at Hofstra University, developed a nutrition workshop at Stanford University Continuing Education Program for Doctors and Nurses, and served as nutrition consultant on the Committee of the Accrediting Council for Continuing Education and Training, Washington, DC.

A columnist for many health publications over the years, Betty has had hundreds of nutrition reports published. Articles written by or about Betty have appeared in the New York Times, Chicago Tribune, San Francisco Progress, Prevention Magazine, Baltimore Sun, and many other local and national publications. A full page photo of Betty and one of her grandchildren appeared in the March 1998 issue of Time Magazine.

But never mind all the credentials. Betty says her children describe her most aptly when they say, "Mom? She's just the oldest health nut in the country" — to which Betty responds: "If you have to be the oldest anything, 'health nut' is not so bad."

ACKNOWLEDGMENTS

Special thanks to these wonderful people for their caring and sharing:

Serafina Corsello, MD
Denise Fletcher
Daisy Lee & Francesco Garripoli
Burton Goldberg
Kathi Kamen Goldmark
Christopher Hegarty
David Hennessy
Paul Kamen
Si Kamen
Perle Kinney
Rabbi Rita Leonard
Michael Rosenbaum, MD
Janis Van Tine

Illustrations

Dorothy Beebee

Cover Design

Raylene Buehler

Also From Betty Kamen

BOOKS

~ **The Remarkable Healing Power of Velvet Antler**
~ **Hormone Replacement Therapy: Yes or No?**
   How to Make an Informed Decision
~ **Kamut**
   An Ancient Food for a Healthy Future
~ **Everything You Always Wanted to Know About**
   Potassium But Were Too Tired to Ask
~ **New Facts About Fiber**
   How Fiber Supplements Can Enhance Your Health
~ **The Chromium Connection**
   Diet & Supplement Strategy for Blood Sugar Control
~ **Startling New Facts About Osteoporosis**
   Why Calcium Alone Does Not Prevent Bone Disease
~ **Germanium**
   A New Approach to Immunity
~ **Siberian Ginseng**
   Up-to-Date Research on the Fabled Tonic Herb
~ **Sesame—The Superfood Seed**
   How It Can Add Vitality to Your Life
~ **Nutrition In Nursing—The New Approach**
   A Handbook of Nursing Science
~ **Osteoporosis**
   What It Is, How to Prevent It, How to Stop It
~ **In Pursuit of Youth**
   Everyday Nutrition for Everyone Over 35
~ **Kids Are What They Eat**
   What Every Parent Needs to Know About Nutrition
~ **Total Nutrition for Breast-Feeding Mothers**
~ **Total Nutrition During Pregnancy**
   How To Be Sure You and Your Baby Are Eating the
   Right Stuff

TAPES

~ Table Talk Tapes: Lessons in Nutrition
   Six 1-hour Audio Cassette Tapes
      1. Supplements, 2. Food & Immunity, 3. Memory,
      4. Remedies, 5. Antioxidants (OPCs or Pycnogenol),
      6. Osteoporosis
~ Nutrition Breakthroughs
   Six 1-hour Audio Cassette Tapes
      1. Supplements, 2. Heart Health, 3. Scaling down,
      4. Immunity, 5. & 6. Common Problems
~ Individual Audio Tapes
      Locker Room Logic: For Men Only
      Things Your Mother Couldn't Tell You
      Hormonal Feedback
      Feminine and Afflicted
      Lactoferrin
            Helper Cells, Antioxidants, Immunity
      Cytolog
            Infopeptides and Cell Signaling
      Germanium
            Immunity, Alertness, Acuity

See www.bettykamen.com for details on all tapes, and for Betty Kamen's newsletters and special reports on new products.

ONE-LINE ONLINE DAILY NUTRITION HINT

Betty's free Table Talk nutrition hint-of-the-day has been an overwhelming success. Betty e-mails a free online, brief, one-line daily Table Talk Nutrition Hint if you e-mail a request to betty@well.com. Just write "hint" in the subject area.

The last ten hints, with expanded information and source references, are always available at the website.

CONTENTS

Figures

FOREWORD

You've gotta have it! This **book**, that is, if you want the full story about female sexuality. Betty Kamen writes about women's sexual health with the same incisive and all-encompassing approach that has firmly rooted her as an icon in the field of nutrition and women's health. "She's Gotta Have It" tracks the life stages of female sexuality from early pubescence to postmenopause with detailed accounts of the inner workings of the female sexual experience from arousal to climax and bliss. Finally, she suggests a few easy strategies for enhancing that experience.

Sexuality is intimately glued to environmental health. In the chapter "Enemies Among Us" Dr. Kamen tells a disturbing—yet compelling—story about the disastrous health effects of chemical pollution on women's health. I have been captivated by this story as it has unfolded over the past forty years, beginning with the seminal eye-opening book "Silent Spring" by Rachel Carlson and accelerating menacingly in the past five years with an array of information warning about the global threat to sexual integrity for humans and animals alike by this "chemical menace." Betty provides a deft summary of the literature about chemical estrogens and hormone disruptors. As Betty explains, these chemicals are ubiquitous. For a woman, the chemical menace may cause or promote an array of female health problems including PMS (or to be politically correct—the new phrase "premenstrual dysphoric disorder"), fibroids, ovarian cysts, fibrocystic breasts, irregular menses and the most dreaded conditions—breast and uterine cancer.

Women can seize control of their sexual health with determined lifestyle choices including the judicious use of natural hormone replacement with an emphasis on progesterone. Dr. Kamen wrote a provocative book about progesterone several years ago that earned her widespread acclaim: "Hormone Replacement Therapy: Yes or No? How to Make an Informed Decision." And now in this this new book, she provides a summary and update about estrogen dominance, as well as hormone therapies that work and those that don't.

But it's not all bad news. The book offers helpful information to enable us to breathe a bit easier: strategies that may help stem the tide and enhance female sexual health.

Betty Kamen has few peers in the nutritional arena. She is privy to information about new, cutting-edge nutritional supplements for sexual wellness that she willingly shares in "She's Gotta Have It."

That's why you've GOTTA HAVE IT!

Michael E Rosenbaum, MD
Corte Madera, CA

INTRODUCTION

"…the sexual life of adult women is a dark continent of psychology."

~ Sigmund Freud, 1926

It was my first day of class as a sophomore at Brooklyn College. The subject was Psychology 101.

After introducing himself, the young, handsome professor asked a question that cast a veil of discomfort over the fifty women filling the room. (The male students had gone off to save the universe. It was 1942, and we were smack in the middle of World War II.)

The professor had asked: "How many of you think your breasts are too small?" Since we were thrown into tongue-tied immobility on being challenged to discuss something so personal in an open forum, the professor had to repeat his question. On his second try, four women raised their hands, albeit timidly, finally breaking the spell. He then asked: "How many of you think your breasts are too big?" Three hands went up, more quickly this time, but accompanied by barely audible snickers of embarrassment. The final question received no response at all: "How many think your breast size is just right?"

On the last day of the semester, the professor asked the same three questions. This time, every one of us responded. (For those of you who are curious, the results appeared to be evenly divided among the too-bigs and too-smalls, with only a scant number of just-rights.)

During the many months between the first and last days of that class, the professor taught us how to be more comfortable when talking about our own bodies. He taught us that *everyone* has a "torn coat lining," the hidden secrets we carry around, something that would embarrass us, or that we don't care to share with anyone. He taught us that we *need* to be active, but first we *need* to eat and to rest and to sleep and to have love and esteem for the maintenance of our health. He taught us that we all have a continuous desire to fulfill potentials. He taught us about the hierarchy of those needs and about self-actualization. The professor was *Abraham Maslow,** who went on to world fame as the founder of humanistic psychology! We had no idea how lucky we were to have such a mentor, or how famous he would become. He shared his views with us as he was laying the very cornerstone of his groundbreaking theories.

In the half century-plus that passed since those beginnings, I learned that sexuality is so much more than mere sexual bodily function. Some of the lessons were hard to come by because it took more than one brilliant professor to break down the barriers of communication concerning a woman and her body, and especially about a woman and her sexuality. But it was a good start.

For much of human existence and in many societies, women have been considered to be the "property" of men. In the 1880s, my grandmother risked being beaten when she stole her brothers' books and ran into the woods to teach herself to read. She raised a daughter who, in the early 1900s, became a "bloomer" girl, an active member of the successful suffrage movement.** And just as my mother helped women gain political rights, so my daughter, two generations later, worked to help women gain sexual rights.***

Even in this new millennium, when we are all supposed to be more enlightened and open about sexual matters, *fear, prejudice, and problems abound.* The purpose of this book is to help women understand these problems, and, with easy (yet unusual) strategies, to fully enjoy the sexual experience.

It is my sincere hope that my young granddaughters and their peers will grow up free of sexual hang-ups and the disrupting environmental problems faced by most of today's women.

Hopefully, this book will shine a little light on that "dark continent" of Freud's, and help women to realize that their sexuality is not something to be ignored or to be feared, but something to be celebrated!

Betty Banoff Kamen

* See Appendix A for a short biography of Abraham Maslow.

** My mother was one of the first women to be fitted for a diaphragm by Margaret Sanger. Mom was 18, newly married, and Sanger had just been released from prison. *She had been jailed for promoting contraception, which at that time was against the law.* See Appendix B for a short biography of Margaret Sanger.

*** See Appendix C for a short biography of Kathi Kamen Goldmark.

"Not tonight, honey — I've got dyspareunia."

Chapter One

FEMALE SEXUALITY: WHAT'S WRONG DOWN THERE?

The philosophy professor gave his class an assignment: "Write a 250-word essay titled 'Is an Hour of Pleasure Worth a Lifetime of Regret?'" A young co-ed in back of the class raised her hand and asked, "How do you make it last an hour?"

Times, They Are a Changin'... Or Are They?

When no one is looking, you may be using the Internet to explore some of the over-abundance of sexual information that lurks only a mouse-click away. Unlike your mother, you may be discussing intimate details of the once-taboo subject of female sexuality with your friends or your doctor. You may even be attending workshops to learn "how to do it better."

Are you old enough to remember—or perhaps even to have been part of—the swift, boisterous sexual revolution of the sixties and seventies? Did you experience first-hand the sexual freedom of those seven years between Roe vs. Wade and the onslaught of the AIDS epidemic? It was an era of sexual revolution that was unequalled in the past, and is not likely to be duplicated in the future.

Coupled with the quieter and slower continued progress of the eighties and nineties, these sexual transformations have had a major impact for your benefit, both culturally and socially: *Female sexuality has finally been recognized as an important part of a woman's health, her quality of life, and her general well being.*

But don't get too excited. Despite the fact that we've come such a long way, it is apparent that we haven't come far enough. Today, 40 percent of women of all ages have serious sexual problems, and a much higher percentage confesses to at least one or more minor difficulties. In fact, a recent research project, reported in *Family Practice*, revealed that a total of 98.8 percent of women surveyed claimed to have one or more sexual concerns![1] Have we really come a long way, baby? It may not have been much different in Grandma's days, but she'd probably drop her knitting if she heard our frank conversations about sex.

Unfortunately, not enough women *are* talking about sex. In fact fewer than half of female patients' sexual grievances are known by their physicians, so the average doctor is not aware of how common some of these problems are.

The list for the causes of discontent is surprisingly long, with the most frequently reported being decreased libido, vaginal dryness, pain during intercourse, declining sensation in the genitals, and difficulty or inability to achieve orgasm.[2] Here's how some of the prevalent obstacles break down:

Problem	Percent with problem
Lack of interest in sex	87.2%
Difficulty achieving orgasm	83.3%
Inadequate natural lubrication	74.7%
Difficult or painful coitus	71.7%
Body image concerns	68.5%
Unmet sexual needs	67.2%
Ignorance of basic information about sexual issues	63.4%[3]

Other studies show even higher rates. One group of researchers found that the percentage of women reporting difficulties achieving orgasm was as high as 92 percent! You are part of a very large majority if you picked up this book because you would like to improve your ability to achieve orgasm. (The numbers are much more than most people would guess, based on the cultural illusion we have that all women have orgasms almost every time.)

Yet the most common sexual stumbling blocks cited in the medical journal *Sex and Marital Therapy* are "too little foreplay before intercourse" and "partner chooses inconvenient time."[4] (For most men, *any* time appears to be a convenient time!)

And these problems are not specific to the United States. Women in other wealthy, industrialized countries are suffering right along with us. In England, for example, vaginal dryness and infrequent orgasm are also among the most widely reported female difficulties.[5]

It's interesting to note that two groups of women have significantly fewer complaints. These are:

~ older women, ages 55 to 71

~ menopausal women who are not on hormone replacement therapy[6]

Reasons for these unexpected facts are explored later.

Is it surprising that today's successful career women are among those expressing grievances? The sexual dysfunction and disorder patterns of both married working and nonworking women were compared in couples who had undergone sexual and marital therapy at the Masters & Johnson Institute. You would think that women who had an opportunity to pursue their dream career would have it all, a healthy sex life included. But results indicated that these women were **twice as likely** to complain of inhibited sexual desire than women who were employed in jobs requiring less creativity or who were not employed outside the home at all.

Career women were also significantly more likely to develop vaginismus. (Vaginismus is a spasmodic contraction of the vagina, often rendering intercourse nearly impossible.)

Not that the women on the other side of the equation were entirely home free. Those who were not career-oriented, or had less demanding jobs, were found more likely to complain of concerns related to orgasm.[7] It seems we can't win either way.

So Is There Any Good News?

Yes, the good news is that most of the obstacles to sexual enjoyment are treatable. The bad news is that most women are not aware of where or how to get help. There is at least one self-help strategy that offers an easy solution to many of the problems just outlined. (Okay, skip ahead to chapter nine if you must know tonight!)

Unfortunately, even in our medical schools, a medical student's attitude plays a significant role in how the doctor-to-be responds to sex education, and, eventually, how he or she will deal with future patients' sexual issues. The erotophobic students (those with negative attitudes toward sexuality) have significantly lower levels of sexual knowledge and are less likely to participate in sexuality courses than the erotophilic students (those with positive attitudes toward sexuality). According to *Academic Medicine*, most medical schools get a failing grade when it comes to preparing young physicians for treating patients with sexual problems.[8]

To compound the difficulty, would you believe that many obstetric and gynecologic texts still contain outdated and erroneous views about sexuality, portraying women in stereotypical roles? Women's sexuality is depicted from a purely heterosexual perspective, with a distinctly Victorian view of marriage and motherhood as the only "natural" aspiration of all women.[9] If Betty Friedan or Gloria Steinem had aspired to be physicians, they might have reshaped those medical books as they have women's attitudes.

The fact remains that sexual problems are a modern epidemic.

Sexual problems are classified into four categories:
    (1) sexual desire disorders
        hypoactive sexual desire
        sexual aversion disorder
    (2) sexual arousal disorders
        not sexually responsive
    (3) orgasmic disorders
        inhibited female orgasm
    (4) sexual pain disorders
        dyspareunia
        vaginismus

Current psychological treatment may include one or more of the following components:

~ sensate focus exercises
~ cognitive-behavioral therapy
~ relaxation training
~ hypnosis
~ guided imagery
~ group therapies

Do today's women have time for any of this?

Techniques, such as directed self-stimulation, the stop-start and squeeze techniques, the sexological examination, systematic desensitization, and Kegel exercises (explained later), are added therapy when appropriate. Medical management may include drugs to correct endocrine dysfunctions or to alter the progression of the sexual response, or, as described in chapter seven, lifestyle change involving beneficial nutrient supplementation. The new adage may well be: "*Sexuality* is what you eat."

Which problems are resolved after therapy? None make the Dean's list routinely, but when it comes to sexual desire disorders, long-term success is at the bottom of the barrel.[10] That leaves the most common female sexual dysfunction as the hardest to treat![11] Whether this loss of sexual desire should be seen as abnormal or simply as a variation of normal has long been debated.

Exploring The Process

Despite the "information revolution" of the modern age, there is still a fundamental lack of knowledge about exactly what happens physiologically when a woman is "turned on." But just as most of us drive cars without understanding exactly how the engine works, it may not be necessary to be explicitly aware of what goes on under the covers in order to have good sex. Although we may not necessarily need to know how the biological pathways of *desire* start in our brain, how *excitement* results in dilation of our blood vessels, and how *orgasm* is produced by the contraction of certain genital muscles, such understanding can be invaluable in helping to circumvent problems. By the time you finish this book, you'll realize the importance of that last statement. And you might even be a little more familiar with a very important part of your body.

Although reduced sexual desire and female orgasmic disorder are prevalent problems, experts agree that the major complaints center on women's dissatisfaction with such non-genital behavior as expressing affection, communicating, and non-genital touching, as well as issues of attraction and passion.[12] Those currently studying female sexuality tell us that women suffer more from a lack of sexual desire and from a deficit of sexually stimulating feelings than from insufficient genital functions.[13] As Portuguese researchers concluded after studying women who believed they were living with sexual disorders, these women were simply not "living their sexuality."[14]

Researchers remind us that human beings are truly a "cognitive" species who use imagery and language. Sexuality is very much in the frontal lobes, and what we *perceive* as eroticism is probably much more important than the actual sexual expression.[15] They go on to tell us that self-image and body image are precursors of sexual activity: Overall satisfaction with oneself relates to frequency of sex, orgasm, initiating the sexual encounter, trying new sexual behaviors, and confidence in giving one's partner sexual pleasure.[16]

But these views are not entirely unanimous. Another large group of researchers, expressing their findings in *Current Opinions in Neurobiology*, offers valid scientific reasons for the decline in libido based *entirely* on physical metabolic disturbances. They suggest that "recent advances in the neurobiology of sexual behavior have helped to refine our understanding of the systems that are responsable for sexual stimulation. New knowledge has emerged concerning complex pathways, including hypothalamic, limbic, and brainstem structures, neuropeptides, brain monoamines, and nitric oxide."

Behind the big words, we are learning that these factors affect partner preference, sexual desire, erection, copulation, ejaculation, orgasm, and sexual satiety.[17]

No doubt sexual dysfunction is diverse and results from a complex interaction of biological, psychological, and social factors—nature *and* nurture. Even in a case with a clear biological cause (for example, in the case of diabetic neuropathy), the treatment and long-term consequences of the sexual disorder, initiated because of the disease and its treatment, will be affected by psychosocial implications.

Sexual functioning can be strongly influenced by your own sense of self and competence.[18]

Time for a
QUICKIE

Until recently, female sexual fantasies were generally associated with psychopathology or negative qualities. Sexual fantasy is now regarded as a normal occurrence.

When and How Women
Learn About Their Sexuality

"Contributions to knowledge of female sexuality are provided by direct observations as early as during the second year of life concerning genital self-stimulation and masturbation in girls. Girls are capable of vaginal masturbation and possibly of experiencing vaginal sensation and stimulation very early in life."

Source: Heiman M.
Sleep orgasm in women. *Journal of the American Psychoanalysis Association* 1976;24(5S):285-304.

~~~

The Most Important Advance
In Female Sexuality

"The most important advance in the study of female sexual function is the recent surge of interest in this relatively unexplored field."

Source: Davis AR.
Recent Advances in Female Sexual Dysfunction.
Current Psychiatry Report 2000;2:211.

On the Campus

A study describes sexual behavior over a ten-year period in a female student population. The use of condoms at first intercourse increased from 40 percent to 77 percent. Sexually transmitted diseases decreased from 26 percent to 14 percent, and abortions from 11 percent to 5.5 percent.

One-fourth of students had had anal intercourse, and 86 percent had performed oral sex. Half of the women had read pornography. The majority of women with experience of oral sex graded it as positive, whereas they graded anal sex as mostly negative. Twelve percent of the women had been sexually harassed, mainly by their male peers (80 percent).

Source: Tyden T et al. Improved use of contraceptives, attitudes toward pornography, and sexual harassment among female university students.
Womens Health Issues 2001 Mar-Apr;11(2):87-94.

And Baby Makes Three:
Sexual Desire Following Childbirth

During pregnancy, coital frequency and orgasmic capacity decrease. While there is a wide range of individual responses, a general decline in sexual interest, activity, and satisfaction takes place as pregnancy progresses. The desire for body contact, however, remains at a very high level throughout. Some changes in sexual sensitivity may occur. Although about 72 percent of women experience a waning of sexual desire while pregnant, a few women show an increase.[19,20]

Sexual problems are common for a period of time after childbirth. Problems more prevalent at one month following delivery include breast symptoms, vaginal discomfort, hot flashes, and extreme fatigue. Women with vaginal deliveries have a higher incidence of hemorrhoids, vaginal discomfort, pain during intercourse, and difficulty reaching orgasm. Recovery from childbirth often requires more than the six weeks traditionally allotted. Health status following delivery appears to be affected by the route through which the baby entered the world, the nutrition status, and work status.[21]

Even after three months, 83 percent of women still experience stumbling blocks in sexual activity, declining to 64 percent at six months—*but never seem to reach pre-pregnancy levels.* At six months, the association with type of delivery is no longer significant.

Painful intercourse before pregnancy and current breastfeeding do exert their influence, however.[22] As a woman takes on the roles of mother and housewife, it is not unusual for the importance of the lover role to diminish. Women, either instinctively or through learning (though certainly not unnaturally), make the responsibility of being a mother a high priority.

However, rapid and intense sexual responsiveness is not unusual after the birth of *several* children. One contributing factor is the increased vascularity of the pelvic area that occurs after childbirth.

Breastfeeding stimulates sexual feelings in both mother and baby. This could be related to differences in hormone levels or in feeding behavior. Women who go on to breastfeed were found to be very similar on sexual behavior to those who go on to bottle-feed. The method of feeding is the major influence on the hormonal status, and the experience of painful intercourse reported by breastfeeding mothers may be related to low estrogen levels. Cessation of breastfeeding is associated with an improvement in mood, fatigue, and sexuality.

For those currently pregnant, it has been scientifically validated that intercourse during late pregnancy is associated with a reduced risk of preterm delivery. Similar decreased risk for preterm delivery was found with female orgasm. If you are pregnant now, take advantage of these facts. The party may soon be over—for a while, anyway.[23]

Time for a
QUICKIE

The following factors were de-terminded to be responsible for rigid stereotyped sexual behavior for both partners in dysfunctional groups:

~ traditional/religious upbringing

~ early familial disruption

~ current religious attitudes of male

~ prejudices concerning normal sexual behavior

~ sexual ignorance

~ communication problems

Whether emotional, cultural, or physical, simple solutions can turn things around for the majority of women—regardless of causes, regardless of relationships, regardless of how long the diffi-culties have been in place.

But more about that in chapters seven and nine.

Russian President Putin called President George W. Bush with an emergency: "Our largest condom factory has exploded. It's our favorite birth control method. We need help at once."

"The American people would be happy to do anything within their power to help you," replied the President

"Could you possibly send one million condoms ASAP?" asked Putin.

"Why certainly! I'll get right on it," said Bush.

"Oh, and one more small favor, please?" said Putin.

"Yes?"

"Could the condoms be red in color and at least 10" long and 4" in diameter?" asked Putin.

"No problem," replied Bush. Bush hung up and called Freecondoms.com.

"I need a favor. You've got to send one million condoms to Russia right away."

"Consider it done," said the President of Freecondoms.com.

"Great! Now listen. They have to be red in color, 10" long and 4" wide."

"Easily done. Anything else?"

"Yeah," said the President. "Print 'MADE IN AMERICA, SIZE SMALL' on each one."

Ch-Ch-Ch-Changes:
Sex and Menopause

Physical changes in later years, specifically of the genitalia and the breasts, are obviously more noticeable in women than in men—and are clearly brought to our attention when we stop menstruating. Menopause, however, does not relate to reduced libido.

If you use it, you won't lose it.

This adage is most appropriate for women of menopausal age and beyond. Regular sexual activity helps a woman to maintain responsiveness, regardless of advancing years.

One problem present with aging or menopause is lubrication difficulties. So it's a surprise to learn that the most prevalent sexual problem expressed by older women does *not* happen to be insufficient lubrication resulting in painful coitus. Again, lack of tenderness and of sexual contact tops the complaint list. The effect of hormonal changes at menopause is smaller than psychological, societal, and partner-related factors.[24] Menopause status has less of an impact on sexual functioning than a woman's health or her mate's responses.[25]

This does not mean that physiological changes are unimportant or should be neglected. A woman should experience no loss of sexual desire if she's in good health. But this is not the case for the average woman.

In fact, there is overwhelming evidence to suggest that many postmenopausal women experience relief of symptoms when they receive testosterone therapy, indicating that perhaps these women aren't producing enough. Chapter four explains this in-depth.

Ovarian hormones—estrogens, androgens, and progesterone—affect our nervous systems in myriad ways. Alterations in the circulating levels of androgens play an important role in psychological and sexual changes that occur after menopause.[26] It's almost as though nature provided means for us not to have children at a late age (for obvious reasons) by reducing the estrogen, but didn't want us to miss out on a little fun or well being. Healthy women produce enough androgens to keep the sexual furnace burning, even when the grey hair looks like snow on the roof.

If it puzzles you that you require a male hormone to be a sexually active female, note that young boys, as they approach puberty, require estrogen to initiate the development of their masculine traits. As for adult men, they should know that their brains use no testosterone —it's all made into an estrogen first. Brain estrogen limits the activational effects of testosterone in females, but enhances them in males. *Brain estrogen contributes to male-typical sexual motivation.*[27,28] (And yet, they still won't stop to ask for directions!)

Finally, note that depression is common in middle-aged women, but it is not specifically associated with the hormonal changes occurring at menopause.[29]

The Real Golden Years: Sex and Aging

Research on sexual behavior in the second half of our life span is sparse, especially when it comes to older women left without their lifelong partners, or in their second go-round with someone new.[30]

Claire, a 72-year-old woman whom I knew quite well had a 75-year-old boyfriend. (Her husband of almost fifty years had died a few years earlier.) She lived alone, but her sister routinely stopped in for a quick cup of coffee every morning. Whenever this gentleman stayed at her apartment overnight, he hid in her closet while the sister paid her daily visit. Although far less conservative than her sister, Claire was not willing to face the criticism the overnight stay would evoke. In our culture, taboos about sex in general are minor compared with those placed on the sexuality of elderly people.

People who have been sexually energetic on a frequent basis throughout their lives show a lower rate of decline in activity in later years than the less sexually active. There is no question that most physically healthy men and women can and do remain sexually alive on a regular basis into their eighties. And most of these older folk enjoy the experience. What form this sexual activity takes could include solo and mutual masturbation, oral sex, and penetrative intercourse. It's not easy for younger people to relate to this, but they should be aware that elderly people may have just as wide a range of interests and preferences as they do.[31]

Currently, the average life expectancy is 78.9 years of age for women, 72 for men. By the year 2030, it is estimated that elderly people will make up approximately 17 percent of the total United States population. The responsibility of physicians is, therefore, very clear. The care of this population must provide an acceptable quality of life and allow elderly people to enjoy living. This is where the question of sexuality plays an important part.[32]

> **Time for a QUICKIE**
>
> Women with loss of desire can still have good sexual functioning. They just don't initiate sexual contact.

Sexual function in a community of middle-aged women with partners was examined. Here is a summary of the results:

> The participants were a randomly selected community sample of 436 women with partners. They were questioned about frequency of sexual intercourse and orgasm with their partners, plus attitudes toward their sexual relationships. For men, frequency of sexual intercourse, orgasm, and enjoyment of sexual activity was most closely associated with younger age and better general marital adjustment, with their partners' ages also appearing to influence frequency, and the duration of the relationships affecting enjoyment.

Women's satisfaction with their sexual relationships was most closely associated with marital
adjustment and bore no relation to age of either
partner.

Some associations were found between higher
socioeconomic status and frequency of orgasm
and enjoyment of sexual activity. Sexual behavior
was largely unrelated to gynecological symptoms.
Little difference was found between age-matched
groups of pre- and postmenopausal women in the
frequency of sexual behavior and attitudes toward
their sexual relationships.[33]

Another study, reported in the *Journal of the American
Academy of Psychoanalysis*, validates that the **loss of
sexual drive is not an inevitable aspect of aging**, and
shows that the majority of healthy people remain sexually
active on a regular basis until advanced old age. However,
the aging process does bring with it certain changes in
the physiology of the male and the female sexual response, and these changes, along with a number of
medical problems that become more prevalent in later
years, play a significant role in sexual disorders.

The typical patient over 50 has only a partial degree of
biological impairment, which may be escalated into a
total sexual disability by a variety of cultural and
relationship stressors. However, these problems are
frequently amenable to a therapeutic approach that
emphasizes the improvement of the couple's intimacy
and the expansion of their sexual flexibility.[34]

Becoming familiar with the information cited in chapters seven through nine can also be of invaluable help. Studies do suggest that sexual activity is associated with well being and longevity.

Here's the percentage of the sexually active in advanced age groups, with the majority reporting that they enjoy the experience:

~   50 to 59 years – 93%
~   60 to 69 years – 81%
~   70 to 79 years – 65%[35]

The passionate love stage of relationships that are biologically based lasts three to four years. This is different from the later stages of long-term committed partnerships in which sexual activity continues as a form of exercise and fun.[36] Isn't it nice to know you can look forward to a pleasurable sexual and orgasmic old age?

The reasons for sexual decline in older people include:

bad state of health
decrease of fitness
genital atrophy
gynecological surgery
partner problems

On the other side, sexuality can be maintained up to an advanced age. In any case, the demand for affection, tenderness, love, and sexual relations is nearly always present, and its realization should not be inhibited.[37]

Hysterectomy:
An Advantage?

One in three women in the United States has had a hysterectomy. According to experts, far too many of these operations were unnecessary. There is, however, one advantage: hysterectomy seems more likely to result in *improvement* rather then *deterioration* of sexual functioning. Although I am certainly not advocating this commonly performed surgery (there are often better ways to eliminate ovarian and uterine problems), women report that sexual activities increase and health problems decrease after they have recuperated from their surgery. The rate of pain during coitus drops from 18.6 percent before hysterectomy to 4.3 percent at twelve months after the operation, and to 3.6 percent twenty-four months later. That's significant! The rates of experiencing orgasm increase, as do libido rates. And fewer women report vaginal dryness after a hysterectomy.[38,39]

But that still leaves about one in five women with a downward slump in sex drive following the surgery. These women regard the uterus, menstruation, and fertility as fundamental to their femininity—especially if they are under forty.[40] And for most women, although coital frequency increases, the incidence of desire and multiplicity of orgasm remain unchanged. Sexual activity prior to surgery is more important in predicting post-operative sexuality than is the occurrence of difficult or painful disease.[41]

But why should 79 percent of women experience improvement? After all, the ovaries are no longer contributing their half of the testosterone supply. The trend in medical research is to study the problems, not the successes. Not only is the source of previous discomfort gone, but the fear of pregnancy is also gone, —making sex more pleasurable.

Time for a QUICKIE

There appears to be a syndrome of headaches associated with sexual excitement where no organic change can be demonstrated, analogous to both benign cough headaches and benign exertional headaches.

For many women who do not experience sexual advantages following a hysterectomy, transdermal testosterone is currently prescribed by many physicians. The percentage of women who have sexual fantasies, masturbate, or engage in sexual intercourse at least once a week increases two to three times with its use—but only when high doses are administered. The positive well being and depressed mood also improve.[42] But chapter five will explain why this isn't a viable solution, and why this is NOT in your best health interst.

Depression may be a predictor of sexual dysfunction after hysterectomy.[43] See the segment later in this chapter for information on depression and its effects on sexuality.

Magic Button:
Understanding The "G" Spot

Women have a small sensitive area in the anterior wall of the vagina, which seems to trigger "deeper" orgasms.[44]

Ancient East Indian texts in sexology (kamasastra), from the eleventh century onward, prove that their authors knew about the area (later termed the "Grafenberg zone" in Europe), as well as about the female ejaculation connected with its stimulation. The Grafenberg zone is a sexually arousable zone in the front part of the vagina, situated beneath the clitoris, stimulation of which can lead to the discharge of liquid from the urethra, a phenomenon that is described as female ejaculation.

This zone was detailed for the first time in Western medicine in 1950. Since the 1980s the so-called Grafenberg zone—popularly termed the "G spot"—and female ejaculation have been controversially discussed medically as well as in popular literature, first in the United States, then in Europe. Both phenomena have meanwhile been accepted as facts in many medical manuals and reference books.[45]

Forty percent of women report having a fluid release (ejaculation) at the moment of orgasm. Eighty-two percent who report the sensitive area (Grafenberg spot) also report ejaculation with their orgasms.[46]

Even though there is skepticism concerning the actual existence of the G spot, it seems reasonable to accept that women possess a zone of tactile erotic sensitivity on the anterior vaginal wall. It also appears that some women emit a fluid through the urethra at orgasm, although its true nature and anatomical origin are still unclear.[47]

Figure 1

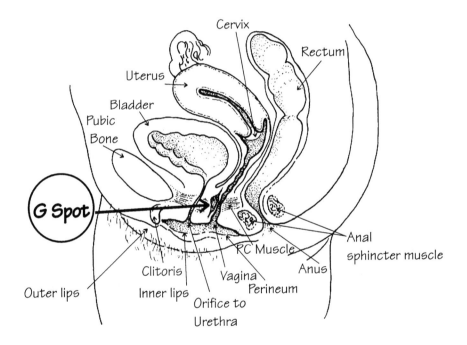

The G Spot

This diagram gives you an idea of the location of the G Spot in relation to the other female genital parts.

Bedroom Blues:
Depression and Sexual Desire

Our high incidence of sexual dysfunction is often a symptom of depression. Antidepressant treatment, however, only exacerbates the problem. In this lose-lose situation, antidepressant medications are associated with a wide range of disorders of desire, arousal, and orgasm, as well as with the occurrence of sexual pain.[48]

SSRI is the acronym for "selective serotonin reuptake inhibitor." This refers to antidepressive drugs that promote transmission of nerve impulses along pathways using the neurotransmitter *serotonin*. (A neurotransmitter is an agent that crosses from one nerve cell to another.)

SSRIs are clearly related to absent or delayed orgasm. Sexual dysfunction caused by these drugs is almost universal, yet it is poorly understood. The problems appear to occur in more than half of those treated with SSRIs.[49] Their effects on sexual function seem strongly dose-related.[50]

The purpose of one study published in *Biological Psychiatry* was to determine whether or not three SSRI drugs affected sexual function in anxiety disorder patients over a three-month period. For men and women, orgasm quality was lower and orgasm delay was longer after the first, second, and third months. Lubrication, libido, and sexual frequency were not appreciably changed after three months. Orgasm appears to be the primary sexual function affected by these drugs.[51]

For those Familiar with the Drugs

Data was collected on patients with previously normal sexual function who were treated with antidepressants alone or with antidepressants plus benzodiazepines.

The overall incidence of sexual dysfunction was 59.1% when all antidepressants were considered as a whole. There were relevant differences when the incidence of sexual dysfunction was compared among different drugs. Among the results:

~ fluoxetine (Prozac),57.7%

~ sertraline (Zoloft), 62.9%

~ fluvoxamine (Luvox), 62.3%

~ paroxetine (Paxil), 70.7%

~ citalopram (Celexa), 72.7%

Men had a higher frequency of sexual dysfunction (62.4%) than women (56.9%), although women had higher severity. About 40% of patients showed low tolerance of their sexual dysfunction. The incidence of sexual dysfunction with SSRIs and venlafaxine is high, ranging from 58% to 73%, as compared with serotonin-2 (5-HT2) blockers (nefazodone and mirtazapine), moclobemide, and amineptine

A variety of tactics has been found useful in the management of SSRI-induced sexual dysfunction. These include waiting for tolerance to develop, dosage reduction, drug holidays (stopping on Saturday or Sunday), adding or switching to a different antidepressant (perhaps a non-SSRI drug like Wellbutrin), and strategies with additional drugs.[52]

> **Time for a QUICKIE**
>
> Sexually unresponsive women describe themselves as more timid, more reserved, plus more inhibited.

One SSRI-like drug, Celexa, claims to have little or no sexual dysfunction effect but it does have other side effects. And Wellbutrin is actually a sexual stimulant.

Depression *can* be dealt with minus harmful drugs, and sexual dysfunction *can* be remedied more naturally, too. (Again—solutions are explored in chapters seven and nine.)

Fewer sexual dysfunctions have been reported with some drugs (Wellbutrin, Serzone, and Remeron) than with others (monoamine-oxidase inhibitors, tricyclic antidepressants, selective serotonin-reuptake inhibitors, and effexor). As many as half of all patients treated with SSRIs report delayed orgasm, and virtually all patients treated with clomipramine (a tricyclic) do not experience orgasm at all.

Sexual dysfuntion is probably underreported and may result in the patient secretly not taking the drugs, and relapsing.[53]

The book, *Your Drug May Be Your Problem: How and Why to Stop Taking Psychiatric Medications*, explains that the adverse effects of SSRIs haven't been proved to be reversible.[54] The possibility that SSRIs could permanently affect sexual function is one good reason why no one should turn to this class of drugs before trying other, safer measures.

Perhaps knowing that chronic adrenal stress creates a hormonal imbalance that ultimately affects sexual desire might encourage people to seek counseling or attend workshops to learn stress relaxation techniques.

Ginkgo biloba extract, derived from the leaf of the Chinese ginkgo tree, is noted for its cerebral enhancing effects. In an open trial, it was found to be 84 percent effective in treating antidepressant-induced sexual dysfunction predominately caused by SSRIs. Women are more responsive to the sexually enhancing effects of ginkgo biloba than men, with relative success rates of 91 percent versus 76 percent. Ginkgo biloba generally has a positive effect on all four phases of the sexual response cycle—again, desire, excitement (lubrication), orgasm, and resolution (afterglow). Dosages of ginkgo biloba extract ranged from 60 milligrams daily to 120 milligrams twice a day (average = 209 milligrams a day) in this study.[55] Generally, more than 240 milligrams a day is necessary.

A simple program of regular aerobic exercise can substantially improve the problem in those with moderate to severe major depression, despite prior failures with drug therapy. Investigators studied the effects of aerobic exercise on depression in patients with serious depressive episodes ranging from twelve to ninety-six weeks in duration. Most of these people were characterized as having hard-to-manage depression after failing to improve during treatment with at least two different classes of antidepressants for at least four weeks during the current episode.

The intervention consisted of interval training (walking speed) on a treadmill for thirty minutes a day for ten days. Overall, exercise training caused a clinically significant drop in depression.[56] Knowing that depression plus the associate drugs depress libido should inspire *everyone* to spend that half hour a day moving aerobically.

Time for a
QUICKIE

Belief that her vagina is too small may be one of the reasons for a woman's fear of vaginal penetration.

Chronic Illness

We know that certain medical conditions have their impact on sexual desire. We have already cited the example of depressive illness, which usually dramatically reduces desire, as do stress and fatigue. The more debilitating the illness, the more affected the sexuality. Any condition or illness can result in decreased sexual function. For example, a woman with arthritis may have difficulty using her hands to pleasure herself or her partner. She may not be able to find a sexual position that minimizes the pain.

Conditions and drugs that cause the production of too much prolactin have a direct effect on reducing sexual drive. How the prolactin hormone relates to sexuality is explained in chapter five.

Any health problem that might affect sexual anatomy, the vascular system, the neurological system, or the endocrine system, must be considered. Indirect causes are conditions that can cause pain during intercourse. Here are just a few examples of illnesses and their relationship to sexuality.

Hypertension

Hypertension is a common problem among women of all ages. Whether medicated or not, women with hypertension report significantly decreased lubrication and orgasm as well as increased pain compared to non-hypertensive women.[57]

Diabetes

Sexual dysfunction is common in diabetics, and both sexes suffer from libido, arousal, and orgasm problems.[58] It affects all aspects of sexuality. As part of a diabetic woman's day-to-day life, sexuality may impact in ways that are detrimental to her health, her relationships, and her self-esteem. Problems reported are fatigue, changes in perimenstrual blood glucose control, vaginitis, decreased sexual desire, decreased vaginal lubrication, and increased time to reach orgasm.[59,60] This is caused by neuropathy of pelvic nerves and reduced circulation.

Celiac disease

Celiac disease is a chronic disorder where the intestinal lining is inflamed in response to the ingestion of protein known as gluten. Gluten is present in many grains, including wheat, rye, oats, and barley. Symptoms include abdominal distention, pain, and fatigue. Treatment is avoidance of gluten-containing foods.

It's hard to be sexy when you have a bellyache. Untreated celiac patients have a significantly lower frequency of intercourse and a lower prevalence of satisfaction with their sex life. After one year of dietary treatment, celiac patients show improved values for all indices of sexual behavior. Differences are significant for intercourse frequency and satisfaction prevalence. Sexual difficulties are even rampant in those with subclinical celiac, a problem more common than most people realize.[61] (Pay attention here if you have belly bloat.)

Back pain

Sexual dysfunction increases in both sexes with back problems. Fatigue and pain are shared symptoms, but there is markedly less sexual dysfunction in the male. For many females, back pain serves to "legalize" previously latent sexual dysfunction.[62]

Drugs that can affect your sexual function include:

~ Antiandrogens
   (Cyproterone, Gonadotrophin
   releasing hormone analogues)
~ Antiestrogens
   (tamoxifen, contraceptive drugs)
~ Cytotoxic drugs
~ Psychoactive drugs
   (sedatives, narcotics, antidepressants,
   narcoleptics, stimulants)[63]

These are just a few demonstrations of how the lack of optimal health affects sexuality.

It doesn't have to be that way!

Dietary treatment as described in chapter seven, plus the solution outlined in chapter nine, are part of the answer for any chronic illness.

Does this mean you may have to watch your diet, take your supplements, and do that dreaded exercise to maintain sexual vigor after all? Well, maybe ... but maybe not!

Let's **(Not)** *Drink to That: Alcohol and Sexuality*

Alcohol consumption has a significant hold on both women's and men's sexual judgments. Under its influence, many find themselves behaving more sexually and in a less inhibited manner. Intoxicated participants usually exaggerate the meaning of cues when making sexual judgments.[64] (As if we needed a scientist to tell us that. Just imagine what a coup it must have been for the researchers who got a grant to do that study!)

But let's not get carried away. When the male alone is an alcoholic, his female partner neither desires nor enjoys sex during his drinking bouts, though she often accepts sex reluctantly. The male alcoholic reports satisfaction with sex while drinking, despite awareness of his partner's negative emotional reactions during sex.[65] (Is there some double entendre to the term "bottoms up"?)

Worse, female-initiated sexual activity appears to be inversely related to alcohol use—with women proposing significantly fewer sexual activities following the consumption of larger amounts of alcohol. Contrary to the facts, women believe alcohol enhances sexual desire, enjoyment, and activity. This data suggests that women view alcohol as an aphrodisiac despite their physiological and reported behavioral responses.[66]

Most women drinkers (heavier drinkers) report that drinking lessens sexual inhibiton and helps them feel close to others. Only 8 percent report becoming less particular in sexual partner choice, 22 percent report they are more sexually assertive, but over half (60 percent) are targets of other drinkers' sexual aggression. *The heaviest drinking women have the highest rates of lifetime sexual disinterest and lack of orgasm with a partner.*

Time for a QUICKIE

Approximately 59 percent of women in the US drink alcohol, and 6 percent consume two or more drinks daily—an amount considered to be heavy drinking for women. The age when girls first begin drinking has shifted downward. The percent of female college students who drink is now nearly equal to their male peers (75 to 79 percent).

Women become intoxicated more quickly and with lower consumption.

So the negative side of "Cheers" is that virtually all aspects of the human sexual responses are adversely affected by alcohol (and by recreational and prescribed drugs, too):

~ Desire (libido) is reduced.
~ Performance is impaired (impotency).
~ Dissatisfaction ensues.

These effects of alcohol and drugs can be understood and illustrated by examining the phases of excitement, plateau, orgasm, and resolution in the sexual response.[67]

Sobriety, even of relatively short duration, improves sexual function in alcoholic women.[68]

"We Must, We Must, We Must Increase Our Lust!": Positive Effects of Exercise

Although the sexual response is a form of physical exercise, not much research has focused on the subject. There's no question that exercise and the orgasmic response are closely related.[69]

Regular exercise significantly increases vaginal pulse amplitude and vaginal blood volume, which means that physical activity stimulates increased blood flow throughout the entire body. We all know that it increases heart strength and vascular health, which produce a stronger pulse. However, for women who do not experience orgasm, these responses may not occur, and may even be reversed.

A technique that measures the strength of vaginal muscular contractions shows that women who experience orgasm have stronger vaginal musculature than women who do not. The same is true for women who exercise regularly. Could it be that muscular activity of *any* kind influences blood flow and neuromuscular activity in all contractile (muscle) tissue, making it easier to achieve orgasm?[70]

The effects of acute exercise on sexual arousal was studied in two experimental sessions. Women viewed a neutral film followed by an erotic film. In one session, the women were exposed to twenty minutes of exercise before viewing the films. Acute exercise significantly increased vaginal pulse amplitude and vaginal blood volume responses to an erotic film among sexually functional women and even those with low sexual desire.[71]

Psychostimulants

Women experience enhanced levels of arousal, orgasmic sensation, and excitement during the resolution phase (afterglow) of the sexual response cycle when they are on psychostimulants.[72] The effects of ginkgo biloba have already been described.

Twenty sexually functional women participated in two experiments in which self-reported and physiological sexual responses to erotic stimuli were measured after administration of either ephedrine sulfate (50 mg) or a placebo. Ephedrine significantly increased vaginal pulse amplitude responses to the erotic films but had no meaningful effect on subjective ratings of sexual arousal. The researchers concluded that ephedrine can facilitate the initial stages of physiological sexual arousal in women.[73] But the physical effect does not always result in sexual stimulation.

Time for a
QUICKIE

Throughout history, with very few exceptions, women have had little or no power until the early 20th century.

Not Just for Bob:
Viagra for Women?

Sildenafil (Viagra) has become the number-one drug. Although mostly an erectile stimulant and so seemingly only for men, there are actual sexual benefits to this new drug for women as well—but not without risk.

One project examined women with self-described sexual dysfunction who were treated with Viagra for three months, using the drug three or four times a week. After twelve weeks of use, clitoral sensation improved by 31.3 percent, lubrication by 23.2 percent, and orgasm by only 7.4 percent. And there were unpleasant side effects: clitoral discomfort and "hypersensitivity," headache, dizziness, and digestive problems. Overall sexual function was not enhanced significantly. The role of Viagra in treating sexual dysfunction in women does not appear to be a viable solution.[74]

We do credit Viagra, however, for shedding light on the "hidden" sexual lives of older people.

Androstenedione, a precursor to testosterone—available in creams and mouth spray—can inhibit human endometrial cell growth and secretory activity. The problem is it may also be partially converted to estrogen. Infertility and miscarriage associated with high androgen levels may be due to an adverse effect of high androgen levels on the endometrium. (More about this later.)[75]

In Summary

As so eloquently stated in the Women's Health Book Collective, OUR BODIES, OURSELVES: FOR THE NEW CENTURY:[76]

> "Our powers to express ourselves sexually last a lifetime—from birth to death. Whether or not we are in a sexual relationship with another person, we can explore our fantasies, feel good in our bodies, appreciate sensual pleasures, learn what turns us on, give ourselves sexual pleasure through mastur-rbation. If we were taught to be embarrassed or ashamed of our sexual feelings, we may have spent a lot of energy denying them or feeling guilty. Women are learning to experience our sexuality without judging it and to accept it as part of ourselves.

> "We are all sexual—young, old, married, single, with or without disability, sexually active or not, transgendered, heterosexual, bisexual, or lesbian. As we change, our sexuality changes, too. Learning about sex is a lifelong process."

"I ate a dozen oysters last night before a hot date."

"Smart move. I hear that oysters are a good aphrodisiac."

"Not really. Only five of them worked."

Chapter Two

"WAS IT GOOD FOR YOU?"

Organizers of the first national "Orgasm Week" march were very disappointed with the turnout. Over half the marchers just pretended to be there.

Orgasm: What Is It?

We all know that orgasm is the height and climax of sex. The word itself comes from the Greek *orgasmos*, meaning "swelling" or "to swell." Vaginal engorgement in women remains at a high level after an initial orgasm, thus setting the physiologic stage for consecutive orgasmic responses.[1] Women, unlike men, are naturally multiorgasmic (making up somewhat for PMS, the pain of childbirth, and cellulite!).

The female genitals are richly endowed with blood vessels. When you are aroused, your brain sends signals to specific cells, directing them to bring blood to your pelvic area. This causes swelling of the clitoris and the vaginal lips. When you reach the orgasmic stage, contractions of the PC muscle take place. (PC is short for pubococcygeal, the muscle sling that surrounds the anus, vagina, and urethra.) The beating or pulsating sensations of the orgasm, although centered in the pelvic area, begin to radiate outward. The result is incomparable pleasure.

Female sexual arousal relates mainly to the vagina (thickening of the vaginal wall due to vasodilation, lubrication, and widening of the vaginal cavity). Orgasm is brought about by stimulation of the skin of the clitoris. (See figures 2 and 3.) Muscles contract against the engorged vaginal tissues (particularly the tissues in the forefront of the vagina) to produce the female orgasm.

Sexual intercourse itself does not produce the degree of intense physical stimulation for women as does direct clitoral manipulation, and most women are aware of this. In fact, only women who have a low orgasmic threshold are able to experience an orgasm with penetration alone. Vaginal stimulation is also effective. A third site, the cervix, is another area known to elicit orgasm in some women.[2] (Keep all this in mind when you read about the selective strategy in chapter nine.)

Masters and Johnson (1966) described three to fifteen rhythmic contractions of the "orgasmic platform" in the outer third of the vagina as the physiological basic of female orgasm. A more recent study (1994) registered up to thirty-four additional irregular pelvic contractions during longer orgasms. In a sample of one hundred female health professionals and counselors, orgasmic contractions were reported in 80 percent of the women.

Figure 2

The Sexual Response of the
Clitoris and Labia

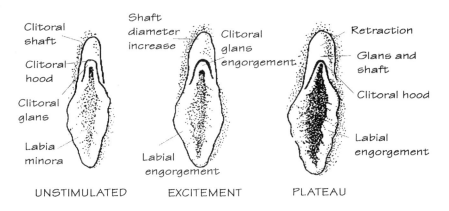

Clitoral
shaft

Clitoral
hood

Clitoral
glans

Labia
minora

Shaft
diameter
increase

Labial
engorgement

Clitoral
glans
engorgement

Retraction

Glans and
shaft

Clitoral hood

Labial
engorgement

UNSTIMULATED   EXCITEMENT   PLATEAU

The clitoris is similar in origin and function to
the penis, and has just as many nerve endings as
the head of the penis, only it occupies a much
smaller space.

The glans of the clitoris corresponds to the glans
of the penis, just as the outer lips of the vagina
correspond to the scrotum.

Here you see the changes that take place in the
clitoris and labia during the sexual response. On
the next two pages, you can see a more total
picture of the genital changes. In the plateau
phase, the clitoris seems to disappear, but it is
actually quite engorged.

Figure 3

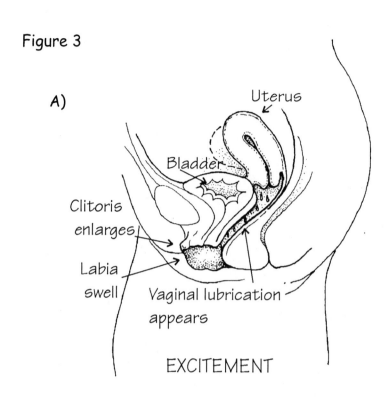

A)

Uterus

Bladder

Clitoris
enlarges

Labia
swell

Vaginal lubrication
appears

EXCITEMENT

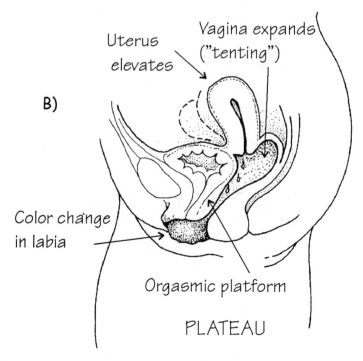

Uterus
elevates

Vagina expands
("tenting")

B)

Color change
in labia

Orgasmic platform

PLATEAU

C)

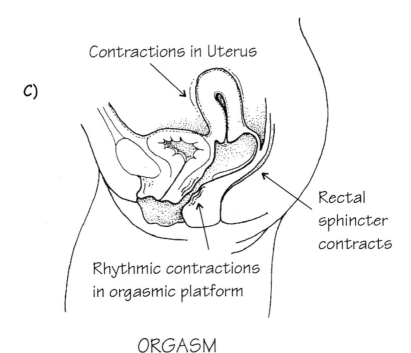

Contractions in Uterus

Rectal sphincter contracts

Rhythmic contractions in orgasmic platform

ORGASM

D)

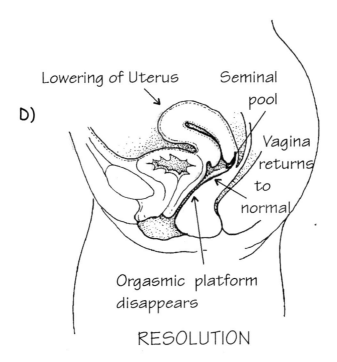

Lowering of Uterus

Seminal pool

Vagina returns to normal

Orgasmic platform disappears

RESOLUTION

Although contractions seem to accompany female orgasm frequently, they do not always go hand in hand. Some women experience orgasm regularly without vaginal contractions and some report experiencing them only occasionally during orgasm.[3]

There are always exceptions. Women who are sexually responsive and have good quality sex with imaginative foreplay leading to orgasm can do so without penetration. The contractions can occur not only on attempted penetration but also on anticipated coitus or foreplay.

The strength and degree of gratification provided by an orgasm are not related to how it is induced or to the location of the pulsating sensations.[4]

The following report, published in *Archives of Sexual Behavior*, clarifies several other issues concerning orgasm:

> Human female orgasm was studied by collecting and analyzing the subjective orgasmic histories of women, ages 18 to 59 years. Virtually all of the 93 percent who reported they had experienced orgasm also reported some level of conscious control over whether or not they reached orgasm. Women differed widely as to preferred types of physical stimulation and/or mental activities to facilitate orgasm. Orgasms were experienced as centered in the clitoral and/or vaginal areas. Women over 40 were more likely to have experienced orgasm in more than one anatomic site

than were women aged 18 to 29. Marital status, religion, occupation, educational level, experiences of pregnancy and childbirth, various reported characteristics of relationships with partners, and early sexual experience were not associated with where orgasm is experienced within the body or with other variables of adult orgasmic experience. The variation among women as to how orgasm is best reached, differences in where it is experienced within the body, and the reasons why individual women experience orgasms differently over time remain poorly understood phenomena.[5]

Time for a
QUICKIE

About a third of women masturbated fifty years ago. Today the number is closer to half.

But what about those women—the third or two-thirds or more (depending on which study you read) of American women who do not experience orgasm?

Although orgasm can be achieved in many ways with or without a partner, partner involvement is a noted preference. If you are among those who consider orgasm of little relevance and are content without it, you are not alone. An important issue is your partner's understanding of the female orgasm. Men tend to evaluate female responses by their own standards. They often feel that women couldn't possibly fully enjoy sexual activity without orgasm, since for men this is normally true.

This may put pressure on a woman to achieve orgasm. Those women who are orgasmic agree with the men, confirming that nonorgasmic women are "missing out" on one of life's most pleasurable experiences. (That's why the simple solution outlined in chapter 9 is so important!)

Interpretations of arousal or pleasure are complex and differ greatly from person to person.

A working definition of "anorgasmia" would be an involuntary inhibition of the orgasmic reflex. A woman may have a strong sexual desire with significant sexual arousal, but she may then hold back even though the stimulation should be sufficient for orgasm. The therapists tell us these women often have a deep-rooted fear of losing control over their feelings and behavior—conscious or unconscious. An example of a situational anorgasmia is a woman who can achieve orgasm by solo masturbation but not when having sex with her partner.

Among the factors that modify a woman's ability to achieve orgasm is the age when her periods started. Women who started menstruating after age sixteen generally are less able to achieve orgasm than those who had their first period around age eleven.

Giving women "permission" to use vibrators to assist with access to genital areas and stimulation is often helpful.

Orgasm Boosters

Knowledge is Power

There's an interesting correlation between sexual knowledge and the ability to achieve orgasm. Familiarity with facts about sexuality is significantly related to orgasm potential, and the greater the knowledge, the *more* orgasm experience.[6,7]

Say "When"

Sexually assertive women confirm increased frequencies of sexual activity and orgasm. They claim to have more habitual subjective sexual desire. They also report greater marital and sexual satisfaction.[8]

I *Think* I Can

Physical genital stimulation is not always necessary to produce orgasm. Some women experience orgasm from imagery alone. Orgasm from self-induced imagery or genital self-stimulation generates significant increases in blood pressure, heart rate, pupil diameter, and even pain tolerance—just as it would with a partner.

The physical responses in self-induced imagery orgasm are comparable in magnitude to those in the genital self-induced stimulation-produced orgasm.[9]

Timing Is Everything

Some studies show that women are more arousable just prior to their periods. There really is no single series of events related to the menstrual cycle that correlate with every woman's sexuality. A group of women free of PMS reported a peak of sexual interest in the premenstrual phase; those with PMS experienced this in the ovulatory phase.[10] The time of the month influenced how women *think* about their own sexuality. Women who are questioned about sexual feelings during the post-ovulatory phase report less desire to engage in sexual activity and less frequent activity. But these *same* women tell a different story about themselves during *other* phases of their menstrual cycle.[11]

Give Yourself a Hand

Masturbation had been practiced by 74 percent of college women queried. For most, the practice began as an accidental discovery. The women who were orgasmic in masturbation were more likely to continue the behavior.[12] Frequency of masturbation and of intercourse are not related. Nor is masturbating to orgasm related to orgasm ability in intercourse.[13]

Why Not Take All of Me?

Researchers studied vaginal erotic sensitivity with women complaining of coital anorgasmia (no orgasm during intercourse), but who were readily orgasmic at self- or partner-performed external genital stimulation.

They concluded that the entire anterior vaginal wall, rather than one specific spot, was found to be erotically sensitive. Sixty-four percent of these women learned how to reach orgasm by direct spccific digital stimulation (using their fingers) and/or coital stimulation of this area.[14]

The XXX Factor

Contrary to expectations, orgasmic and anorgasmic women do not differ significantly on either the frequency of use of sexually explicit films or on arousal when viewing sexaul activities in these films.[15]

Head Start

Married women who reach orgasm most of the time or always during sexual intercouse usually had their first coitus earlier than those who do not.[16]

Time for a
QUICKIE

Witchcraft was practiced in the 15th century to overcome sexual difficulties. One remedy for men was to place the testicle of a rooster under the victim's bed. Another was to abstain from intercourse for three days and three nights. Then perform it, and thus all diabolical power is destroyed.[17]

Orgasm Busters

Butt Out

Smokers experience a lower score for orgasm than do nonsmokers. Like so many other metabolic phenomena, the precise reasons are not fully understood.[18]

You Booze, You Lose

As indicated in the previous chapter, *the heaviest drinking women have the highest rates of lifetime sexual disinterest and lack of orgasm with a partner.*

Mind Over Matter

In response to being unable to conceive, many women feel emotions such as anger, panic, despair, and grief, and these may have serious effects on sexual activity.

Not Giving Yourself a Hand

Absence of masturbation is a frequent finding in the histories of women who later complain of orgasmic difficulties.

Time for a QUICKIE

Freud assumed vaginal stimulation triggered orgasms. Masters and Johnson demonstrated that it is stimulation of the clitoris.

What's Going On?
How Orgasm Affects Your Body

Orgasm produces its own distinct set of effects—changes that occur in your nervous system and your glandular system.[19] A specific deeply satisfying female orgasm is also associated with a particular type of respiratory pattern and uterine pressure change.[20]

Orgasm also increases levels of the hormones *adrenaline* and *noradrenaline*. These hormones, produced by your adrenal glands, are usually secreted in response to excitement, exercise, or stress. They cause an increase of cardiac output and vasodilation of small arteries. Vasodilation increases the diameter of a blood vessel, causing an increase in blood flow—just what is needed here! But obviously, the adrenaline burst must be very brief. Otherwise, we would not be relaxed after sex.

For those who have orgasms frequently, mortality risk (for a specific age and lifestyle) is reduced by 50 percent compared with those who don't—with evidence of a dose-response relationship. (The greater the number of orgasms, the greater the health benefit.) The results are most remarkable in their correlation to preventing death from coronary heart disease.[21] Never mind going to the gym, reducing fat intake, cutting out sugar, eating five portions of green vegetables daily, taking all those supplements, or lowering cholesterol! Have we been overlooking this most powerful tool for protecting our coronary health?

Think of the implications. Compliance rates would zoom if the doctors were prescribing frequent orgasm as part of their treatment protocol.

Sexual excitation also produces small increases in testosterone concentrations. These results concur with those observed in men.

Masturbation-prompted orgasm also induces these increases in the adrenalin hormones, in addition to prolactin in the blood of both males and females.[22]

Orgasm and Oxytocin

You may recognize oxytocin as the hormone responsible for initiating childbirth, in addition to functioning as the letdown reflex when lactating. (The letdown reflex is an involuntary reflex that occurs during breastfeeding causing the milk to flow freely.) Oxytocin also plays a role in female sexual responsiveness, and is released during orgasm.[23] Research on nonhuman mammals demonstrates that oxytocin is important for maternal behavior and the formation of adult pair bonds. It has been speculated that social stimuli may induce oxytocin release and that oxytocin may make positive social contact more rewarding for humans, too.

Oxytocin levels in women are elevated in response to relaxation massage and decreased when experiencing unpleasant emotional reactions.[24] One minute after orgasm, oxytocin levels are significantly higher. So this hormone plays a major part in the human sexual response.[25] Orgasm intensity correlates significantly with increased levels of oxytocin in multiorgasmic women only. This association and other positive metabolic reactions are consistent with a possible functional role for oxytocin in the human sexual response.[26,27] (More about oxytocin in chapter nine.)

A mother heard a humming sound coming from her daughter's bedroom. When she opened the door she found her daughter naked on her bed with a vibrator. "What are you doing?" she asked, rather surprised. The daughter replied, "I'm 35 and still living with my parents and this is the closest I'll ever get to a husband."

Later that week the father heard the same humming sound. "What are you doing?" he asked. She replied, "I'm 35 and still living at home with my parents. This is the closest I'll ever get to a husband."

A couple of days later the mother heard the humming sound again, this time in the living room. She found her husband watching television with the vibrator buzzing away at his side. "What are you doing?' she asked. He replied, "Watching a football game with my son-in-law."

Tone Your Zone:
The Benefits of "Kegel" Exercises

Kegel refers to the name of a pelvic floor exercise, named after Dr. Arnold Kegel, who discovered it. These exercises are said to improve orgasm consistency. The muscles involved are attached to the pelvic bone and act like a hammock, holding in your pelvic organs. To try and isolate these muscles, try stopping and starting the flow of urine.

Kegelites (those who promote and confirm kegel benefits) advise tightening and relaxing the muscles about two hundred times a day. That's a basic kegel. Among the variations: elevator kegels involve tightening the muscles slowly in increments going in and out, like an elevator stopping on several floors; you can hold the muscles tightened for five seconds; you can bulge the muscles out at the end of each exercise.

To identify the proper muscle group, place your finger in your vagina and squeeze around your finger. If you feel pressure, then you are squeezig the right muscles.

There are many other modifications, all explained on the Internet. Just use your search engine and key in "Kegel"[28] For starters, you might want to try this website:

http://www.childbirth.org/articles/kegel.html

Figure 4

PC Muscle

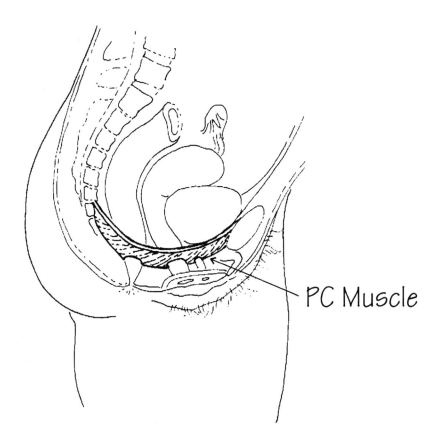

PC Muscle

Dr Kegel believed that having good muscles was a necessary condition for orgasm. Some doctors claim there is a high correlation between orgasmic capacity and pelvic muscle strength.

"Kegeling" is also known to:

~ condition these muscles, making birth easier, so your perineum (the region between your vulva and rectum) will more likely be intact
~ help to prevent prolapses (displacements) of pelvic organs
~ help prevent urine leakage when you sneeze or cough
~ help to prevent incontinence that is common among older women
~ enhance sexual enjoyment for both partners

As for orgasm, kegel exercises are reported to:

~ induce a state of excitement during the performance of the exercises because of the involvement of increased pelvic muscle tension
~ help during masturbation, not only to enhance the excitement but to distract the woman from intrusive thoughts and inhibition
~ enhance orgasm, in that the female learns to be an active participant in her own sexual response
~ induce an increase in awareness of the clitoral-vaginal sensations that lead to orgasm
~ produce an increase in pelvic vascularity (bringing more blood to the area)
~ produce an increase in muscle tone with a corresponding increase in direct clitoral stimulation during intercourse

You can practice your "kegels" any place, any time—even in a crowded subway or at a boring cocktail party.

Helen Singer Kaplan, MD, who is well known for her rational information on sexuality, is explicit in describing the role of the "circumvaginal muscles" in human orgasm, and she endorses the use of kegel exercises both as a general aid, and specifically during intercourse to trigger orgasm. She wishes there were more studies to validate the importance of these exercises.[29]

The problem, however, stems from the difficulty many women have in their efforts to kegel correctly. It's not easy to do these exercises the right way without good instructions.[30]

Then there's the other side of the coin. Although some studies show that the physiological state of the PC muscle (described earlier) in relation to female orgasm appears to be significant—demonstrating an important difference between orgasmic and anorgasmic women[31]—other researchers refute this. For example, about a hundred women from a university community were examined in a controlled investigation. Contrary to experimental hypotheses, PC strength was *not* found to be positively related to frequency or self-reported intensity of orgasm. Furthermore, women with higher PC strength did not report that vaginal stimulation contributed more to attainment of orgasm, nor did they rate vaginal sensations during coitus as more pleasurable.

Only in the case of pleasurability of orgasm through clitoral stimulation was a significant relationship obtained.[32] (But, hey—that sounds significant enough to me!)

It turns out that favorable consequences are just as frequent with PC exercises as they are when women practice relaxation exercises or learn attention-control techiques.[33]

It just may be that PC exercises are not of specific value for women with normal muscle tone, but may be beneficial for women with poor muscle tone. Since muscle tone may decline as we get older, we have nothing to lose by learning to kegel.

Another advantage is that the pelvic floor muscle exercises help to combat postmenopausal incontinence, a very common problem (evident by the Depends commercials).[34]

Time for a
QUICKIE

With sexual experience, and after child-bearing, women develop a large complex venous system in the pelvic area that enhances the capacity for sexual tension and improves orgasmic intensity, frequency, and pleasure.

There's a First Time For Everything: Orgasm and the First Encounter

The proportion of young people having sexual intercourse before age sixteen is increasing. Intercourse before that tender age, however, is often regretted.

When a woman looks back on her "first time" with a seasoned view and without the emotional or physical stress of the moment, her outlook is quite different. Rueful thoughts result after re-evaluation from a more mature perspective.

Among a group of girls aged six to eighteen, those who reached orgasm during their first sexual intercourse were orgasmic mostly or always in their future encounters. Statistically significant differences were noted among those who did and did not experience orgasm initially:

~ Orgasmic girls were more frequently waiting anxiously for their first sexual intercourse.

~ Those who did not have a first-time orgasm had sex because of curiosity or in an effort to satisfy their partners.

~ The majority of nonorgasmic girls experienced the first sexual intercourse as unpleasant and reported frequent occurrence of vaginal bleeding.

~ In this group, most girls for whom the experience had not been pleasant had lost their fathers during the first six years of their lives.[35]

Compared with orgasmic women, anorgasmic women report:

~ greater discomfort in communicating with a partner about sexual activities involving direct clitoral stimulation

~ more negative attitudes toward masturbation

~ greater belief in common sex myths

~ greater guilt regarding sex

Again, there is little doubt that the absent capacity of women to attain orgasm in sexual intercourse is caused by factors of both biological and psychosocial nature.[36]

Time for a
QUICKIE

Sexual interest at different stages of the menstrual cycle can follow a pattern, but it varies depending on whether or not there are mood swings. With no mood swings, interest is often greatest at the post- and premenstrual phases.

"After You": *Orgasm and Timing*

Because failure to reach orgasm through sexual intercourse is such a commonly reported complaint in women, sex educators and therapists are eager to increase awareness of timing factors in order to influence satisfying sexual relationships. This involves time spent on foreplay. Other timing factors are significant, too. For example, women who usually experience orgasm *following* the orgasm of their male partners perceive less physiological and psychological sexual satisfaction.[37]

On the other hand, women retain more sperm if their coital orgasm occurs *after*, rather than *before* male ejaculation—important information for women trying to conceive. Women can learn to regulate the amount of sperm accepted or rejected by manipulation of coital orgasm timing. So here's another hole in the theory that there is no functional role except pleasure assigned to a woman's coital orgasm. It has also been shown that frequency of orgasm after a partner's orgasm remains a powerful predictor of the desire for pregnancy.[38]

The duration of an orgasm as normally reported by women turns out to be far shorter than the actual time. The average orgasm duration as tested in one study was 19.9 seconds, but it was greatly overestimated by the women involved.[39]

The Pretenders:
The Phenomenon of Faking It

The phenomenon of women often "faking" an orgasm is becoming more common in sexual relationships for many couples. More than one-half of women who were queried reported pretense of orgasm. Among these women, the pretenders and non-pretenders did not differ in attractiveness—either rated by those doing the questioning or self-rated by the women themselves.[40] Another survey showed that nearly two-thirds of all women fake orgasm, and that those who have done so became sexually active at a younger age and were also more sexually explorative.[41]

Couples who care about each other want to please each other. If a woman admits to not having an orgasm, she may feel that her partner will think his "performance" was not adequate. In addition, the media surrounds us with images contributing to the pressure for women to have sex to completion. Faking may relieve the pressure, and the prevalence of doing so indicates that this is a common attitude. The solution offered in chapter nine has the potential to reduce, if not eliminate, this phenomenon!

Women who experience greater distraction during sexual activity with a partner report *higher incidence of pretending orgasm.*[42]

In Summary

Inhibited female orgasm is caused by many factors—both biological as well as psychological.[43]

Clinical research issues in female sexuality can now be investigated with physiologic measures, so we can be certain of a few facts concerning orgasm. These include:

~ Vaginal engorgement in women remains at a high level after an initial orgasm, thus setting the stage for consecutive orgasm.

~ Arousal can be measured with acceptable degrees of reliability and specificity.

~ Muscle contractions during orgasm can also be measured with high levels of precision.

~ Women respond directly to erotic activity physically much the way men do.[44]

~ Women who practice masturbation are more likely to have more exciting sexual experiences and more frequent orgasm with a partner.

There appears to be a stigma about not experiencing orgasm. Every woman with whom I have ever discussed the subject informally (that is, not as a therapist or nutrition counselor), claims to be multiorgasmic. However, that doesn't quite fit the statistics. Female sexual problems are rampant, but there is a simple solution. (Chapter nine again.)

"Why do so many women fake or-gasm?

"Because so many men fake fore-play."

Chapter Three

HERS AND HIS: UNDERSTANDING FEMALE vs. MALE SEXUALITY

Love is when intercourse is called "making love." Lust is when intercourse is called "fooling around." Marriage is when intercourse is a town in Pennsylvania.

Alike, But Different

It has generally been assumed that a man's orgasmic experience is very different from that of a woman's. To determine whether or not this is actually so, a questionnaire consisting of 48 descriptions of an orgasm (written by 24 males and 24 females) was submitted to seventy judges. The judges were professionals (obstetrician-gynecologists, psychologists, and medical students), and they were asked to decide whether each statement was written by a male or a female.

The judges could not correctly identify the sex of the writers! Furthermore, none of the three groups did better than any of the others, nor did the male judges do better than the female judges. These findings suggest that the reactions and feelings of the experience of orgasm for males and females are essentially the same.[1]

But differences do occur extensively in many other aspects of female vs. male sexuality. Some of our beliefs are mythical, others factual, and some are simply caused by innate or cultural diversities.

A common gender stereotype is that men are more interested in sex than women. Not unlike the divergent views of the causes for female sexual problems, there are those sociobiologists who claim that this difference is biologically determined, while many others attest to cultural causes. So, like other aspects of sexuality, there's little doubt that nature *and* nurture, or biological *and* social factors, act in concert, combining their influences for the responsibility of female/male differences.[2]

Following are the results that reveal the differences.

TURNING ON

~ For most men, sexual desire can be aroused under exciting (erotic) circumstances during their entire lives, whereas female desire is less consistent. Although a woman's orgasmic potential is greater than a man's, her sexuality is more readily and easily disturbed. It doesn't take as much to distract her as it does him.

~ Subjective sexual arousal increases significantly in both men and women during an erotic film, with the arousal eliciting an increase in blood pressure for both sexes. But the hormone secreted by our adrenal glands in response to excitement (noradrenaline) rises in females only.[3]

~ Absorbed states of consciousness accompanying sexual arousal (sometimes called altered states of consciousness or a sexual trance) can impact on sexual responses. Absorbed states have different effects on females and males. It appears that there is a necessary pathway to high sexual arousal and to orgasm in many, perhaps all, females. But this is not so with most males.[4]

HAVING A HARD TIME

~ Fifty million American women endure reduced sexual responsiveness, but only fifteen million men experience erectile dysfunction out of a population of 284 million.

~ Women report greater cognitive distraction during sex than men. These women also claim relatively lower sexual esteem, less sexual satisfaction, less consistent orgasms, and higher incidence of pretending orgasm.[5] Not so for men!

~ The proportion of males experiencing sexual problems increases with age. Not so for women![6] Unlike many men, elderly women often remain capable of enjoying orgasms.

~ Impotency is identified as the major sexual impediment for senior men, whereas relationship problems are those most reported by women.[7]

~ It is predicted that ideas and practices will change as women continue to become freer, lessening the gender gap in physical sexual satisfaction.[8]

~ The greater sexual dissatisfaction among women compared to men may be due to any one or combinations of the following:

- late start to sexual activity

- conservative sexual attitudes

- unimportance of sexuality

- lack of sexual assertiveness

- fear of pregnancy

- fear of disease

- restricted use of sexual techniques

- family responsibilities

- career stress

~ For men, the most common complaints regarding general interpersonal difficulties are:

- intercourse occurring too infrequently

- failure of partner to reach orgasm

- concern with own sexual adequacy

~ For women, interpersonal problems are:

- difficulty becoming sexually aroused

- difficulty achieving orgasm [9]

~ Reports of desire disorder have increased in sex clinics, and males outnumber females when it comes to such problems.[10]

~ Men today are very concerned with partner satisfaction and are the primary initiators for sex therapy.[10,11]

HERE'S LOOKING AT YOU

~ When men meet a new female acquaintance, they tend to perceive much more sexual tension between them than women generally do at a first meeting. Men appear to be more sexually attracted to an opposite-sex partner.[12]

~ The importance of sexuality in life, love, and the use of sexual materials is connected directly to physical sexual satisfaction among men but only indirectly among women.[13] (Few men ever find a hidden stash of porn under their girlfriend's bed!)

~ Language pertaining to female sexuality generally is the product of a male value structure and, as such, reflects patriarchal prejudices about female sexuality. For example, the word testosterone is based on the gland that produces this hormone in men, the testes. The word estrogen means *producing frenzy*.

~ More men than women report that they and their partner were equally willing to have sex for the first time— 77 percent for males, 53 percent for females. Mutual willingness of both partners was greater for those who reported that it was also the first time for their partner.[14]

~ University students participated in a study showing that among the sexually active adults, 67.4 percent of males were psychologically satisfied after their first sexual experience, compared with only 28.3 percent of females. 80.9 percent of males and 28.3 percent of females reported current psychological satisfaction with their sexual experiences.

Significant differences between genders focused on male dissatisfaction with infrequent opportunities for sexual intercourse, lack of variety of sex partners, and insufficient oral-genital stimulation, whereas females expressed concerns relating to lack of stimulation to their breasts, painful sexual intercourse, lack of orgasm during intercourse, and feelings of guilt and fear.[15]

Needless to say, a great deal of this relates to the fact that women are the ones who fear getting pregnant.

~ Timing of the first experience of sexual intercourse was considered "about right" by 49 percent of men and 38 percent of women. Many women (54 percent) reported that they should have waited longer, and this rose to 70 percent for women who had had intercourse before age 16. For both sexes, subjects who were older at first intercourse were more likely to report that it was about the right time. The proportion of men who thought they waited too long was not related to age.[16]

GETTING STARTED

~ For women (but not for men), an early start to sexual life correlates with later enjoyment of sex. (But not too early, as already indicated.)

~ In adolescent males, testosterone directly affects sexual motivation, with social factors exerting little or no influence. In adolescent girls, by contrast, societal and peer pressure play a pivotal role in sexual behavior, much more so than their hormonal metabolism.[17] (Hence the slang phrase "Horny as a teenage *boy*.")

~ When asked about the importance of romantic acts, young girls judged physical intimacy as more important than boys did.[18]

~ Boys usually ejaculate more rapidly than they expected during a first intercourse encounter. Girls can have the most arousing sexual experience without intercourse, but as a result of stimulation of breasts and clitoris, whereas the initial coital experience is usually disappointing.

Time for a QUICKIE

In 1776, arguing against contemporaries who believed that all women were given to hysteria, the Dutch physician Antonius Ludgers wrote: "Hysteria is not an idiosyncrasy that we can attribute to the female portion of the population; it is obviously a major symptom of this deeply-rooted disease [endometriosis].

SOCIAL HANG-UPS

~ Women are more sexually influenced by cultural and social factors than men. Some anthropologists attribute the gender difference to evolutionary, biological forces. Gender roles powerfully shape behavior, and hetero-sexuality is a more important element of the male role than the female role.[19] The female sex drive is more flexible than the male's in response to sociocultural and situational factors.[20]

IT'S IN THE GENES

~ The clitoris is a sense organ and a transformer of stimuli. Only the human female has an organ that functions both to initiate and increase sexual tension. No such organ exists in the human male.[21] (The function of the clitoris is explained in more detail in chapter 9.)

~ Testosterone rises more for women than men during the sexual experience.[22]

~ Women are more responsive to the sexually enhancing effects of ginkgo biloba than men, with relative increased responsiveness of 91 percent versus 76 percent.[23]

~ It is theorized that changes in the brain which enable girls to fall in love for the first time, appear to be a biological prerequisite, and are more important for the beginning of full sexual life in pubescent girls than hormonal development manifested by the first menstrual period. Hormonal development is more significant for young boys.[24]

Time for a
QUICKIE

The French writer, Simone de Beauvoir, said, "Men fall in love with what they see; women fall in love with what they hear."

~ Findings indicate that women experience increased sexual arousal and sexual pleasure as they progress from the menses to the time just before their period, suggesting that human sexual behavior may be influenced by hormone fluctuations and cognitive factors associated with the menstrual cycle.[25] No such cycle exists for the men.

SO WHAT ELSE IS NEW?

~ Individual women will exhibit more variation than men in sexual behavior.[26]

~ Sexual variations are referred to as paraphilias, a neutral term for behavior formerly called deviant. Paraphilias can be defined as conditions in which a person's sexual gratification is dependent on an unusual sexual experience revolving around particular sex objects. Paraphilia is much more common in men than women.[27]

"But I Read It In Cosmo!"
Common Myths About Sex

Many myths come from one's family and friends. Most tend to be intergenerational and are often based on religious dogma and/or cultural beliefs. Sadly, these myths may lead to practices that diminish the quality of the sexual experiences both for women *and* men.

~ Men with bigger penises make better sex partners.

~ Sex should be how it is in the movies—dramatic, passionate, and perfect.

~ Once two partners see a decrease in the frequency of their sexual encounters, there is no going back.

~ Women prefer affection to sexual intercourse.

~ A woman who enjoys sex is "loose."

~ A woman who doesn't want sex is "frigid" and she is "uptight."

~ In sex, as elsewhere, it is performance that counts.

~ An erection is essential for a satisfying sexual experience for a man.

~ All physical contact must lead to sex.

~ Intercourse equals sex.

~ Good sex must terminate in orgasm for both partners.

~ Sex should be natural and spontaneous.

~ You shouldn't have to touch yourself at all during sex. Let your partner do the touching.

~ The only way to get full satisfaction is for the man to be on top and the woman on bottom.

~ On the whole, the man must take charge of and orchestrate sex.

~ A man wants and is always ready for sex.

~ Frigidity is a medical term.

~ Sex is "dirty" and "animalistic."

~ If the woman takes the lead in sex, it can damage her partner's ego.

~ Having to tell your partner what you want isn't necessary.

~ You should be available to your partner anytime he or she wants you to be.

Time for a
QUICKIE

One physician reported that sexual intercourse is a potential treatment for intractable hiccups.

STUDY REVISES LENGTH OF MALE ORGAN

An interesting Penis Survey conducted by a condom company concludes that the average length of an erect penis is shorter than you probably think. A report titled "Penis Survey Comes Up Short" posted the results on the Internet:

"For those of you who don't like to deal in raw numbers, at 5.877 inches, the average penis is about the size of a Nestle Butterfinger candy bar (unwrapped) or a grande (medium) cup of coffee at Starbucks (with the sip lid). Most men vary in size between a Twix bar and a Peter Paul Mounds (with the wrapper extended).

"According to the study, the average erect penis had a girth of 4.972 inches. About 75 percent of men were between 4.5 and 5.5 inches. Of course, once again, the frail male ego comes into play, and while condoms come in large, studded, ribbed and flavored varieties, you don't see small or petite or narrow models."

Survey conducted by LifeStyles Condoms.
Source: http://a142.g.akamaitech.net/7/142/622/
30001103769734/abcnews.go.com/images/
abcnewscom_83x20.gif

CAUSE & EFFECT

Forty-eight female college students were asked to complete a sexual attitudes questionnaire in which a frequency of masturbation scale was embedded. Twenty-four of the women (the experimental group) then individually viewed an explicit film involving female masturbation. One month later, all subjects again completed the same questionnaire. Subjects in the experimental group also completed a questionnaire evaluating aspects of the film. Results indicated that the experimental group reported a significant increase in the average monthly frequency of masturbation, as compared to the control group (the group that didn't view the film). The experimental group, however, reported that the film had no effect on their sexual attitudes or behavior. The inconsistency of these results is fascinating![28]

"Did I hear you say
you wanted two men
at once?"

"Yes. One to cook
and one to clean!"

Chapter Four

ENEMIES AMONG US: ENDOCRINE DISRUPTERS

We used to look for sex without fertility. Now we have fertility without sex.

Swinging Terns and Other Odd Tales:
The Estrogen Imposters

The environmental biologists were confused. "Why," they asked, "are all these terns laying six eggs at a time, instead of their usual three? Don't these birds know about the worldwide trend of decreased fertility?

The scientists were puzzled for good reason. They tell us that no plant or animal any place on this earth has escaped reproductive setbacks. And they mean *all* living things—whether dwelling on the plains of Africa or the tundra of the North Pole; whether Armani-clothed on Wall Street or loin cloth-covered in the bush; whether the smallest creature or the most enormous. So why not these birds? Why did they appear to be even *more* prolific than their ancestors?

They weren't! The terns resolved what was actually a male fertility dilemma with altered social behavior: *polygamy* and *communal living*! What the biologists discovered was that two female terns were sharing a nest with a single male.

But aren't we humans doing the same thing? Okay—so we don't usually share our nests and our lovers (well, maybe in the seventies!), but we do co-op our eggs and sperm. Sperm banks and borrowed eggs for implantation reflect our way of handling a similar problem.

> **Time for a QUICKIE**
>
> An Israeli law that barred women, except those undergoing infertility treatment, from donating their ova, will be replaced by a law that encourages such donations. The original law was instituted to prevent the sale of ova.

The adult human male has suffered a 50 percent decrease in both sperm count and quality over the past thirty years. There has been a sharp increase in testicular and prostate cancer. And the steady growth in the incidence of benign prostate enlargement sends forty thousand positive specimens to the laboratory every year.

The operation to relieve the symptoms of an enlarged prostate is the second-most commonly performed surgical procedure among American men.[1]

Unfortunately, it's an equal opportunity dilemma. PMS, fertility difficulties, endometriosis, breast cancer, and menopausal problems have been escalating in women at the speed of epidemics.

Why is this happening?

Endocrine disrupters, new to human existence, are the culprits.

The immune signal that transmits the *danger-afoot-so-let's-get-rid-of-it* message to your protecting cells does not seem to apply to these mischief-makers that surround us. Your macrophages and T cells simply don't always perceive endocrine disrupters as dangerous. Perhaps it's because they resemble "self." Perhaps it's because they are incredibly sneaky. Perhaps it's because there are so many of them. Perhaps it's because—well maybe we don't know enough to theorize *why,* just yet.

What are endocrine disrupters, anyway?

Endocrine disrupters are compounds cooked up in test tubes (or byproducts of these compounds), produced for daily industrial, agricultural, or domestic purposes.

They have estrogenic or other hormonally active properties which adversely affect the reproductive health of both women and men. The resulting disorders can include cancer development in hormonally sensitive tissues and structural alteration of reproductive organs.[2]

These unwelcome guests are found everywhere—in almost everything you swallow or use or touch *every single day*. They are released from plastics—furniture you sit on, clothes you wear, toys your baby plays with, plastic you wrap your food in, baggies you transport your vitamins in, eyeglasses on your face, the water bottle you store your water in, and water itself because of its chlorine content. They come from herbicides and insecticides sprayed on food you eat, parks you walk in, and the golf course you spend your weekends on. (Golf courses are the greatest consumers of agricultural chemicals.) They are even released from auto exhaust, filling the air, and then your lungs, with unnatural chemistry.

Unequivocal evidence validates that very many of these substances are present in our aquatic environment. They are found in surface waters and water sediments because of microbial breakdown of industrial surfactants, as in detergents or paints.[3]

Environmental contamination by endocrine-disrupting chemicals used as plasticizers have been shown to be emitted from plastic products.[4]

Sadly, we know from experiments with test animals that the negative effects show up in the grandchildren of those exposed. They can cause gene imprinting, resulting in a change of the gene expression.[5] DES exposure (explained later), if it occurs during critical periods of prenatal development, can affect reproductive performance over several generations.[6] Our mothers give us more to worry about than fat thighs!

Xenoestrogen is the name for an endocrine disrupter that is or emits a synthetic estrogen. (Xeno meaning "foreign.")

In wild animals abnormal sexual development has been associated with exposure to *mixtures* of endocrine disrupters.[7] Wildlife from ecosystems contaminated with these chemicals may display strange alterations or modifications. Some of these animals are not quite male or female, and they may even be both. Or neither. Scientists have been so confused, they keep repeating test after test, hoping to prove themselves wrong. No such luck! Here are some specific examples:

~ Alligators in Lake Apopka, Winter Garden, Florida, have anatomy that lies somewhere between that which is not quite male and not quite female. These reptiles have very low levels of testosterone.

~ Same-sex couples—female seagulls—are sharing nests together on Santa Barbara Island, off the coast of Los Angeles. On closer observation, the gulls are discovered to have both testes *and* ovaries.

~ Male sex organs of otters living in the lower Columbia River in Portland, Oregon, have been steadily decreasing in size, at measurements that correspond directly to the amount of pesticides and industrial chemicals found in their livers.

~ The masculinization of female mollusks exposed to an anti-fouling agent and the feminization of male fish exposed to estrogenic chemicals in waste matter from sewage-treatment plants has been documented, demonstrating physical sex reversal.[8]

~ Many of the remaining members of the endangered Florida panther population suffer from reproductive, endocrine, and immune-system defects, including congenital heart problems, abnormal sperm, low sperm density, and thyroid dysfunction.[9]

~ Male fish in polluted English rivers are producing a protein normally found only in fish eggs.[10]

~ A bird species feeding on contaminated salmon in the Great Lakes area is exhibiting mysterious behavioral changes. Adult bald eagles that migrate to this area and feed off the fish for more than two years are having problems producing viable offspring.

~ Humans living near the Great Lakes have polychlorinated biphenyl amounts significantly greater than the background level found in the water.

Polychlorinated biphenyls (PCBs) are a group of manufactured chemical compounds that were used widely as coolants and lubricants in transformers, capacitors, and other electrical equipment before they were banned in the US. It was found that PCBs build up in the environment and cause harmful effects.

Products containing PCBs include old fluorescent lighting fixtures, electrical appliances with PCB capacitors, and hydraulic fluids. They persist in the environment for long periods of time, and they are bioaccumulants. These compounds readily enter the lipid (fat) stores of plants and animals, thus easily and rapidly migrating into our food chain. This enables the bioaccumulation and biomagnification of the PCBs in our bodies.

PCBs keep piling up because they are retained in our tissues and are not degraded, placing a burden on metabolic processes.[11]

They may even initiate tumors.

Time for a
QUICKIE

Chemicals that disrupt endocrine function during critical stages of fetal development can produce profound reproductive alterations in both wildlife and humans. Of the tens of thousands of chemicals in existence, few have been tested for their ability to disrupt the endocrine system.

How Endocrine Disrupters Work

Endocrine disrupters work by mimicking normal substances, particularly the action of sex hormones. Because they masquerade with such conniving cunning, they slither into your estrogen receptor sites with ease— camping out in your brain and heart and skin and uterus and vagina—wherever receptor sites are located. But since the disrupters are not the real McCoy (the stuff you produce in your blood, organs, glands, and bones), your body can't use them effectively or efficiently. Worse, these alien hormones block the receptor-site doorways, preventing the real stuff from getting through.

These body wreckers affect your immune system cells by diminishing their ability to get rid of viral and bacterial toxins, allergens, and tumor antigens. And they interfere with *sexual function*.[12] Included in the long list of subversions is the fact that **they make testosterone less available but estrogen more so.**

AHA !

Why this is so critical to sexual function is one of the most important messages in this book.

Testosterone levels plummet, while estrogens are supercharging everywhere—in both males and females.

What about the argument that the amount of natural estrogen in your body is usually much greater than that of compounds that mimic estrogen? Does this mean we don't have to worry about these estrogen immitators, as some representatives of industry would have us believe? No! Most of your natural estrogen gets tied up—that is, it gets bound by cells—called sex-hormone-binding globulin (SHBG)—in your blood. But these particular cells are incapable of finding and binding estrogen mimics. This increases the effective dose of the mimics! (It is also one reason why testing your blood for estrogen is an ineffective measure for determining your estrogen needs.)

The estrogen receptor cells, however, bind to many compounds in addition to natural estrogen. These include phytoestrogens *and* xenoestrogens. For this reason, the estrogen receptor is sometimes called *promiscuous*.[13]

Because reproductive tissues readily respond to steroid hormones, they are particularly vulnerable to the effects of these compounds. Endocrine disrupters are increasingly implicated in:

~ infertility
~ menstrual irregularities
~ spontaneous abortions (miscarriages)
~ birth defects
~ endometriosis
~ breast cancer

And only a fraction of these chemicals has been adequately examined for toxicity or for synergistic effects due to multiple exposures.[14]

Of all the hormones we know, the estrogens are the most potent. One-tenth of a trillionth of a gram can bring about changes. You can get biological effects from estrogen at levels so low you cannot measure them by any analytical method.[15] It's like one salt crystal in an Olympic-size swimming pool.

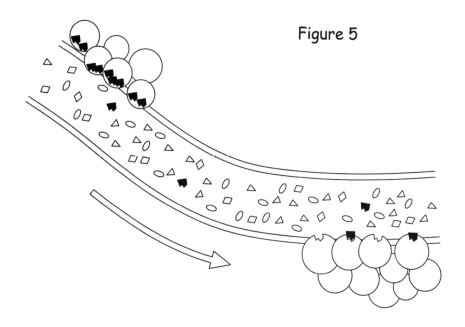

Figure 5

HORMONES:
FROM GLAND TO TARGET ORGAN

A small concentration of a hormone affects tissue at remote locations. The circles at the upper left represent cells produced in a gland. Hormones are represented by the black particles. The hormone enters the bloodstream and will only exit when it meets a matching receptor, as represented by circles at the lower right.

The First Endocrine Disrupter: DES

The first endocrine disrupter, diethylstilbestrol (DES), has been linked to cancer and changes in uterine structure that reduce or completely destroy reproductive ability. Until recently, little was known about the metabolism involved in the anomalies associated with DES. Knowledge garnered from modern molecular science has helped us to understand what has been happening.[16]

DES, a synthetic estrogen administered between 1945 and 1971 to help prevent miscarriages, was also given to mothers who were encouraged NOT to breastfeed, in attempts to dry up their milk. It carried with it, however, a high risk of vaginal cancer in girls whose mothers had DES treatment. (Turns out it was a useless and needless drug anyway.) Males whose mothers were exposed developed with undescended testicles. They may appear physically less masculine because an undescended testicle interrupts the production of testosterone, and they may also have decreased semen volume and sperm counts. Testicular cancer is the commonest malignancy in men aged fifteen to thirty-four, and its incidence is rising. The risk of testicular cancer increases tenfold among those born with undescended testes.[17] Exposed females may be masculinized (deeper voice, facial hair).[18] When prenatal hormone balances are atypical, powerful influences come into play.[19]

Estrogens block a signal, transmitted in the brain by the pituitary gland, called *luteinizing hormone*, which stimulates testosterone. Because DES blocks this process, which causes impotence, it has been referred to as a *chemical castrator*.[20]

These disrupters can also be responsible for neuro-behavioral deficits in children. And Mom doesn't even have to swallow DES anymore during pregnancy for these adverse effects. *Endocrinology Metabolism* reports that approximately one in three fetuses in the Los Angeles area is exposed to endocrine *environmental* contaminants in utero, the consequences of which remain unknown at this time.[21]

The incidence of abnormalities in the reproductive tracts of the daughters and sons of DES-treated women is much greater than the incidence of cancer. The US is the largest user of pesticides in the world.

The anti-estrogen tamoxifen, the most common therapy for breast cancer, has similar effects as DES. Very little is actually known about drugs that modulate estrogen receptors. Although tamoxifen doesn't stimulate breast tissue, it does increase the risk of endometrial cancer of a more virulent kind than usually seen. Minor side effects are hot flashes, fatigue, and depression.[22]

Time for a
QUICKIE

Even xenoestrogens that aren't strongly attracted to receptor sites can disturb endocrine systems when we're exposed to them in high concentrations.

HORMONES IN YOUR FOOD

ABSTRACT: In the absence of effective federal regulation, the meat industry uses hundreds of animal-feed additives, including antibiotics, tranquilizers, pesticides, animal drugs, artificial flavors, industrial wastes, and growth-promoting hormones, with little or no concern about the carcinogenic and other toxic effects of dietary residues. After decades of misleading assurances of the safety of diethylstilbestrol (DES) and its use as a growth-promoting animal-feed additive, the United States finally banned its use in 1979, some forty years after it was first shown to be carcinogenic. The meat industry then promptly switched to other carcinogenic additives, particularly the sex hormones estradiol, progesterone, and testosterone, which are implanted in the ears of more than 90 percent of commercially raised feedlot cattle. Residues of hormones are not detectable, since they cannot be differentiated from the same hormones produced by the body. The relationship between recently increasing cancer rates and lifetime exposure to dietary residues of these and other unlabeled carcinogenic feed additives is a matter of critical public health concern.

Epstein SS
The chemical jungle: today's beef industry.
International Journal of Health Services,
1990, 20(2):277-80.

Gone But Not Forgotten: DDT and PCBs

The organochlorine pesticide DDT, and its common breakdown product DDE, are also examples of endocrine disrupters with hormonal properties.[23] DDT is an androgen receptor antagonist, which means that it blocks the function of male hormones. (Recall that androgens are essential for libido in both men and women.) This disrupter can markedly interfere with erectile function and can persist after only a single dose.[24] DDE has been shown to delay puberty, reduce sex accessory gland size, and alter sex differentiation in test animals.[25]

Although now banned in the United States, these endocrine disrupters will remain in our environment for generations. DDT is still being used in the developing world, especially for mosquito control for reducing malaria. But DDT does not stay at home. It makes its way into the upper atmosphere and travels around the world with the wind. DDE is now surfacing in some Great Lakes fish and even in some Arctic species. Eggshell thinning from DDT was observed in bald eagles on the Columbia River in Washington State. Its half-life in temperate regions is fifty-nine years. (Half-life is the time it takes for 50 percent of the substance to disappear.)

Dioxin

Dioxins, another group of toxic chemical compounds created by industry, suppress progesterone secretion.

Thus these compounds can cause adverse reproductive effects, including early pregnancy failure.[26] (And you already know that anything that decreases progesterone can decrease libido.) After discovering its widespread harm by 1998, the World Health Organization drastically reduced the amount of dioxin it previously thought was safe in 1990.[27] Dioxins are released into the air from processes such as commercial or municipal waste incineration and from burning fuels (like wood, coal or oil). They can also be formed when household trash is burned, and from forest fires. Chlorine bleaching of pulp and paper and other industrial activities can create small quantities. Cigarette smoking can also be responsible for the emission of small amounts into the environment.

Like DDT and PCBs, dioxins are extremely persistent and will also be around for years. They may be transported long distances, so they, too, travel around the world (in less than eighty days). You swallow most of your dioxins with your food: Ninety-five percent comes from the animal fat on your plate. Smaller amounts come from the air you breathe and through skin absorption.[28]

Hormones and related synthetic chemicals, commonly used for birth control and treatment of certain hormonal disorders and cancers, have been turning up in our waterways.

DDT blocks testosterone.
PCBs imitate estrogen.
Dioxin suppresses progesterone.

Time for a
Q U I C K I E

There's no escape. DDT, dioxin, and PCBs can be found in the tissues of the blackfooted albatrol, far out in the middle of the Pacific Ocean, on Midway Island, as well as in marine mammals and in people living in remote Arctic regions.

In 1995, a neurotoxicology workgroup identified PCBs and dioxins as affecting nervous system function.[29] In addition to declining sperm counts,[30] endocrine disrupters may influence thyroid hormone metabolism by reducing their levels.[31,32] (PCBs are particularly noted for this action.)

Food is the major source for PCBs and dioxin. The accumulated amount of PCBs and dioxins found in toddlers was discovered to have come from dairy products.

Extracts of paper for household use was tested. Twenty different brands of kitchen rolls, nine made from recycled paper and the remainder from virgin paper, were obtained from retail shops. A marked estrogenic response was observed in nine of the extracts, seven of which were made from recycled paper and two from virgin paper. Recycled kitchen rolls contain bisphenol A and other xenoestrogens. Other types of food packaging may contain these same estrogenic substances.[33]

The use of recycled paper for the manufacture of food contact materials is widespread. The FDA has stated that contaminants in recycled paper intended for food packaging could be a risk to public health.[34]

Many additional studies confirm that chemicals with anti-androgenic properties have been detected in the environment, and that these chemicals affect the development or function of sex glands.[35] Twenty-five years of data from the Swedish Twin Registry failed to identify a genetic component to endometrial cancer and suggest that environmental factors play the largest role in terms of endometrial cancer risk, as reported in 1999 in the *International Journal of Cancer.*

Many compounds of plant origin with the ability to bind to the estrogen receptor have also been identified in the last decades.[36] **But don't confuse the xenoestrogens with the phytoestrogens.** Plant estrogens are short-lived. Pollutant xenoestrogens, like chemical Methuselahs, appear to live on, seemingly forever. Phytoestrogens are safe and protective, just as phytochemicals are beneficial. Too bad the longevity is not the other way around.

> The simple fact is, anything that interferes with your hormones interferes with your libido, interferes with the health of your reproductive organs, interferes with your energy levels, and even interferes with your mood.

The Ubiquitous Phthalates

Doom and gloom were predicted with the use of phthalates *more than forty years ago*. Now we know why. But it's still taking forever to ban their use. Phthalates are compounds used to make plastic more pliable. They are used in vinyl floors, food wraps, cosmetics, medical products, and toys. In spite of extensive and long-term use, most have not been adequately tested for toxicity.[37]

They are also commonly used in soap, shampoo, hair spray, and many types of nail polish. Phthalate has many industrial uses, as a solvent and vehicle for fragrances and cosmetic ingredients—substances that come in contact with your skin. (These chemicals *can* be absorbed through your skin.)[38] Polyvinyl chloride plastics made flexible with phthalates are used in a wide array of medical devices. They are used in "bendy" plastics such as blood bags and tubing. Hospitalized patients can be exposed to a high dose while receiving respiratory therapy or during hemodialysis, when they are more likely to be vulnerable to the potentially ill effects.[39]

The first national US report on human exposure to environmental chemicals, produced by the Centers for Disease Control and Prevention in Atlanta, Georgia, has shown surprisingly high levels of phthalates in our blood and urine. Human blood concentrations of organochlorines reach estrogenic levels.[40]

Phthalates are known to cause hormonal disruptions and fetal malformations. The US Consumer Product Safety

Council recommended that toy manufacturers stop using phthalates as softening agents in toys and teething rings, but it was a recommendation and not a ruling.

A first demonstration that phthalic acid binds to the estrogen receptor with high affinity and mimics the actions of the estrogen hormone was published in January 2001 in *Toxicology Letters*.[41] The phthalates cause malformations that appear to result from antagonism of androgens in utero.[42] (Here we go again—another disrupter disrupting our libido.) Dibutyl phthalate is an environmentally dangerous hormone that interferes in the pathways of testicular differentiation in male animals.[43]

A form of phthalate, bisphenol A, carries with it a long list of problems. This plastic has properties making it tremendously useful in many applications. It, too, is used in the packaging, storing, and preparation of foods and beverages, including water jugs, bottled beverages, baby food, and juice containers.

The release of bisphenol A from resin into saliva has aroused concern regarding exposure by dental treatment. Researchers found the substance in the saliva of patients one hour after a sealant was applied to their teeth. Leachable amounts from dental equipment are small, but it's another source of exposure, and a very direct one.[44]

Many food cans are lacquer-coated with a plastic lining. The food in some of these cans contain substantial amounts of bisphenol A. The plastic coating in a single can of peas has been shown to contain a disrupter that is 300 million times higher than the natural action of estradiol (the most potent form of estrogen).

Test animals exposed to bisphenol A not only had an overall earlier onset of puberty, but also an increased risk of obesity compared with unexposed animals.[45] Bisphenol A is structurally similar to DES, and can cause some of the same ill effects.

Now the researchers are telling us that estrogen tissues in humans that are targets for bisphenol A may be subject to greater exposure than the tissues of the test animals used for assessing estrogenicity of xenobiotics.[46]

On the very day I am writing this, May 10, 2001, the UK government's food watchdog announced that the seepage of "the estrogen-mimicking compound bisphenol A into canned food is widespread. Nearly two-thirds of canned food assessed by the Food Standards Agency's Committee on Toxicity including baked beans, tuna and fruit cocktail, were found to contain bisphenol A [in brands familiar to all of us in the US]. Animal research has shown that bisphenol A enlarges the size of the prostate gland in mice, advances the onset of puberty in females, and reduces fertility in rats."

The vagina is especially sensitive to the estrogenic actions of the xenoestrogen bisphenol A. Continuous exposure to microgram levels is sufficient for exerting estrogenic actions.

Estrogen Overload and Libido Loss

Do the scientists agree that the endocrine disrupters are affecting libido? You'd better believe it!

~ *Clinical Endocrinology Metabolism*:
    "The emerging adverse trends in human repro-
    ductive health and the ubiquitous presence of
    endocrine disrupters in the environment, support
    the hypothesis that disturbed sexual problems
    could be caused by this increased exposure to
    these environmental endocrine disrupters."[47]

~ Michael Rosenbaum, MD:
    "Sperm is down for the same reason that libido is
    down: free testosterone has declined, often the
    result of environmental estrogens going up."

~ Dr. Theo Colborn, editor of *Chemically Induced Alterations in Sexual and Functional Development*:
    "Xenoestrogens are persistent, additive, synergis-
    tic, and unpredictable. Their quantity over-rides
    their low-level emission. The hormones that tell
    your body what to do are getting too many mes-
    sages from xenoestrogens, turning systems on and
    off at the wrong time."[48]

~ Dr. Louis Guillette, Professor of Zoology, University
of Florida:
    "There is not an animal in the world that does not
    have sperm problems."[49]

~ David Feldman, MD, in *Estrogens from Plastics*:
  "New chemicals with endocrine disrupting potential continue to be discovered, unanticipated
  pathways of exposure continue to be found, and
  concern about the cumulative effects of these
  agents continues to grow."[50]

"When it's bad enough to scare us, it's bad. And when I
sit down and think about this, it scares me stiff," said
Charles Facemire, a Fish and Wildlife Service toxicolo-
gist in Atlanta who has investigated contaminants for
nearly twenty years.

Organochlorine pesticides are still widely used by farms
and households to kill insects and weeds—the very substances that mimic estrogen or inhibit testosterone. We
cannot overemphasize that because of the endocrine
disrupters:

  ~ too much estrogen pervades

  ~ progesterone is curtailed

  ~ androgens are blocked

  ~ thyroid hormone production is reduced

These are hormones that control sexuality.
They are our sexual messengers.

New World Disorders:
In Summary

As explained in chapter one, the female sexual response cycle is initiated by increased pelvic blood flow, vaginal lubrication, and clitoral and labial engorgement. These mechanisms occur through a combination of events. Physiological processes that interfere with these normal female sexual responses result in:

> ~ diminished sexual arousal

> ~ reduced libido

> ~ lack of vaginal lubrication

> ~ curtailed genital sensation

> ~ limited ability to achieve orgasm[51]

We have never had to deal with so huge a number of chemicals in any evolutionary span. The most menacing aspect is that the damage easily goes undetected, even to the knowledgeable. **And the entire world population has been exposed.**

We may be winning the fight over sexual hang-ups. But now we have to fight the battle of the disrupters. How do we deal with exposures that started about fifty years ago? We must think and act globally, but each of us must also act locally. Chapters seven and nine tell us how to do this.

"You sound like you have a terrible cold."

"I do. And every time I sneeze, I have an orgasm."

"Oh my! What are you taking for it?"

"Pepper."

Chapter Five

HORMONE HELPERS: DO THEY REALLY HELP?

What's six inches long, two inches wide, and drives women wild?
A bar of chocolate!

What's In a Name?
Hormones—Why We Need Them

T he word hormone stems from the Greek
hormaein, meaning *to excite*. As hormones jour-
ney through your body, many of them control
the actions of your organs and tissues. Some help cells
create protective "coats of armor." Others instruct molecular switches to turn on or off—including those that
arouse your sexual feelings. They may mandate immune
processes to grapple with invaders, and order receptors
to stoke fires that require more fuel. They can be responsible for glands inducing *differentiation*, prodding
a cell which appears to be able to turn into *anything*
during the fetal stage, to turn into *something very specific* years, even decades later—like those that are responsible for your sexual maturity.

Only certain cells of certain organs or tissues have their chemical receptors "tuned in" to respond to the effects of a particular hormone as it swims by. For example, your ovaries and adrenal glands secrete hormones that cause reactions in both your vagina and in your brain.

Figure 6

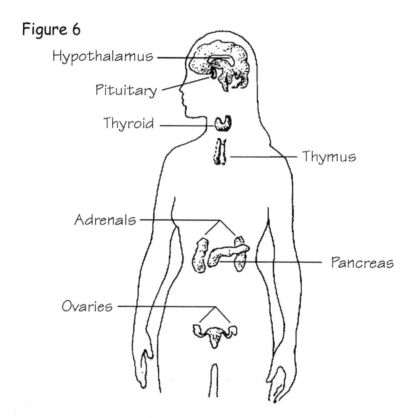

Hypothalamus

Pituitary

Thyroid

Thymus

Adrenals

Pancreas

Ovaries

Major Hormone-Producing Glands

Different types of hormone-secreting cells make up the endocrine system, influenced in part by the nervous system. The female and male sex hormones are referred to as steroids.

As demonstrated by figure 5 (page 94, chapter four), your body doesn't physically direct a hormone to a particular tissue or organ, but the hormone travels until it is recognized by a receptor shaped to fit it, in much the way pieces of a jigsaw puzzle fit together. In the case of the xenoestrogens (also described in chapter 4), these "estrogen imposters" are similar enough to fool receptor sites, encouraging them to be less selective and to have something of an "Open Door" policy—allowing these harmful compounds to enter without recognizing their dangerous difference.

It's amazing how few hormone molecules are required to produce a major effect! For those hormones secreted in comparatively higher amounts, there is only one hormone molecule for every fifty billion molecules in the fluid compartment of your blood. At the low end of the concentration scale, there may be one hundred times fewer hormone molecules for those produced in lesser quantities—one in every five zillion. That's five thousand billion!

Keep this in mind when you consider intervening by taking hormones from an outside source—for example, when undergoing hormone replacement therapy (HRT).

The multiple interrelationships between various hormones and other nutrients make the subject of female sexuality interesting—but also complex—and create a good deal of controversy in attempts to maintain optimal health.

Sex hormones are produced in your sex glands, in your adrenal glands, and in your brain. *Testosterone, estrogen*, and *progesterone* are the three principal sex hormones.

The word testosterone identifies the hormone made in the male *testes*. As indicated earlier, there's no such identity for the word estrogen! Again, this word comes from the Greek, meaning "producing frenzy." Coined in 1927, it has been suggested that the differences in terminology reflect the bias of the male researchers involved. If these men had known that estrogen is also essential for males—in fact, necessary for their very maleness—no doubt the hormone would have a different name.

Aside from the fact that both sexes create *both* hormones, there's another discrepancy involved in referring to estrogen and testosterone as strictly male and female. Testosterone is one hormone of a general class of hormones called *androgens*.

Androgens, taken as a group, include testosterone. Estrogen, unlike testosterone, but like androgen, is the name for the class of hormones consisting of several closely related substances associated with females. If this is starting to sound a little like a "who's-on-first?" routine, just be aware that it's a common practice to be loose with the jargon, even among the profesisonals.

Androgens contribute to muscle strength, appetite, a sense of well being, and sex drive for both men and women!

For total clarity, let's summarize:

> Testosterone is only one of a broad class of hormones, the androgens—the term used for the dominant male sex hormones. Estrogen—the term used for the dominant female sex hormones—refers to an entire class of female hormones. These may be estrone, estriol, or estradiol.

Confusion also abounds concerning the proper use of the term progesterone. Progesterone, or natural progesterone, refers to one specific hormone—the one manufactured by your adrenal glands and ovaries. Progesterone is natural; progestins are not. A natural hormone (found in humans or anywhere in nature) cannot be patented by a pharmaceutical company.

Progestins may also be referred to as progestens, progestogens (also spelled progestegins in the medical literature), gestagens, or progestational agents. *All progestins are synthetic hormones.* Only progesterone is the natural form, but—to confuse us further, even physicians misuse the nomenclature.

Time for a
QUICKIE

Rates of coitus and orgasm are unrelated to the changing levels of circulating hormones.

The Latest Hot Flashes on Hormone Replacement Therapy

Much emphasis has been placed on estrogen, and for good reason. Estrogen has myriad effects on your libido through your nervous system and sensory organs, which include the oil and sweat glands of your skin, key receptors for external sexual stimuli. Estrogens are also responsible for the action of the key cells and metabolism involved in the changes leading to vaginal lubrication, essential for pleasurable sexual experience.[1]

Some researchers make the assumption that the weak xenoestrogens in our environment are unable to compete with the powerful actions of our own estrogens. But too much research demonstrates that interactions between those we produce and environmental estrogens can promote sexual dysfunction and disease, as detailed in chapter four.[2]

Another important condition contributing to loss of libido involves changing hormonal patterns. For example, although poorly understood, it is well known that loss of desire is more common with premenstrual tension and just after giving birth. It also declines around the time of natural menopause. Add to that the number of women who have undergone surgical menopause (hysterectomy) in their twenties and thirties, and you can see how altered hormone ratios can have a huge impact. The usual therapy prescribed is the look-alike—yet dangerously different—*hormone replacement therapy.*

In a book about the prostate, Patrick C Walsh, MD, writes: "Ninety percent of men on hormone therapy lose sexual drive."[3] We know the same is true for women. It's an old adage: *You can't fool Mother Nature.* But ten million women a year are taking synthetic estrogen, the most prescribed drug for decades—until Viagra knocked it into second place. It still reaches ten million or more women annually!

As indicated earlier, contrary to what many women believe, synthetic HRT does *not* have any significant positive effects on sexuality.[4] Women who use oral estrogen have lower concentrations of bioavailable testosterone than nonusers—a major reason for their diminished libido.[5] (Bioavailable refers to the amount of a substance that is usable in your body.)

Furthermore, when we start to ingest a hormone, our cells send signals to each other. The message is: "Hey, we don't have to work so hard to produce any of this stuff any more." This causes your own endogenous supplies (your internal sources of estrogen) to begin to dwindle.

What makes matters worse is that estrogen therapy has little value other than temporary relief of symptoms, and even that benefit is not universal. Abundant research contesting the value of synthetic estrogens shows how we've been "taken in" when told HRT is safe and that it will relieve many of our health problems. Just the opposite is true, as the following examples show:

~ In opposition to popular press reports, results from the largest and longest studies to date indicate that estrogen does *not* have any therapeutic role in the treatment of Alzheimer's disease. The doctors involved in the research stated: "The findings are a reminder that there is no simple translation from laboratory experiments to clinical application."[6,7]

~ Hormone replacement is highly associated with hysterectomy, since 58.7 percent of those who have undergone hysterectomy were using hormone replacement therapy compared with only 19.6 percent of women who had not undergone hysterectomy.

~ A cross-sectional study in Germany indicates that use of HRT does *not* protect against osteoarthritis.[8]

~ More adverse cardiovascular events were reported in women on estrogen therapy than in control groups. (Those in the control group were on a placebo, an inert pill with no active ingredients). The researchers involved concluded that the recommendation of postmenopausal therapy as a method of preventing cardiovascular diseases is *not* justified at this time.[9]

~ HRT reduces the sensitivity of mammographic screening, increasing the risks of both false-negative and false-positive results.[10] The reason that mammograms are less accurate in women who use hormone replacement therapy than in nonusers is that estrogen makes breast tissue thicker, so the mammogram can't read through.[11]

~ There is a significant subgroup of women whose sexual difficulties respond initially to HRT but who subsequently revert to their initial problems, especially when the difficulty has been loss of libido. Sexual difficulties remain unresponsive for women on HRT (unless they take testosterone).[12]

~ Even *low-potency* estrogen formulations increase the relative risk of endometrial cancer to the degree that close surveillance of those on the therapy is essential.[13]

Why ten million women agree to swallow a drug that requires medical monitoring is difficult to understand, particularly when there are safe alternatives.

~ Administering progestin (synthetic progesterone) along with estrogen may have significant negative consequences for the development of cardiovascular disease and osteoporosis.[14]

~ While the role of estrogen in breast cancer has long been recognized, new research findings now suggest that this hormone may also contribute to the development of non-small cell lung cancer.[15]

~ Your doctor may tell you that estrogen slows bone loss. The truth is that once we reach age seventy-five, women who have been on estrogen therapy have as much chance of hip fracture as those women who have never been on the therapy.

~ Osteoarthritic knee problems *increase* with bone density and current use of hormone replacement therapy.[16]

~ It may also fly in the face of traditional thinking that women with *lower* amounts of bone mineral density appear to have a major health advantage because they are at the *lowest* risk for breast cancer. Bone mineral density represents a composite measure of exposure to many different factors throughout one's lifetime, including HRT and the environment.[17]

~ Women taking HRT after going through menopause could face an increased risk of blood clots. In three separate studies published in the medical journal *Lancet*, doctors reported HRT users were two to four times more likely to develop blood clots in the leg and lungs.

~ Changing levels of thyroid hormone, rather than estrogen deficiency, may be responsible for some women's menopausal woes. *Menopause and thyroid disease share many markers.* This may be one reason for HRT failure! Undiagnosed thyroid disease is twice as prevalent in the US as previously suspected.

Thirteen million Americans have thyroid disease but half don't know it.[18]

~ Estrogen treatment (either for oral contraception or hormone therapy) suppresses DHEA (dehydroepiandrosterone) concentrations in both premenopausal and postmenopausal women.[19] DHEA is a very important adrenal hormone found in young people, and it is associated with vitality and youthfulness.

Adding progestins increases the problems:

~ Using progestin as an adjunct to HRT, substantially increases the risk of developing breast cancer. Even giving progestins to women who no longer have a uterus is not advisable because of the added breast-cancer risk.[20]

~ Progestins combined with estrogen therapy worsen mood, and have no influence on sleep or libido.[21]

Ten things men understand about female sexuality:

1.
2.
3.
4.
5.
6.
7.
8.
9.
10.

~ When a woman agrees to have her hormones manipulated with drugs, she becomes the passive recipient of her doctor's choice of treatment. The doctor may or may not explain that the following measures must be taken because of the risks involved:

(1) Annual tests for blood evaluation are needed.

(2) Breasts have to be examined on a regular basis.

(3) Periodic biopsies for early detection of pre-malignant or malignant endometrial changes become indispensable. (Endometrium refers to the lining of the uterus.) This is done via pap smears, which can be invasive.

These procedures are mandatory because of the high probability of negative side effects caused by hormone replacement therapy.

Using natural progesterone, on the other hand, may have an overall beneficial effect. One study, cited in my book, *Hormone Replacement Therapy—Yes or No: How to Make an Informed Decision,* demonstrates how the application of natural progesterone directly on the breast itself actually reduces the proliferation of cancer cells.[22]

There is a vast difference between hormones that are natural (or identical to what you produce in your body) and those we create or manipulate in test tubes.

Summary of Side Effects of Synthetic Estrogen Hormone Replacement Therapy

Abdominal cramps
Amenorrhea (no periods)
Bloating
Cystitis-like syndromes
Depression
Elevated blood pressure
Endometrial cancer
Gallbladder disease
Hair loss
High cholesterol
Jaundice
Nausea and vomiting
Prolonged vaginal bleeding
Reduced carbohydrate tolerance
Reduced glucose tolerance
Skin rashes
Thrombophlebitis (inflammation
     of a vein associated with
     clot formation)
Undesirable weight gain or loss
Lung tumor growth
Vaginal candidiasis

Kamen B. *Hormone Replacement Therapy—Yes or No: How to Make an Informed Decision.* Nutrition Encounter, Novato, CA, p 104.[23]

Healthy-User Syndrome

Articles on the hazards of postmenopausal HRT are beginning to appear in medical journals. They emphasize that healthy profiles among users may inflate the apparent benefit of treatment.[24] Note these comments about healthy-user syndrome published in *New England Journal of Medicine*, a most prestigious journal:

> Studies have reported reduced mortality among women taking hormones, but many have had flaws that limit firm conclusions. Women for whom estrogen is prescribed are often healthier initially, and those who continue to take hormones tend to be free of disease. For example, women in whom cancer is diagnosed often stop taking hormones. Thus, lower mortality among hormone users may be attributed erroneously to the hormone itself. Expected mortality advantages are, in part, offset by the risk of breast cancer.

> Women discontinue hormone use when symptoms of a fatal disease develop. This must reflect the selection of healthy women for estrogen therapy, a potential "healthy-user" effect.[25]

The British Medical Journal discusses the fact that pooled data of clinical trials "do not support the notion that postmenopausal hormone therapy prevents cardiovascular events." These researchers looked at 22 trials involving 4,124 women. They conclude:

> There have been hundreds of trials studying the impact of hormones on various physiological phenomena, laboratory values, osteoporosis, symptoms, or various health problems, but few fully report adverse effects.

> In many trials, women were lost to follow up, and even more trials gave no data on reasons or numbers of dropouts or losses. Most trials had selected only healthy women. Therefore, the effects of postmenopausal therapy on sick women cannot be inferred from these results.

> Carcinogenic effects or slow tumor promotion may take years or decades to show up. (These studies were not long-term.) Studies failed to report adverse effects fully, if at all.[26]

And from the *American Jouranl of Epidemiology:*

> Women who elect to use ERT (estrogen replacement therapy) have a better cardiovascular risk factor profile **prior** to the use of ERT than do women who subsequently do not use this treatment during menopause, which supports the hypothesis that part of the apparent benefit associated with the use of ERT is due to pre-existing characteristics of women who use ERT. Beware of the "healthy-user" syndrome.[27]

It has been shown that when people know they are part of a study, they begin to take better care of themselves. They may begin eating better or exercising more. Such changes alone could account for the apparent benefits.

Check out www.bettykamen.com for more information and updates on the subject.

Time for a QUICKIE

The average number of times people have sex in Britain has risen recently from 70 to 77 times a year. Men purchase most of the condoms, the most frequently used contraception in the UK.

Testosterone And Other Androgens For Women

Although libido does not increase with estrogen therapy, it may be improved with *testosterone* therapy.[28]

The job of producing testosterone in women is split evenly between the ovaries and the adrenal glands, and it is produced *throughout your life.*[29,30] But the levels do go down the drain considerably with menopause.

Female test animals receiving testosterone show an increased preference for sexually active males than those given estrogen.[31]

When women complain of fatigue, low libido, and diminished well being, symptoms are frequently attributed to psychosocial and environmental factors. When there is low circulating testosterone, replacement with this hormone may result in significant improvement.[32]

Again, the predominant symptom in women with androgen deficiency is loss of sexual desire. This is quite apparent after surgical menopause.[33]

T i m e   f o r   a
Q U I C K I E

Women produce 3/10ths of one milligram of testosterone daily. Men, more than 20 times as much—or about 7 mgs per day.

Testosterone Levels Fluctuate Morning, Noon, and Night, Literally

~ Testosterone in the bloodstream is highest in the morning just after you wake up, and can fall significantly throughout the day.

~ Levels change over periods of minutes and hours in response to social stimuli.[34]

~ Average testosterone levels are correlated with masturbation frequency, but not with sex involving a partner.

~ An association between testosterone and lifestyle is evident (i.e., full-time jobs or housewife duties tend to decrease the production.)[35]

~ Sexually active young female teenagers have higher testosterone levels than their less sexually busy female peers.[36]

~ Female trial lawyers have testosterone levels higher than non-trial female lawyers.[37] (Of course we don't know yet which is the cause and which the effect.)

Adipose (fat) tissue is one of the sites where andros-tenedione, a precursor for the production of testoster-one, gets converted to estrogen. This, plus other meta-bolic alterations, causes greater than normal amounts of estrogen to be available in overweight women. So not only do the overeaters have more estrogen, they also have less testosterone.[38] There goes the libido.[39]

Sexual activity affects testosterone levels more than initial testosterone levels affect sexual activity.[40]

Levels of hormones produced during the different phases of the menstrual cycle provide further evidence of the importance of androgen in women's sexuality. Andro-gen levels are higher at times of greater sexual desire. The relationship between menstrual cycle phases and sexuality is very clear. This is not so for the phases of the cycle that produce various mood changes.[41]

Time for a
QUICKIE

Hormones are the necessary—but not the only—factors to maintain a satisfying li-bido.

How Estrogen Depletes Testosterone

Testosterone is carried in the blood, most of it attached to a protein known as "sex hormone binding globulin," or SHBG. Only a small amount is unattached, or "free" to produce its effects on tissues. Both testosterone and estrogen are carried on the same protein. Estrogen stimulates the production of more SHBG, which then binds up still more testosterone, leaving less testosterone "free" to work on cells.

That's why taking extra estrogen ties up a little more of whatever testosterone we may still have, causing testosterone deficiency.

Recall that the consumption of alcohol is associated with elevated sexual interest. This effect may be due to known alcohol-mediated testosterone elevations.[42] Isn't it amazing how the puzzle pieces fit together when we have enough information to understand *why* some of these physiological events occur?

Androgens may be critical for the maintenance of optimal levels of sexual functioning in postmenopausal women, too.[43] Not unlike other hormone production, the little glands that churn out testosterone will power back their assembly line output as we age—especially when health is not optimal. So if there is a critical reduction in ovarian testosterone at the time of menopause, this is sometimes associated with a syndrome of specific changes in sexual desire and sexual response.

Estrogen replacement could exacerbate the symptoms of androgen loss. Postmenopausal women who use oral estrogen have lower concentrations of bioavailable testosterone.

Okinawans have the longest disability-free life expectancy. Hormones decline as Okinawans age, as with all other populations, but they decline more slowly, especially when compared with North Americans. According to *The Okinawan Program* (Clarkson Potter Books, 2001), Okinawans are also more active in the bedroom. In any case, they seem to preserve their testosterone levels much longer than we do. The authors attribute this to their superior diet.

We know that in low-cancer-risk Asian populations, serum levels of testosterone and estrogen have been found to be 20 to 50 percent lower than in Western women. There's no discrepancy here. There is a level above and below which problems unfold.

Now the downside of testosterone therapy:

There are important reasons why testosterone hormone therapy is *not* the way to go! Testosterone, when administered exogenously (from an external source), can produce serious consequences.

Testosterone is a possible pathogenic cofactor in endometrial cancer, as recently reported by the European Society of Human Reproduction and Embryology. All of the women in a study group had undergone hysterectomy and ovariectomy for endometrial cancer or for benign gynecologic conditions. *It was determined that testosterone was the only hormone that was "significantly higher" in patients with endometrial cancer.*

No studies have been done on the long-term effects of offering women testosterone, either to swallow, to inject, or to apply with a patch. Literature documenting the benefits and safety of testosterone replacement is scant.

Not only is our understanding of its actions in women incomplete, but there is no consensus as to what constitutes either biochemical or clinical deficiency. The focus of the limited research on testosterone replacement has been on sexuality—sexual desire.[44] Based on the few studies that have been done, plus the observations of clinicians, plus experience with other exogenous hormones, we can be pretty certain that testosterone replacement (that is, methyltestosterone) is not without serious risk.

And here are the specific problems we know about:

~ Oral doses of methyltestosterone (synthetic testosterone) could have a masculinizing effect.

~ Women treated with testosterone need to be monitored for increased facial oiliness, acne, hirsutism (abnormal hairiness), and alopecia (baldness, loss of hair).[45] The side effects of hirsutism are dose-related.[46]

~ Some forms of testosterone initiate hepatic (liver) or lipid (fat) imbalances.[47]

~ Recent studies provide strong evidence that the risk of developing breast cancer in postmenopausal women is increased by high serum levels of testosterone and estradiol.[48]

~ Supplementary testosterone stimulates red blood-cell production in bone marrow. Those with certain forms of heart disease and older people may have more narrow blood vessels. If the blood becomes "too thick," it could put these people at risk for potential heart attack or stroke.[49]

~ Testosterone has an anticoagulant effect. People taking an anticoagulant (such as Coumadin) need to be aware that adding testosterone can further thin out their blood.

The current body of evidence does not support the routine addition of androgens to postmenopausal hormone therapy.[50]

Hormones and Menopause

There is little agreement among physicians regarding the direct effect of estrogens on sexual behavior at menopause. They do agree, however, that sexual life is not just a matter of the ebb and tide of hormones.[51] Many recognize that psychological, social, and cultural influences are of prominent importance. The xenoestrogen debacle doesn't seem to have "caught on" just yet; most doctors neglect to mention the significance of their accumulation over the years in older people, and how this can decrease libido.

Menopause is confirmed after twelve months of amenorrhoea (the time that your periods stop) resulting from your ovaries scaling down its business. The average age of US women at menopause is fifty-one years. Perimenopause, a time when the pace of hormone production in your ovaries begins to slow down, precedes final menstruation by several years. The transition to menopause is not well understood from a biological standpoint.[52] But just ask the women—they'll tell you hot flashes begin in the perimenopausal years. They don't really care why. They just want them to go away. Theoretically, they should also experience increased libido because their supply of androgens is not subjected to annihilation as much as estrogen.

But the investigators continue to explore the exact relationship between sexual function and changes in hormonal status during menopause. Women for whom progestins had been prescribed should know that their use contributes to vaginal dryness and dyspareunia (recall that this is vaginal pain during intercourse).[53] To remedy this discomfort requires restoration of vaginal cells, pH, and blood flow. The approach described in chapter nine is the best solution we have ever discovered for accomplishing this goal.

Time for a QUICKIE

Healthful guidelines for the management of impotence are commonly forgotten, and just as sildenafil (Viagra) is considered an easy solution, so is estrogen. Of course, these measures never address the causes of the problems, or the serious side effects of these drugs.

Estrogen, because it is the hormone associated with female reproduction, is given first consideration in treating complaints of dysfunction, especially dyspareunia. However, as already stated, simply restoring some, or all, of the estrogen of the premenopausal years does not lead to improvement in overall sexual functioning. Decreased libido is often still present in situations that appear to be anatomically satisfactory.[54]

Loss of estrogens and—specifically—of androgens deprives female libido of major biological fuel. But the biological losses can be more than compensated for by so many other factors, as indicated throughout these chapters.[55]

Oxytocin and Female Sexuality

Many animal studies suggest that the hormone oxyto-cin initiates a variety of reproductive behaviors, includ-ing sexual arousal, orgasm, and even birthing and spe-cific maternal behaviors such as breastfeeding and bond-ing between mother and infant. These actions are ap-parently facilitated by the "priming" effect on certain cells by sex and steroid hormones. *Oxytocin has a po-tential aphrodisiac or prosexual effect on women.*[56] More on oxytocin in chapter ten.

The Pros of Prolactin

Prolactin is a multifunctional hormone closely related to growth hormone. It helps the ovarian structures that secrete progesterone, the "pregnancy" hormone. *Proges-terone enhances female libido.* Prolactin is another marker of sexual arousal and orgasm.[57]

The prolactin receptor is also involved with immune processes. The functions of this hormone demonstrate how various metabolic pathways are related—includ-ing those responsible for our sexuality.

Eighty percent of women with too much prolactin have reduced sexual drive and inability to reach orgasm. The underlying mechanisms are as yet unknown. The initial symptoms are menstrual disorders. Most sexual disor-ders in both sexes regress after plasma prolactin levels return to normal.[58]

What Happens When You Eat Hormones?

Meat, fish, and even fruits and vegetables contain all the hormones and enzymes used to regulate the life processes of these foods when they were living organisms— before they became your food. If their blend of chemical signals suddenly becomes mixed with *your* hormones and enzymes, the result would be disastrous. It would be like trying to run a Mac program on a PC. So immediately after hormones are digested in your small intestines, they are passed through your liver, which helps rid your body of these unnecessary hormones.

One of your liver's most important jobs is to break down foreign hormones or keep them out of your bloodstream by returning them to your digestive tract.

There's an interesting design feature here. Your liver returns the unwanted hormones to your digestive tract at the entrance to your small intestines, where they could get reabsorbed! It's like placing the sewage outlet upriver from where the town gets its drinking water. Did nature miss something at this juncture? No! This method of disposal works because the hormones, *first time around*, are converted by your liver into water-soluble forms. They now bind with other substances, making them difficult to get absorbed through your intestines the second time around.

In fact, the materials that cause the hormones to return to your digestive tract to make them able to be excreted, may also act on newly ingested hormones on their first pass through your intestines, so some ingested hormones don't get absorbed even once. This process is called *first-pass liver removal.*

These reactions are fine if your only outside hormone sources came from natural foods. But you are also affected by the xenoestrogens that entered our food chain —stressing this conversion system to the hilt. (Recall our sensitivity to very small quantities of hormones.)

Among the unwelcome characteristics of hormone-like pollutants is their persistence in the environment and their ability to accumulate and to *biomagnify* in individual food chains. Many experts believe these compounds are associated with the increased incidence of breast cancer and other estrogen-related cancers in women due to increased proliferation of breast epithelial cells.[59] And you already know about their effects on libido!

First-pass liver removal is also responsible for the extreme variations women have with hormone replacement therapy prescriptions. The doctor doesn't really know just how effective or ineffective your first-pass detoxifying liver responses will be. Your personal reactions are more significant than the not-so-accurate hormone tests currently available. (You will be hearing more about the failings of saliva tests in the near future.)

How natural foods affect your sexuality (and they do!) is explored in chapter seven.

Oral Contraception (the Pill) and Its Hormonal Influence

Most women agree that men should share contraception as well as conception. But for too long oral pills swallowed by women have been seen as synonymous with contraception in general, helping to maintain ignorance of alternative methods.

An article in *Lancet* summarizes the situation:

> Despite calls for increased involvement of men in contraception, only the century-old methods of withdrawal and the condom remain available.

> As such, the gulf between these and the steadily improving range of female methods continues to widen. Although it has been doubted that women would trust men to use regular contraception, there in fact seems to be considerable enthusiasm for the burden of contraception to be more evenly shared.

> Even after the introduction of combined oral contraceptives brought about the revolution of sex without fear of pregnancy forty years ago, there is still demonstrable unmet need.[60]

Oral contraceptives have a negative effect on mood and behavior in many women, inducing depression and loss of libido.[61] On the plus side, oral contraceptives reduce acne because they lower the production of adrenal and ovarian androgens.[62]

So there you are with the fear of pregnancy gone and a gorgeous complexion—but no sex drive! (See chapter seven for safer ways to get your skin to glow and look youthful.)

More seriously, note these side effects that come along for the ride with oral contraceptives:

~ Major risks are cardiovascular problems.[63]

~ Its use is a well-established acquired risk factor for thrombosis.[64,65] A thrombus, or blood clot, is abnormal, as opposed to one that forms to prevent bleeding. When blood clots form within an artery, it may eventually block the artery, preventing blood and oxygen from reaching the organ or tissues it services. This is *not* what we want in our genital areas! (Or anyplace in our body!)

~ Risks of malignant-type fatal viruses are increased in women on oral contraceptives.[66]

~ An enhanced risk for breast cancer was found in women older than forty-five years of age who had been using oral contraceptives for more than five years.[67,68]

~ The most frequent negative interactions of oral contraceptives occur with antibiotics or anticonvulsants.[69,70]

~ Oral contraceptives increase blood pressure and tri-glycerides, dose-related: the higher the hormone levels of the contraceptive drug, the greater the increases. The drug also lowers levels of carotenoids (protective agents found in vegetables of deep color and in palm oil tocotrienols).[71]

~ Studies indicate an increase in Lupus with the use of oral contraceptives.[72]

~ Once you pass age forty, you are at greater risk for serious side effects from the Pill.[73]

~ Long-term use of hormonal contraceptives can accelerate the progression of periodontal disease.[74]

~ On average, it takes from one to two months longer to conceive once going off the Pill than it does for women who have not been on the Pill.

~ Oral contraception is contraindicated in women who have varicose veins, clots in veins (frequently in the leg), any form of heart disease, hepatitis or other liver disease, heavy smokers (twenty or more cigarettes a day), women who are breastfeeding or who have given birth within six weeks, any cancer of the reproductive organs, hypertension, or diabetes.

Sexual activity ironically decreases in those on birth control pills.

Hormones and Aging

It's not all bad news: not every gland shows a decline in hormone production with aging. Thyroid hormones usually remain unchanged, and the activities of the hypothalamic-pituitary-adrenal axis seem to be increased.[75] (These glands get Oscars for their supporting roles in sexual excitation.)

Granted, aging in general produces changes in our sex organs, in the production of hormones, in the strength of the sexual urge, and in other physiologic sexual responses. But our sexual interests and thoughts do *not* disappear.

Having a partner, thinking sexual thoughts, and retaining youthful attitudes are important elements of sexuality at any age.

All authorities agree that regular sexual activity is the essential factor in maintaining capacity and performance for both men and women. Those who struggle with sex problems should know there are solutions, and should seek help to overcome them.[76]

Hormonal Highs and Lows

It's no easy task to get an accurate reading of the hormone levels floating through your body. Perhaps some day medical science will develop equipment sensitive enough to accurately measure these infinitesimal amounts. To confound the problem, quantities may vary with the time of day. Morning and evening salivary hormone concentrations may differ, and all kinds of changes occur during the menstrual cycle.[77] Some hormone levels go up or down depending on social interaction as well as sexual intercourse. Sometimes the hormone will hide in cells (as is the case for estrogen concealed in fat cells), and because of nutrient deficiencies (in this case, lack of vitamin E), the hormones may not get released into the blood.

Seasonal changes and nutrient intake come into play, too. Add to this the fact that synthetic testosterone cannot be measured.

So neither a blood test or a saliva test can accurately reveal what is really going on.

In Summary

Too many people are getting prescriptions for health-destroying hormone therapy based on inaccurate evaluations. If your physician recommends hormone therapy, ask about the side effects so that you can make an informed decision concerning the risk-benefit equation involved. And it's always a good idea to get a second opinion.

Keep in mind that bias in medicine may be hazardous to your libido (and to your health)!

Want a quickie?   As opposed to what?

Chapter Six

WAM, BAM, THANK YOU, YAM

A young man asked his ladylove, "Am I the first?"
She answered, "Why does everyone always ask me that?"

Estrogen Dominance

The ill effects of estrogen dominance in the body range from bloat to weight gain to depression to *loss of libido* to life-threatening cancer. If you are swallowing or "patching" a hormone under strict doctor's orders, hopefully you are doing so only as a temporary measure until natural alternatives "kick in." *My attitude against the use of any exogenous hormone remains fixed.* But there is one exception: the application of a cream containing a very low dose of progesterone, combined with Mexican yam extract and specific tried-and-true herbs.

The xenoestrogens described in chapter four contribute to a problem referred to as "estrogen dominance," creating an imbalance between estrogen and progesterone.

This specially formulated progesterone cream, which helps to normalize the ratio, has become a necessity in today's world.

Estrogen and progesterone are in competition with each other. In the presence of enough progesterone, estrogen is displaced in receptor cells, canceling any effect that may be caused by an estrogen overload. But if progesterone levels are low, or if estrogen is excessively high, estrogen "dominates," a description coined by John Lee, MD.

Using very specific herbs helps your body to naturally produce its own quota of progesterone. The herbs may also act as phytohormones, filling receptor sites with their natural constituents—literally evicting the undesirable toxic xenoestrogen substances. This, in turn, helps to prevent estrogen dominance.

But aren't doctors now adding progesterone to hormone replacement prescriptions? No! They usully add *progestins*, the synthetic variety. Critical differences between natural progesterone and synthetic progestins are often misunderstood. As noted in chapter five, many

---

Time for a
QUICKIE

Studies indicate a strong association between vaginal douching and an increased risk of pelvic inflammatory disease, bacterial vaginosis, and ectopic pregnancy.

physicians even get the vocabulary wrong, referring to progestins as progesterone. The two are as different as day and night.[1]

Time for a QUICKIE

The strongest predictor for the use of hormone replacement therapy in postmenopausal women is sociodemographic, not clinical.

The addition of progestins to estrogen therapy exacerbates problems. It not only worsens mood and fails to influence sleep or libido as originally thought,[2] but it increases the risk of breast cancer. Yes, adding progestins to estrogen *increases the risk of breast cancer relative to the use of estrogen alone.* For every five years that a woman takes estrogen, her risk of breast cancer goes up six percent. But for every five years that she uses the more commonplace combination of estrogen and progestin, her risk jumps twenty-four percent.[3,4] The evidence that progestins are *mitogenic*—causing unwanted and hazardous increases in the number of cells in breast tissue—grows every day.[5]

Among 121,700 American nurses participating in an extensive ongoing study, deaths from breast cancer increased by 45 percent in women currently taking postmenopausal hormones for five years or more.[6] The risk of cardiovascular disease associated with oral progestins increased significantly, and so did venous thromboembolism (inflammation of a vein associated with clot formation).[7,8]

EXCESS ESTROGEN EFFECTS	NATURAL PROGESTERONE
creates endometrium problems	maintains endometrium integrity
stimulates breast-cell growth	protects against breast fibroids
increases body fat	helps use fat for energy
increases salt & fluid retention	works as a natural diuretic
creates depression & headaches	functions as natural antidepressant
interferes with thyroid hormone	facilitates thyroid hormone action
can cause excessive blood clotting	normalizes blood clotting
decreases libido	restores libido
impairs blood sugar control	normalizes blood sugar levels
causes loss of zinc	normalizes zinc levels
retains copper	normalizes copper levels
reduces oxygen levels in all cells	restores proper cell oxygen levels
increases risk of endometrial cancer	helps prevent endometrial cancer
increases risk of breast cancer	helps prevent breast cancer
slightly restrains bone building	may stimulate bone building

Both estrogen and progesterone are necessary and important. These effects refer to excess estrogen and to a balanced ratio of progesterone. When the ratios are normal, your natural estrogen can also reverse depression. And if progesterone is in excess (just as with excess estrogen) it can also cause depression and fatigue.

The Dynamic Duo: Progesterone and Herbs

The use of progesterone, the natural stuff, improves mood, can help to prevent breast cancer, and plays a critical role in sexuality.[9] It has a variety of diverse benefits, from your brain to your uterus.[10] In this age of pervasive heart disease, it's also good to know that progesterone protects against cardiovascular problems. You can see why it is so important for your health *and* your sex life.

A compelling study showed that transdermal progesterone significantly increased breast cell progesterone levels when applied directly to the breast. (Transdermal preparations are applied to your skin.) The increased progesterone in the breast decreased breast cell proliferation. That's just the effect we want in the face of breast cancer!

This study also demonstrated that topically applied progesterone is well absorbed, and can reduce the risk of breast cancer. Another intriguing outcome of this research was that the progesterone didn't show up in the blood plasma of the patients in the study, but there was no question that it was certainly present and on active duty! This is another indication of the inaccuracy of using blood tests to determine hormone levels.[11]

Caveat: Synthetic progestins should not be used interchangeably with natural progesterone.

Wam, Bam, Thank You, Yam

The Mexican wild yam extract comes from a tuber known to have progesterone-like qualities. Supplemental *natural progesterone* is usually made from this very extract—manipulated in the laboratory to be the precise equivalent of human progesterone. Since it is molecularly identical to the hormone you make in your ovaries and adrenals, the FDA allows the vendor to label the ingredient *progesterone*—an indication that it is the "real" thing, as opposed to progestin, which is synthetic and does not have the exact molecular configuration.

Although high doses (especially if synthetic, as in birth control pills) reduce sexual desire, low doses of natural progesterone do just the opposite. So you don't want to take more than is necessary, even if the progesterone is natural. If you choose the right low-dose product, the exogenous progesterone won't cause any abnormal reactions. Like most carefully formulated natural products, the herbs added to the cream should function *adaptogenically*. This means they help your body "pull" toward the normal. Adaptogens assist in correcting whatever is out of balance, rather than forcing a physiological parameter in a particular direction, as a drug or a high amount of hormone will do.

The most important aspect of an adaptogen is that it is rarely found in nature as an isolated element. More likely, an adaptogen is a complex substance, just as your body is an intricate chemical factory, carrying out a multitude of highly elaborate chemical transformations.

Unlike drugs, adaptogens:

> ~ do not continue their action when no longer
>   needed
> ~ do not require prescriptions
> ~ are user-friendly
> ~ are nontoxic
> ~ are inexpensive
> ~ are effective against a very wide variety
>   of disorders
> ~ enhance ability to cope with stress
>   (whether physical, emotional, or
>   chemical)
> ~ are not habit-forming

Because we don't fully understand every nuance and subtlety of our life processes—certainly not enough to manufacture products to keep us in optimal health—nature's adaptogenic substances are a requirement.

This is especially true in light of our efforts to combat our current toxic environment. Interestingly, many of these herbs have been used for millennia, and age-old wisdom has demonstrated their effectiveness in helping people prevent disease and stay healthy.

My book, *Hormone Replacement Therapy—Yes or No: How to Make an Informed Decision*, details exactly why the use of a topically applied cream with herbs works so well. The ingredients appear to enhance progesterone activity in a positive way. This phenomenon is known as *synergy*.

A few examples of herbs used to augment the effectiveness of the progesterone and the Mexican wild yam extract are:

~ Siberian ginseng (Eleutherococcus
      senticosus)
~ black cohosh (Cimicifuga racemosa)
~ burdock root
~ dong quai (Angelica sinensis)
~ chaste berries (Agnus castus)
~ chamomile

Some of these herbs contain substances referred to as *phytohormones*. They can improve overall health as well as reduce PMS and menopausal symptoms. They are generally gentle on your body for two reasons:

1. They are absorbed more slowly than single chemical extracts or synthetic drugs.

2. Their constituents have multiple ingredients which are often counterbalancing to the active components in that herb.

The complex nature of herbal medicines also explains their ability to have self-regulating effects on your body. These particular herbs have proved to be extraordinarily safe and effective.

Aloe vera and seed or nut oils may be added to the cream formula to increase absorption. The cream must also have protective agents to prevent the natural ingredients from developing rancidity and creating free radicals. A well-formulated product will contain the least amount and the least obtrusive of these preservatives, but they are a necessity (unless you want to do the extracting, mixing, and formulating in your bathroom sink).

As for the wild yam extract, it isn't just any old yam root that's used. The yam must contain *saponins*. Saponins are reported to mimic the effects of beneficial hormones. Some may even be anti-inflammatory. The Mexican wild yam contains these compounds.

Why transdermal? Why not a tablet or a capsule? Delivery systems can be important. The problem with oral routes is that they involve the first-pass effect described earlier. By avoiding your digestive system, the progesterone can't be sent through your liver for detoxification. You get direct systemic absorption when the cream is applied to your skin, and after a few minutes, no trace is discernible. Because this is a more effective delivery system, transdermal applications are being used for many drugs today.

Time for a
QUICKIE

When your periods have stopped, estrogen production falls about 40 to 60 percent, but progesterone levels may fall even lower in the presence of estrogen dominance. Men have about the same amount of estrogen as menopausal women.

Points for Progesterone

Women who have lost interest in sex often also have water retention, fibrocystic breasts, depression, wrinkled and dry skin, and irregular, sometimes heavy periods.

Is it any coincidence that the symptoms of progesterone deficiency are similar to symptoms experienced in women who have low libido?[12]

Miscarriages are related to lower progesterone levels.[13] Farmers have known for decades that the measurement of progesterone is a potential method of assessing the reproductive status of their animals.[14] Progesterone also intensifies bone formation in test animals.[15] Vaginal application of a progesterone preparation may be at least as effective as daily progesterone injections for achieving and maintaining pregnancy in women undergoing assisted reproductive techniques.[16] The list of benefits is long:

> ~ Progesterone can help reduce, prevent, or reverse the endometrial cancer caused by estrogens.[17]

> ~ Progesterone receptors are essential for effective sexual behavior.[18]

> ~ Progesterone reduces the risk of spontaneous abortion (miscarriage).[19]

> ~ Circulating progesterone is significant during the second trimester of pregnancy. Uterine bleed-

ing during this time is associated with low circulating levels of progesterone.[20]

~ When used on preterm infants, progesterone demonstrates a potentially important role of this hormone for the developing brain.[21]

~ Postpartum blues in the days immediately after delivery are related to the withdrawal of naturally occurring progesterone. There is a direct correlation between decreasing progesterone concentrations from the day of delivery to the day of peak depression.[22]

~ Progesterone helps to modulate the growth of fibroids.[23]

~ No differences in estrogen levels of breast fluid have been found between some normal women and those with breast disease. A possible explanation may be differences in the levels of the estrogen antagonists, such as progesterone.[24]

~ Progesterone inhibits the proliferation of arterial smooth muscle cells, a major factor in the formation of atherosclerotic plaque.[25] Given our high rate of heart disease, this is extremely important!

~ Progesterone is able to induce antibody and cellular immune responses in humans.[26]

~ The progression of a rare lung disease was reduced by progesterone.[27]

~ Both exogenous (that is, from an outside source) estrogen and testosterone cause cell death in the thymus, but progesterone not only inhibits this reaction, it also influences T cell development and thereby immune responses.[28]

~ Hirsuitism (abnormal hairiness) is very resistant to treatment, but progesterone cream application may meet with success.

~ Women using progesterone-releasing IUDs (intrauterine contraceptive devices) have a lower risk of developing problems than do users of other kinds of IUDs.[29]

~ Progesterone cream improves vasomotor symptoms, thereby relieving hot flashes and night sweats.[30]

Progesterone participates in practically every physiological process (in both women *and* men). Biochemically, it provides the material out of which all the other steroid hormones (including *cortisone, testosterone, estrogen,* and even the salt-regulating hormone *aldosterone*) can be made as needed.

By helping to balance hormone ratios, progesterone may compensate for xenoestrogens, preventing the risks associated with estrogen overload. Because it is a master hormone, it gets shunted into other hormone pathways when the need for progesterone is fulfilled. That's one reason why progesterone therapy increases libido.

A Little Goes a Long Way: The Progesterone Potency Controversy

The amount of progesterone necessary in the human body is actually very low. If you are using one of the high-dose preparations (some have as much as 900 or more milligrams of progesterone in a two-ounce jar compared with doses of 50 milligrams), it is a necessity to be under doctor's care. You must be monitored periodically because of the potential dangers. In the case of hormones, more is rarely better. Long-term use of high doses of progesterone can accumulate in your tissues, as indicated by recent laboratory results.

The lower-dose preparations are safer, yet they are just as effective for relieving symptoms (hot flashes, PMS cramps, hormone-related migraines, depression, weight gain, and vaginal dryness in women; loss of libido in both men and women; and prostate problems in men). Again—we may not need a lot of hormone to be beneficial, especially when the hormone is combined with the adaptogenic health-giving herbs. This cannot be stressed enough!

In the last few years, I have lectured on the use of progesterone cream to audiences around the world. I've heard nothing but glowing reports from women, their healthcare practitioners, *and* their partners. One gentleman summed it up perfectly when he said, "Ever since my wife has been using progesterone cream, I'm a better driver." The implication was that his wife was now more relaxed. Progesterone is indeed the feel-good, re-laxing hormone.

Using a well-formulated progesterone cream can help restore normal sex drive in women of all ages. Many women experience immediate relief. Others find that it may take as long as four months. If the remedy appears to be failing, try applying a hot cloth to the area of application before dabbing on the cream. This opens the pores and allows for better penetration. If this doesn't work, try applying the cream vaginally. Vaginal tissues are very sensitive and highly absorbent. (An added benefit of vaginal application: *it will eliminate vaginal dryness!*) Researchers discovered that application of progesterone cream vaginally proved to be effective for stopping the abnormal multiplication of cells in more than 90 percent of patients subject to five months' treatment.[31]

The use of a well-formulated progesterone cream plus the application of the product described in chapter nine offer an unbeatable solution to the vast majority of sexual problems.

When your hormone ratios are out of balance, it goes without saying that other metabolic functions are not working at full capacity, either. *The head bone is connected to the neck bone!* But many physicians who only prescribe treatment for suppressing the overt symptoms you are complaining about ignore this fact of metabolism. No gland "is an island," that is, something that exists in solitude and is unaffected by the rest of your body—a concept ignored by too many practitioners. Products that contain the adaptogenic herbs address *all of you*—your total metabolic system. This is the essence of holistic medicine.

Blood and saliva tests for hormone levels have become very popular, creating confusion and many questions. Some women report that their test results indicate a low level of estrogen, in spite of having symptoms of estrogen excess. Others say the use of progesterone cream eliminated problems, yet test results indicate progesterone deficiency.

The fact is that most tests are not sophisticated enough to reveal exactly what is going on under the hood. Don't be duped by what we refer to as "Science by Press Release"—the headline stories that reveal "new" discoveries about the wonders of synthetic hormones.

Unless the system is overloaded, the body will convert only the amount of progesterone to testosterone that it needs. Hang on to the fact that there may be only one hormone molecule for every fifty billion molecules in your blood plasma! Please consider your intervention with hormones—natural or synthetic—very carefully.

Natural progesterone breaks down to forms that have relaxing properties. Applying it on an ongoing basis assures continued feel-good results.

Fibroids

Uterine fibroids (or myomas), which are benign tumors of the uterus, are the single most common reason that doctors perform hysterectomy. Fibroids are clinically apparent in up to 25 percent of women. Think about that for a moment. One in four of the women you talk to or pass on the street today probably have fibroids!

Fibroid problems may include prolonged or heavy menstrual bleeding, pelvic pressure or pain, and, if the fibroids are big enough, reproductive dysfunction. So both the economic cost and the effect on quality of life can be substantial. Due to their mass, they may cause a dropped uterus later in life when pelvic floor supports weaken, leading to urinary incontinence.

The good news is that after menopause, fibroids routinely disappear.

Surgery has been the mainstay of fibroid treatment.[32] But this invasive procedure doesn't address the *cause.* You may get rid of your fibroids but not the *reason* for their occurrence.

Fibroid tumors, like breast fibrocysts, are a product of estrogen dominance. Estrogen stimulates their growth, but as estrogen declines in later years, lack of estrogen causes them to atrophy. Many women in their thirties begin to have anovulatory cycles (they don't release eggs). As they approach the decade before menopause, they are producing much less progesterone than expected but still produce normal (or more) levels of estrogen. These women retain water and salt, their breasts swell and become fibrocystic, they gain weight (especially around the hips and torso), become depressed and lose their libido, their bones suffer mineral loss, and they develop fibroids. All are signs of estrogen dominance.

Formation of new fibroids remains a substantial problem. Although medications that manipulate concentrations of steroid hormones may be effective, side effects limit the long-term use of any of these drugs.[33]

When sufficient natural progesterone is replaced, fibroid tumors no longer grow in size (generally they decrease in size) and can be kept from growing until menopause, after which they will wither and disappear on their own. This is the effect of reversing estrogen dominance.[34] Natural progesterone is a far better alternative than surgery for fibroid tumors.

So again, it's progesterone to the rescue! Natural progesterone has a favorable effect on the blood vessels involved and increases the blood flow in the walls at the site of the myoma—the fibroid tumor of the uterus. Symptoms can recede in days.[35]

Time for a
QUICKIE

Hormone replacement with estrogens can exacerbate migraine headaches.

From "The Ageless Woman"

"Progesterone is a masterpiece of nature and the female hormone, unfortunately, most neglected by mainstream physicians.

"Progesterone has an anti-estrogenic effect, especially at the breast and uterine sites, where its presence blocks the over-proliferation effect of estrogen that may lead to cancer. Many female cancers and endocrine system problems, including premenstrual syndrome, breast and uterine fibroids, endometriosis, infertility and some of the uncomfortable symptoms that occur around and after the cessation of periods, are the result of too little progesterone and too much estrogen.

"When we stop ovulating, we no longer form a corpus luteum—the predominant site of progesterone production. As ovulation becomes less and less regular, progesterone levels decline rapidly. Progesterone sacrifices itself to produce adrenal hormones under stress, so most urban women unknowingly have deficient progesterone levels even before ovulation becomes sporadic.

"Symptoms of progesterone deficiency can be very surprising—like mid-life asthma. Since progesterone is an involuntary muscle relaxant, its decline can result in constricted breathing in women who have allergies or an inherent lung weakness."

Serafina Corsello, MD[36]

The Science of Profits:
An Unfortuante Reality

Synthetic hormones in wide use today are troublemak-
ers, and yet we do have the technology to create precise
human-matched hormones. Why, then, don't the drug
companies do just that? For good reason! As stated earlier, any substance produced by a human, an animal, or
even a plant, cannot be patented unless its structure is
molecularly altered or its use or function changed. Would
a corporate board of directors allocate millions of dol-
lars to develop and promote a product for hormone
therapy if it could not get patent protection? Not likely!
Your body, however, knows the difference.

Synthetic estrogens have been widely touted by our
medical establishment for many years. It can't be easy
to concede that a drug that has been so enthusiastically
recommended is linked to cancer, in spite of all the
current evidence.

In Summary

In medicine and healthcare, there are rarely "quick fixes"
or treatments without negative side effects, but the low-
dose progesterone cream combined with the herbs
comes very close. This preparation is beneficial, low
risk, and produces immediate and amazing results. It
has become more and more integral to maintaining a
woman's optimum health in today's toxic world.

"What's your
favorite
position?"

"Facing
Bloomingdale's."

Chapter Seven

FROM VITAMIN A TO VITAMIN "OHHHHHH"

A 16-year-old came home from a party announcing she had done something wrong. Mother asked what she had done. "I'm not a virgin any more." "Oh, thank goodness," said Mom. "I thought you were going to tell me you started smoking."

Selective Supplements To Restore Sexual Health

Frequently heard: "Not tonight, honey. I have a headache." Although people report that minor discomforts disappear with a sexual experience, sex is the *last* thing on your mind when the *first* thing on your mind is serious pain or problems. So it's no news that we are more likely to endure sexual dysfunction if we are in poor physical or emotional health. The experts tell us that optimal sexual function depends on the cooperation and integrity of our anatomy, and of our vascular system, and of the neurological, endocrine, and immune systems—a tall order in today's world.

Even if you *are* motivated to become Super-Woman, can you really fit the necessary five portions of deep-colored fresh organic vegetables into your everyday life?

I can't—not usually! Most programs and diet regimens that promote such top-notch health are not easy to follow. They are almost always time-consuming and they demand dedication and discipline. They call for physical exercise and what many regard as cheerless lifestyle changes. True, such behavioral reforms are justified in their own right, and no one can argue against them. But anyone who has attempted to make such adjustments will tell you it's a difficult row to hoe.

When a hunger attack strikes, most of us just don't care how many grams of fat or oxidized lipoproteins a blueberry muffin contains—especially if that muffin is within easy reach and the carrot stick isn't—*even if we know the carrot stick may contain nutrients that will affect our sex drive in a positive way.*

It's difficult to give up a present pleasure for *any* future benefit. Adding to the difficulty is the fact that foods that are not in our best health interest are highly palatable, aggressively advertised and easily available.

Too much of the food within easy readh gives us pleasure rather than health.[1,2] Antioxidants are never added to ballpark hotdogs; airlines pay no attention to a request for complex carbohydrates; and caterers outdo competition by making party food delicious rather than nutritious.

As my children complained when they were younger: "Too bad the vitamins are in the broccoli instead of in the ice cream."

Yet we are told again and again:

(1) Given the right substances, we can keep our immune system at its peak efficiency.

(2) For optimum health, we cannot lose our rapport with nature.

How, then, can we reach that pinnacle of health to optimize our sex life? It is obvious that some other approach is needed to get the proper ammunition and to stay in touch with the natural.

The encouraging news is that there are a few innovative and remarkable user-friendly supplements that can help us to achieve this goal—compensating for what our current lifestyle has been serving up. Certain foods are so rich in nourishment that they can be condensed into easy to take supplements without losing the chemical diversity that makes them so effective.

Unlike the extreme deficiency disorders attributed to the shortfall of a single nutrient—as in the need for vitamin C in scurvy or vitamin B3 in pellagra—most diseases and sexual dysfunctions plaguing us today are *multifaceted*. For example, in recent research pointing to *folate* for avoiding birth anomalies, the entire B complex is demonstrating to be even more advantageous (provided there's enough folate present). Does this mean that if we just take the multivitamin and mineral supplements widely promoted today we will achieve optimum health? Not really!

First of all, food is not a conglomeration of isolated nutrients thrown together in a fashion out of touch with nature's elegance. The laws of nature can never be fully understood when they are cut up and parceled out.

This tendency toward reductionism in nutrition research for the last two or three decades has been misguided. Fortunately, some researchers see "the big picture" of nutritional health, and they are developing natural botanical products and "functional," or adaptogenic, foods.

Furthermore, it has been recognized that food and supplements processed, stored, and consumed under a variety of conditions affect their bioavailability—the proportion of nutrients consumed that is usable by your body.[3] So conclusions that don't allow for these factors (and most of them don't!) can be misleading. A few illustrations follow:

~ Physicians may consider nutrients in your circulating blood serum a benchmark for overall nutrient status. But your body may misinterpret the storage of some nutrients as "enough," even though the quantity measured may be unrelated to consumption or metabolism.

~ Mechanisms of transport play a role in bioavailability. So do many drugs, which can alter absorption, metabolism, utilization, or excretion of a particular nutrient.[4] Plus we have learned that the level of activity of one nutrient is dependent on another and another and another, almost ad infinitum.

~ Whether a spinach leaf is whole, cut in pieces, or minced *before* you consume it affects the absorption of its folate content. The bioavailability of folate from spinach can actually be improved by disruption of the vegetable matrix. So—surprisingly—it's better chopped up than eaten in whole-leaf form.[5]

~ Although heat from cooking destroys many unstable nutrients, the uptake of lycopene—the substance in tomatoes that can reduce the risk of lung cancer and cardiovascular disease—is greater from cooked products than from raw tomatoes or tomato juice.[6] Heat processing increases the bioavailability of lycopene by breaking down cell walls and allowing extraction of the lycopene from the cells that hold the lycopene captive in the raw form. Another surprise![7]

~ A substance in carrots helps to prevent lipid peroxidation, which causes cells to reduce efficiency or, worse, to promote disease. Carrot juice, however, offers no such benefit.[8] In this case, the health-giving substance degrades with the destruction of the food structure.[9]

Time for a
QUICKIE

In 1844, Ralph Waldo Emerson wrote: " Let the stoics say what they please, we do not eat for the good of living, but because the meat is savory and the appetite is keen."

An endless number of factors can tip the scale one way or the other when it comes to translating nutrient make-up. Tests for nutrients and even extensive research projects can't always reveal what is actually going on.[10] Extrapolating data from studies involving one isolated nutrient without looking at total food intake, or the source of the nutrient tested, can blur results.

That is not to say that we shouldn't take isolated nutrients. I wouldn't want to be without my extra vitamin C when I am under stress or when I travel. And I want that mycelized vitamin A on hand when a cold or the flu is brewing. But if our goal is top of the line health, there is a category of supplements that is superior.

Nature knows better. It doesn't offer isolated elements.

Research overwhelmingly validates the amazing performance of nutrient-rich whole foods when contrasted with stand-alone vitamins or minerals, regardless of how dominant a role that single nutrient may play in the metabolic process. For every nutrient discovered to be essential, there are many more yet to be identified.

To this day, the analytical approach has not been able to tell us *everything* about how the molecular pieces are integrated, or exactly how a banana reconstructs into *you*—precisely how one life form transforms into another. It's so much more than a matter of food breaking down into component parts—secrets of nature still hidden from our mortal vision and comprehension.

The point is that many single-substance supplements, although of value for certain therapeutic measures when under doctor's care, provide an incomplete approach when trying to construct the highest level of wellness.

A major breakthrough for optimum health has come with the availability of nutritional supplements that are more *food-like* than *vitamin-like*—nutrient-dense substances containing cofactors and trace elements, as nature provides, with molecular architecture identical to that which your very human body manufactures.

Many of these substances or their derivatives have an eons-long history of alliance with optimal health and the immune system. Unlike today's drugs and pharmaceuticals, they are not new to human existence. Although undeniably old, they have purpose in today's world.

How lucky we are that most are now available to us through the mastery of our current advanced technology—unique extraction techniques, stabilization processing, fast transportation, medical research, dedicated marketing, and so on.

We have gone beyond Grandma clabbering (fermenting) a bottle of milk on her kitchen windowsill, or the farmer collecting the colostrum for his sick child after the birth of a calf.

A trip to the health store brings these products home with their integrity intact!

The greatest lesson I have learned as I have interfaced with the nutrition scientists of the world is that we can no longer survive in a state of total well being without a combination of at least a few of these very unique supplements. Healthful food, exercise, thinking good thoughts, or being a vegan are just not enough any more.

The clinical data and case histories emerging with the use of the supplements described here are compelling— marks of evidence that they perform well, act quickly, and succeed without a lifetime of commitment. At long last, natural remedies with a sharp edge are making medical history.

Best of all, the winning position of these products does not come from pharmacological actions. Unlike a number of "holistic" preparations that may straddle the line between nutrient and drug, these supplements are as natural as the organic foods in the produce section of the supermarket. How they work has been a challenge to scientific imagination—until their modes of action began to be understood. They represent a stunning piece of supplement and immune-enhancing history.

Time for a
QUICKIE

Medical progress did not come from drugs or carefully controlled studies. There is a vast difference between "significant" statistics and maintaining or restoring health.

Selective Supplements:
Why They Work

The food-type supplements that I recommend to improve and retain sexual health are enzyme yeast cells, chlorella, colostrum, organic germanium (Ge132), aged garlic extract, palm oil tocotrienols, and medicinal herbal teas. These supplements have the following general properties in common:

~ With minor exceptions, they contain a multiplicity of known and unknown cofactors that have not been pulled out and taken apart.

~ Their constituents are familair to your digestive and other metabolic systems.

~ They don't have to mimic the actions of healthful foods because they are in the category of healthful foods.

~ Their use requires no compromise of a postindustrial lifestyle that generally rules out obtaining adequate nutrition from "normal" food sources.

~ They have the science to back up the claims cited.

~ They do not require prescriptions and they are safe.

~ They provide special benefit for the functions necessary for optimum sexuality (in addition to optimum overall health).

Each is unique, but there is also some overlap of value.

Just as it is a health advantage to consume a greater variety of foods, so it is with food-type supplements.

ENZYME YEAST CELLS

Common on plant leaves and flowers, yeasts are also found on our skin surfaces and in our intestinal tracts, where they may live either symbiotically or as parasites.

What are yeasts, anyway? They are single-cell living organisms that are classified as fungi. Yeasts have had some bad press, but the negative associations do not apply to certain strains that are in our best health interest, available naturally or as food supplements. Yeast cells are part of our natural microflora, and the right strains contribute to our health in a very postive way.

Some of us know the strain of yeast called *Saccharomyces cerevisiae* better as brewer's or baker's yeast. Baker's yeast continues to germinate within your body and so it is not particularly good for human consumption. Brewer's yeast is heated and often dried into powders, flakes, or tablets, a process that destroys its enzymes and most of its vitamins.

Surely you are familiar with *Candida albicans*, the yeast responsible for the unpleasant "yeast infection." Did you know that this yeast fungus is usually a permanent inhabitant of your body and normally causes no ill effects? If, however, you are pregnant or taking antibiotics, or have a poor diet, an infection of the vagina and vulva caused by this yeast overgrowth is common (referred to as Candida, or candidiasis). Candida of the mucous membranes of the mouth is known as thrush. Candida of the vagina is called vaginitis. Candida also causes disease in those with low immune responses, such as persons with AIDS and in those on chemotherapy.[11]

So you see that yeast can be good or bad. Let's talk about the good stuff, available as a nutritional food supplement—Zell Oxygen in particular, a product I have been taking for more than thirty years. Initially, I learned that yeast is a good food supplement because it is 50 percent protein and is a rich source of B vitamins, including niacin and folic acid, plus enzymes and other important nutrients. The nutrients in Zell Oxygen, now known as *Body Oxygen*, are almost identical replications of the various biological substances which occur naturally in our cells (that is, when we are healthy).

The yeast cells used in Body Oxygen products utilize a unique strain of *Saccharomyces cerevisiae*, along with fresh cell juices of apple, lemon, and grapefruit, plus essential fatty acids from wheat germ. The unusual strain of yeast is prepared with no additives, and has never been dried. The highest temperature reached (32°C or about 88°F) is well below body temperature, and the products are always presented in liquid form. Unlike baker's yeast, the process prevents the cells from reproducing. To facilitate the uptake of these cells in your small intestine, the young enzyme yeast cells have very thin cell walls, so they are readily digested. (Food yeasts usually have thick cell walls, which tend to resist digestion or are at least difficult to digest. Since cell walls contain the allergens, this may be the reason this strain is not likely to be allergenic.)

The yeast cells also have nucleic acids. Other than chlorella, few (if any) supplements can boast this advantage. Eating foods high in nucleic acids provides the material for the repair and production of human nucleic acids, and it is the breakdown of DNA and RNA in our cells that is believed to be one of the main factors in aging and in degenerative diseases.

The cells also contain growth factors—again, an asset not found in most other products. (Chlorella, velvet antler, and colostrum are among the very few supplements containing growth factors.) According to Michael Rosenbaum, MD, growth factors in this kind of supplement may be the key substances to retard and even to reverse the aging process.[12]

To add to the bounty, more than 50 percent of yeast genes are similar to human genes. And the cells contain sulfur amino acids, not only in short supply in our supplements, but especially lacking in the foods we eat today.

These products are fermented with a very gentle biological treatment, allowing the ingredients to remain active. Fermented foods have been included in the foodways of just about every cultural group in the world, past and present—except here in America. Empirical wisdom demonstrates that fermented foods are extremely beneficial by providing friendly bacteria to offset the harmful bacteria that "do us in." Body Oxygen helps to make up for this missing factor in the American diet.

When you start using enzyme yeast cells, don't be surprised if your complexion improves. (Brewer's yeast was the only acne cure we had years ago.) Nail brittleness and hair loss problems may disappear, too!

In addition to helping you feel better and younger, Body Oxygen may enhance sexual function in four ways:

1. This particular yeast strain has an antagonistic effect on *Candida albicans*. Since the vagina is a major site of attraction for Candida, taking a supplement that will help to keep it free of this problem is almost mandatory.[13,14]

2. Facilitating maximum oxygen use of body tissues is one of the major roles of this special yeast preparation. It doesn't supply more oxygen to the tissues per se, but rather the available oxygen is used more efficiently. Many of the micronutrients in Body Oxygen are used by the mitochondria (the powerhouse of the cell), which control energy production in the body. These micronutrients include iron, magnesium, Coenzyme Q10, and select B vitamins.

The fact that oxygen use is maximized was demonstrated scientifically in Hamburg, Germany, by showing an improvement in work capacity and recovery. Participants were subject to an increased load on a bicycle ergometer after they took one to two spoonfuls of Body Oxygen every morning. In each test case, the researchers were able to increase the load, to get better pulse rates, recovery rates, oxygen consumption, and recovery quotients (ratio of the surplus of oxygen consumption during work and recovery). This increase in vitality and performance indicates superior utilization of oxygen by the muscle tissue mitochondria and in energy production.

3. Remember the libido-destroying xenoestrogens described in chapter four? Body Oxygen can help the detoxification process. Glutathione peroxidase and methionine found in this product are the best "garbage disposals" for cleaning up your liver and bowel. Glutathione is probably one of the most effective scavengers of free radicals. It mounts a major enzymatic defense against peroxide accumulation in your cells. (The temperature of Body Oxygen, noted above, never rises high enough to destroy this imporant enzyme.)

Individual vials are now sold in health stores to provide a quick pick-me-up for the serious athlete or the lunch-time aerobic walker—or anyone needing an energy boost.

4. Recall that the sexual excitement phase starts in your brain. Body Oxygen is known for its action in increasing the blood supply to the brain with the immediate result of better cellular respiration. (You might try a vial just before your romantic interlude.)

In Switzerland, this same preparation is used successfully together with a raw food diet to increase the energy levels in patients with chronic fatigue syndrome.[15]

CHLORELLA

Good sexual function requires energy. Chlorella—an algae supercharged with concentrated sunlight and unusual, broad-spectrum nutrients, plus absorption advantages—can help to supply that energy.

We've heard it before and we'll hear it again: "EAT YOUR VEGETABLES." Even if we want to heed Mom's warnings, it's not like it used to be! Some of the veggies and salad stuff available today could travel to the moon and back—slowly—and return looking fresh-picked and table-ready. We all know why: It's the way foods are grown and the additives "embalming" them.

We also know Mom was right—everyone should have green stuff every day. So I try to get organic vegetables whenever possible, but I use chlorella as my *greens-every-day* insurance policy.

Chlorella is a green algae that grows in fresh mineral water pools, usually in the least polluted environment possible. Laboratory and clinical results on chlorella offer a powerful case for its regular use.

A Carnegie Institute study has even proposed that large-scale commercial cultivation of chlorella would eliminate world hunger.

I was introduced to chlorella almost twenty years ago. Because I had entered the nutrition/health arena thirty years earlier, it took something quite special to impress me at that time. Chlorella was just such a supplement!

The first thing I noticed was an improvement in skin tone. So if you're looking for a supplement to help you *look* better, chlorella is among the best. But, of course, it does so much more than that.

Since my introduction to this algae, I have visited chlorella pools in Okinawa, where water and air are unusually pure; checked out chlorella laboratories in Hokkaido; spoken with scientists in Osaka at chlorella headquarters; and had an opportunity to attend an international scientific seminar in Taiwan. The seminar presenters disclosed the results of their studies on chlorella, some of which are noted below. One of the speakers, whose work was especially awe-inspiring, was an ophthalmologist who had experimented extensively, using chlorella to counter the development of cataracts.

Among the reasons chlorella may be so effective in promoting youthfulness is that, like the Body Oxygen, it has a human growth hormone factor.[16] It also inhibits tumor metastasis.[17] In addition, chlorella:

~ helps to remove heavy metals from the body[18]

~ reduces production of substances causing milk allergy[19]

~ helps to prevent gastrointestinal absorption of toxins, including dioxin (remember that nasty number?), and promotes the excretion of any that have already been absorbed into your tissues[20]

~ helps to detoxify unwanted foreign molecules[21]

~ increases production of natural killer activity (production of immune-protecting cells)[22]

~ guards against lipid peroxidation, or production of free radicals[23]

~ may help prevent ulcer formation, mainly through the "immune-brain-gut" axis and through the protection of gastric mucosa[24]

~ enhances resistance to listeria (a parasitic bacteria) through the activation of macrophages (immune cells)[25]

~ can be used as presurgical treatment to help prevent metastasis or tumor progression[26]

~ prevents cholesterol build-up[27]

~ protects against toxic effects of insecticides[28]

~ contains a significant amount of lutein, excellent for eye health[29]

~ helps to prevent psychological stress and to maintain homeostasis in the face of external environmental changes[30]

Of the more than 25,000 species of algae, the most nutritionally valuable is chlorella pyrenoidosa. Perhaps because its reproduction rate is almost unbelievably fast (it quadruples every twenty hours), coupled with its great versatility, chlorella has been tested as a system to help support humans during long-term space travel. Initial results have been positive, demonstrating that it can indeed provide a complete *regenerating* life-support system, essential for future lengthy space travel.[31]

Chlorella has one of the highest nucleic acid content of any known food. Again—when we have a sufficient intake of food rich in DNA and RNA to protect our own cellular nucleic acids, our cell walls continue to function more efficiently. In fact, because of its nucleic acid content, chlorella is used as a prototype for deciphering the complexity of huge plant chromosomes.[32]

The algae has maintained a pure genetic structure for 2.5 billion years, as verifed by examination of fossil remains. Few land animals eat algae as part of their natural diet. This may be due to the difficulties in breaking down the algae cell wall, hampering cell absorption.

But scientists have broken the cell wall in the laboratory. It is only after utilizing the exclusive patented Dyno-Mill™ process, pulverizing the thick outer cell wall without damaging the enzymes inside, that chlorella can be sufficiently digested by humans—insuring all of the natural nutritional value of the organism for optimum assimilation and digestion. The finished product is sold as broken-cell or cracked-cell chlorella.

Unlike drugs, and like so many other food-type supplements, chlorella works slowly, but its changes tend to be more permanent.

But does chlorella really give us what we would get in our dark green leafy vegetables? Yes! *Chlorophyll* is included in its long list of health-building substances. Chlorophyll is the pigment responsible for the deep green color of fast-growing plants.

Green plants make carbohydrates from nothing more than sunlight (solar energy), water, and carbon dioxide—creating bio-organic substances from inorganic chemicals. The process is called *photosynthesis* and chlorophyll is the chemical that makes it possible.

Instead of iron as the focal part of a plant's "blood"—as it is with us—magnesium is the center of the chlorophyll molecule. **More photosynthesis is performed by algae than by land plants.**

Chlorophyll is a powerful cleansing and purifying agent. It is not only therapeutic, but also preventive. Of course, the best way to obtain it is through consumption of dark green vegetables. But chlorella runs a close second. Keep in mind that chlorella is a dark green nutrient-dense food.

Hideo Nakayama, the founder of the Sun Chlorella Corporation of Kyoto, Japan, said to me on one of my many visits to Japan:

> "If we put together the best in Oriental health wisdom with the best of Western health wisdom, the whole world would benefit."

I could not agree more! As for female sexuality, here's a product that offers energy, skin tone enhancement, xenoestrogen detoxification, and an array of other healthful advantages.

Note the similarity between our hemoglobin molecule and the chlorophyll molecule:

HEMOGLOBIN

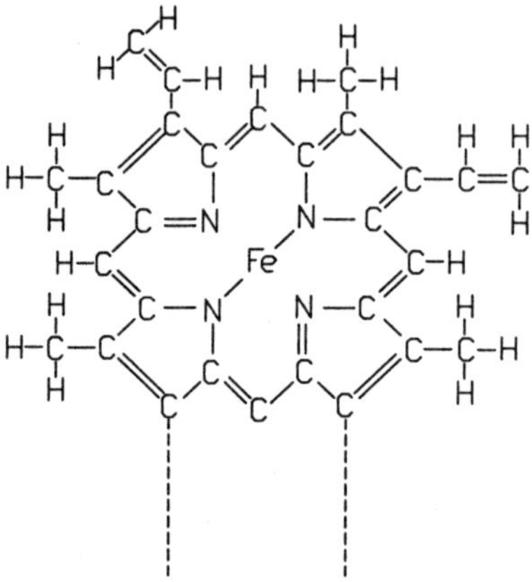

Figure 7

Mg-Magnesium

CHLOROPHYLL

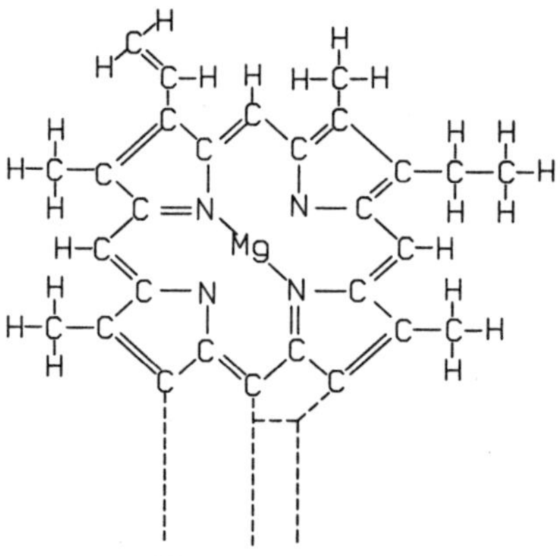

Fe-Iron

An intriguing fact about chlorophyll is its chemical similarity to hemoglobin, the molecule that transports oxygen in our blood. Hemoglobin and chlorophyll share a structure called the porphyrin ring. In hemoglobin, there's an iron atom bonded inside the ring; but chlorophyll has a magnesium atom in that very location instead.

Joe walked into a bar and was astounded to see a little man, about a foot high, playing on a miniature piano. "What's this?" he asked the bartender.

"See that guy over there in the corner?" explained the bartender. "He grants wishes. Give it a try; go talk to him."

Joe came back a few minutes later. "Well, what happened?" asked the bartender.

"I don't know about that guy," Joe said. "I asked for a million bucks, and the next thing you know I was surrounded by a million ducks."

"Yeah," said the bartender, "I guess he is a bit hard of hearing. Do you think I asked for a twelve-inch pianist?"

AGED GARLIC EXTRACT

It's unlikely that Grandma's message about the benefits of garlic have gone unnoticed. We all know garlic is good for us. But did Grandma ever tell you about garlic and your sexuality?

Whatever Grandma revealed, hearing the wisdom of the ages is just not enough anymore. There are questions about the *kinds* of garlic supplements in the marketplace, and how they compare with fresh garlic. And there are certainly questions about the long history of garlic as a sex stimulant, even if you didn't hear it from Grandma.

Garlic and Sex

Both ancient Jews and Romans extolled the aphrodisiac powers of garlic. It was put in the same category as wine. Because it protected against infection and disease, garlic was interpreted as a magical substance. Rabbi Rita Leonard of Hawaii reports that *The Talmud*, the repository of Jewish civil and religious law, sanctioned the use of garlic as an aphrodisiac. She says: "The Rabbis taught five things about garlic: it satiates, it keeps the body warm, it brightens up the face, it increases semen, and it kills parasites in the bowels. In addition, it was said to foster love and remove jealousy."

It has also been noted that garlic should be eaten on Friday because of its "salutary action, and because it would 'spice up' conjugality."[33]

Unlike other aphrodisiacs, which are known to have temporary and immediate arousal effects, garlic is said to provide long-lasting results.

King Tut had placed six pieces of garlic in his tomb 3,350 years ago. Hippocrates suggested that women insert garlic vaginally to bring about menstruation. (It was boiled first, and then cooled.) Pliny (23-79 AD) recommended its use as a menstruation promoter and an aphrodisiac. Its promotion as an aphrodisiac caused much stress among the celibate clergy and politicians, who used the ruse of social "morality" to control women, their sexuality, and their reproduction.

From a medical point of view, garlic's reputation as an aphrodisiac is validated. We now know that garlic increases the enzyme *nitric oxide synthase*.[34] This enzyme is responsible for the mechanism of erection. How it relates to women and sexuality is explained in the last chapter. Clearly folklore is now being proven correct!

Benefits of Garlic

Garlic and garlic supplements are consumed in many cultures for cholesterol-lowering and circulatory benefits. In addition to these proclaimed effects, some garlic preparations also appear to be liver-protective, immune-enhancing, anticarcinogenic, and chemopreventive. Although not all of the active ingredients are known, ample research suggests that several bioavailable components contribute to the value of garlic.[35] Let's see how it plays out scientifically.

A study was done to determine whether people with normal blood pressure consume more garlic in their diets. Sure enough, those with blood pressure on the lower side were avid garlic consumers. (The results were significant for systolic blood pressure only.)[36]

Different types of garlic preparations have different properties, and aged garlic proves to be the most beneficial in several scientific studies. The effects of garlic on the mucus membranes of the stomach, for example, were determined with dehydrated raw garlic powder, dehydrated boiled garlic powder, and aged garlic. Raw garlic powder caused severe damage, including erosion. Boiled garlic powder also caused reddening of the membranes, whereas aged garlic did not cause any undesirable effects.[37]

A report in *Atherosclerosis* in 1997, showed that aged garlic extract resulted in less fatty streak development, less cholesterol accumulation in vessel walls, and less development of fatty plaques—indicating protection against atherosclerosis. Researchers concluded this was the result of aged garlic extract reducing cholesterol uptake into the plaques.

Time for a
QUICKIE

"The greatest mistake in medicine is to seek a single cause for a single disease."
~ Sigmund Freud

Aged Garlic Extract

All these positive results are in keeping with my favorable impression of aged raw garlic after visiting garlic fields and laboratories in Katachi, Japan, a few years ago.

What is aged raw garlic? Aged garlic is extracted from raw garlic through a long-term process. Its constituents include proteins, sugars, amino acids, sulfur compounds, lipids, vitamins, and enzymes.

Extracts of fresh garlic—aged over a prolonged period to produce the special aged extract—also contain antioxidant phytochemicals known to prevent oxidant damage. So it's no surprise that this product was shown to protect against agents used in cancer therapy, against liver toxicity caused by industrial chemicals, and against the damage of acetaminophen, the popular Tylenol analgesic. Acetaminophens are associated with the suppression of neutralizing immune responses.

Substantial experimental evidence also shows that aged garlic has the ability to protect against acute damage from our own aging, radiation, and chemical exposure, and from any long-term toxic damage.

Research supports the fact that garlic also reduces the risk of cardiovascular disease, stroke, and brain cell damage implicated in Alzheimer's disease.[38]

Here are the results of specific studies.

~ Aged garlic inhibited the growth of cancer cells and decreased psychological stress (determined by measuring spleen weight). Aged garlic is an immune modifier.[39]

~ Research shows that aged garlic may protect the small intestine from damage induced by antitumor drugs, a consequence of chemotherapy.[40]

~ Aged garlic may be useful for prevention of atherosclerosis because it can protect against oxidized LDL, the process that causes injury to epithelial cells, leading to heart disease.[41]

~ Aged garlic prevents lipid peroxide damage in a dose-dependent manner. The more you take, the less damage. There's no question that it serves as an antioxidant.[42]

~ Aged garlic extract plays an important role in the survival of neurons in a part of the brain involved in long-term memory storage.[43]

~ A study examined the effect of a major compound found in aged garlic extract on the memory deficit and age-related changes of test animals. These studies suggest that this supplement may reduce age-related learning disabilities and cognitive disorders.[44]

~ Garlic has the potential for the prevention and control of cardiovascular disorders and is beneficial when taken as a dietary supplement.[45]

Many scientific facilities, worldwide, carried out the current research on the positive effects of aged garlic extract. They include:

~ Molecular Genetics School of Medicine, Loma Linda University, Loma Linda, CA.

~ Nutrition and Infectious Diseases Unit, Tufts University School of Medicine, Boston, MA.

~ Clinical Nutrition Research Unit, Memorial Sloan-Kettering Cancer Center and New York Hospital, Cornell Medical Center, New York, NY.

~ Center for Research in Vascular Biology, Department of Anatomical Sciences, The University of Queensland, Brisbane, Queensland, Australia

~ Center for Advanced Food Technology, Rutgers University, New Brunswick, NJ.

~ Graduate School of Pharmaceutical Sciences, The University of Tokyo, Tokyo, Japan.

~ School of Biomolecular Sciences, Liverpool John Moore University, Liverpool, UK.

~ Philadelphia Biomedical Research Institute, King of Prussia, PA.

~ Department of Anesthesiology, Perioperative and Pain Medicine, Harvard Medical School, Brigham and Women's Hospital, Boston, MA.

~ Department of Community Health Sciences, Community Health Centre, Aga Khan University, Karachi.

An extremely important study related to sexual function involves research showing that aged garlic extract is effective in increasing blood flow to skin tissue.

Aged garlic extract widens the blood vessels on the outer edges of your body.

For those of you with cold feet or hands, these results should be especially intriguing. The extract also improves skin temperature. *The most important factor in determining skin temperature is the blood flow directly below the surface of the skin.*[46]

This study confirms that aged garlic extract clinically raises skin temperature and improves such symptoms as numbness and chilling of the limbs and lumbar area (the part of the back between the thorax and the pelvis).

Note these results:

1. Following single administration of the extract, skin temperatures peaked sixty minutes after administration on the backs of the hands and ninety minutes after administration on the tops of the feet.

2. Following fourteen days of continuous administration, higher skin temperature was observed on the backs of the hands and feet.

The thermogram images on the next page graphically demonstrate improvement in blood flow in extremities—in both hands and feet—with the use of aged garlic extract.[47]

Figure 8

THERMOGRAM
IMAGES

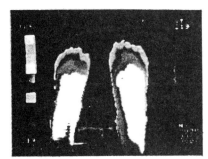
Initial Photo

These results sug-
gest improvement in
blood flow in the ex-
tremities of the
feet.

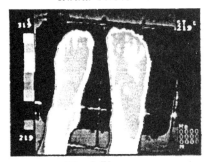
Final Photo

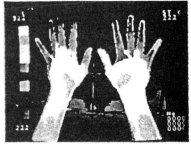
Initial Photo

Here you can see the
improved blood flow
to the hands.

>

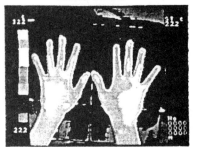
Final Photo

What About Fresh Garlic?

I can hear you ask: How does raw fresh garlic compare with aged garlic extract? First, the odor: We all know that breath mints are no help—they just give you minty garlic breath. And the amount of parsley needed to counteract the smell is unrealistic.

What about other problems? Many people report sensitivities to raw fresh garlic because it can irritate the digestive tract. Studies with animals show anemia and failure to grow.[48,49] So those with digestive problems should use cooked garlic, which is far less irritating. Heating or cooking, however, destroys some of garlic's important constituents.

Raw fresh garlic may increase lipid oxidation (leading to free radicals that damage cells), indicating that some compounds in raw garlic may actually act like oxidants rather than antioxidants.[50,51] In addition, when raw fresh garlic kills certain organisms (*Candida*, for example), it creates a "die-off reaction," which means that the yeast organisms release toxic chemicals. This does not occur with the use of aged garlic. The aged garlic encourages the immune system to get its phagocytes (special immune cells) to knock off the yeast organisms, while avoiding toxic release.[52]

What is done to age the garlic, and why does it have advantages over the fresh cloves? The product is prepared by processing garlic in a special enzyme solution for twelve to sixteen months. During this time, the irritating chemicals are converted to more bioavailable harmless compounds. This "aging" process has been used by the Chinese for thousands of years to render the garlic odorless.[53]

So for health and sociability, it's the odorless aged garlic supplement for me. For flavor, I check my cookbooks.

It is obvious from the research that the aged garlic extract is in accordance with our list of special adaptogenic supplements. It is also obvious from its benefits, especially since it can help bring blood to tissue (its circulatory effects), that it is another plus toward our goal for optimum sexuality.

Time for a
QUICKIE

The theory that vital spirits lost by masturbation caused debility or degeneracy became, along with health food and exercise theories, popular in 19th-century health doctrine. Graham crackers and Kellogg's cornflakes were by-products of the doctrine of sexual abstinence. Under the Comstock Law (1873), which was enforced by police, 19th-century sexosophy negated sexuality so effectively that human psychoneuroendocrine research into sexuality remains muffled and deprived of funds even today.

See Appendix D for details on the Comstock Law, which contributed big-time to female sexual repression in this country.

COLOSTRUM

Colostrum, the first breast fluid expressed after giving birth, is a complex source of unusual nutrients, immune constituents, and bioactive substances, providing unparalleled immune protection for newborns. As short-lived as colostrum is (a new mother produces it only from 24 to 48 hours after her baby is born), it has an impact on health for the baby that cannot be understated. Used for centuries by farmers when family members are ill, bovine colostrum is now available in supplemental form for the benefit of everyone—anywhere—at any age.

Disease is frequently due to a loss of T4 cells, a very necessary component of our immune system in its effort to keep us well. There's no substitute for these cells, despite redundancies and safeguards in the overall design of our immune system. One of the most promising results of recent research with colostrum derivatives, both in the test tube ("in vitro") and in lab animals ("in vivo") is that colostrum increases T4 cells.

Colostrum supplementation can also increase the size of intestinal villi, thereby promoting more surface area for nutrient absorption. Villi are finger-like projections sprouting from the walls of the small intestine, responsible for sucking in nutrients as they stream by. The more prolonged the colostrum feeding, the greater the villus circumference and height. When doctors refer to the ability of the gut to heal, they often mean that the villi are repairing.[54]

Colostrum is also helpful for the lactose intolerant. The long list of people unable to effectively metabolize milk sugar includes most Asians, Jews, Arabs, Eskimos, American Indians, and Africans. If you are not among these ethnic groups, pay attention anyway:

Regardless of your ethnic background, you are likely to be milk intolerant any time you happen to be ill with a fever or when you are malnourished.[55] Colostrum helps to resolve this sensitivity problem.

Let's look at some of the nutrients that make colostrum so special.

 Figure 9

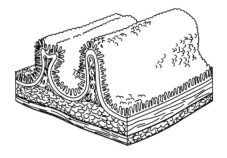

VILLI

The absorptive surface of the small intestine is convoluted by small fingerlike projections called villi (singular, villus). Each villus is lined with cells containing a rich network of blood vessles and lympth vessels. Each cell is covered with much smaller projections, the microvilli. The surface area of the intestine is thereby increased manyfold by the villi and the microvilli. Colostrum increases the size of intestinal villi.

Vitamins In Colostrum

Colostrum is especially extravagant in vitamins A, B12, and E.[56,57] Nutrient absorption declines as we age, but of particular importance is the reduced amount of vitamin B12. Colostrum is one of nature's richest natural sources of this high-powered nutrient. Adequate B12 increases your immune system's ability to fight disease.[58] People who have low levels of vitamin B12, even if the amount is within a normal range, are at increased risk of developing Alzheimer's disease.[59] Few foods offer vitamin B12 today. Is there any question that good cognitive thinking is a sexuality asset?

Colostrum also contains retinoic acid, which helps fight the herpes virus. It also contains a glycoprotein (kappa casein), which protects against the bacteria that causes stomach ulcers.[60]

Minerals In Colostrum

Colostrum contains several minerals in measurable amounts.[61] Zinc is of particular interest because it is associated with sexual function. For starters, zinc levels drop during PMS.

Zinc is important for the production of sex hormones, *including testosterone*. It is also essential for vaginal lubrication.[62] Adequate levels are crucial for a healthy pregnancy—deficiency can cause miscarriage. Zinc plays an important role in maintaining homeostasis, and the risk of deficiency (which is prevalent throughout the world, including the US) seems to increase in proportion to age. Its deficiency actually represents an early sign of disease.[63,64]

The presence of bacteria or viruses may cause your body to rapidly use its stores of zinc. Insufficient protein intake may also cause zinc deficiency.[65] Minerals, like vitamins and enzymes, are often lost when food is processed.

Absorption is the key to why the zinc in colostrum is more powerful than isolated zinc (as found in a multimineral supplement, for example). When zinc status in breastfed babies is compared to those who are formula-fed, the breastfed children have higher zinc levels, even though there is more zinc in the formula.[66] Isolated substances are never absorbed as efficiently as those we consume with natural cofactors intact.

The ability of zinc to retard oxidative processes has been recognized for many years. The zinc content of colostrum may be one reason why this supplement is also helpful for patients who have had heart attacks.[67]

Time for a
QUICKIE

Chlamydia trachoma, a common sexually-transmitted agent, is inhibited by colostrum in a dose-dependent manner.

Growth Factors

Colostrum is awash with growth factors. Growth factors are not just for children—they are potent immune enhancers. Again, they are even considered by some as the only substances that can truly retard or reverse aging. Part of the reason is that we reduce our production of these precious, age-protecting constituents as we get older. Because they stimulate cell growth in the dermis (tissue underlying your skin's outer layers), growth factors improve thickness and elasticity, resulting in firmer, younger-looking, less-wrinkled skin. (Do I have your attention now?)

These are the growth factors found in colostrum:

Growth hormone
Growth hormone can strengthen muscle on a cellular level and help to decrease body fat. It acts by virtue of its ability to generate IGF-1 by your liver. (See below for definition of IGF-1.)

In spite of growth hormone's leverage, it is wrought with problems when taken in supplemental form. If IGF-1 levels are boosted too high, the risks of both prostate and breast cancer are increased. Several studies in test animals and humans demonstrate that isolated growth hormone treatment may actually *shorten* life span.[68] Side effects can include diabetes, fluid retention leading to high blood pressure and heart failure, joint pain, and carpal tunnel syndrome.[69] This is not the case when growth hormone is part of a growth-factor complex in the natural context of a natural substance, as in colostrum.

Insulin-like growth factors (IGF-1 and IGF-2)
These are anabolic hormones resembling insulin. They perform the urgent mission of burning fat and building protein, and (lucky for this overweight nation) they are abundant in bovine colostrum.

IGF-1 is the only growth factor known to stimulate muscle growth and muscle repair all by itself.[70] Colostrum was shown to increase serum IGF-I concentration in athletes during strength and speed training.

It slows protein breakdown and helps to promote collagen.[71] Its concentration in colostrum may be an indicator of growth potential.[72]

Only exercise and very few supplements can get your body to increase its IGF-1 levels to optimum.

IGF-II also stimulates tissue growth.

Transforming growth factors A & B (TGF A & B)
TGF A & B promote the synthesis and repair of DNA, the master code of the cell. Sure, aging happens, but mending your broken-down DNA can postpone this inevitable fact of life.

TGF-B is very effective in wound healing, partly because it stimulates collagen formation.[73]

Epithelial growth factor (EGF)
This one stimulates wound healing and normal skin growth.

Fibroblast growth factor (FGF)
FGF contributes to the increase in cells that help growth and repair.

Because they help to stimulate the repair of nucleic acids (the building mechanisms of DNA and RNA), the presence of growth factors is extraordinary. (Velvet deer antler and the algae chlorella are two other unusual substances available in supplemental form with this capacity.) Studies show that when several of these growth factors are used together, healing is rapid and scarring reduced. *Bovine colostrum was found to contain seven different nucleotides.*[74]

You don't have to remember the specific alphabet growth factor mixes by name—just know that they are present in colostrum in significant quantity, and that they help to promote the reconditioning of your body parts that keep malfunctioning—bones, muscles, nerves, cartilage.

Emerging data from both animal and human studies indicate that combinations of selected growth factors and specific nutrients may improve the growth, adaptation, and repair of the intestinal mucosa. Results of these investigations are defining new methods for support of the intestinal tract.[75] Gastrointestinal problems are increasing in this country. Once again—you don't feel very sexy when you have a bellyache.

Apelin

One other constituent worthy of note found in colostrum is apelin. Apelin is a recently identified substance believed to have bioactive molecules (hormones, neurotransmitters, and cytokines) that transmit signals.[76] *The highest expression of apelin is in the mammary gland.* An especially large amount is secreted in colostrum.[77,78]

Other Nutrients

Colostrum also overflows with *immunoglobulins*—complicated molecules specially configured to bind to foreign cells to facilitate their destruction and removal.[79]

Many other colostrum nutrients, too numerous to mention for our purposes here, are also present. Lester A. Luz, MD, a San Francisco physician, sums it up: "It is remarkable that it has taken us so long to attempt to understand, control, and appreciate a phenomenon [colostrum] that has a history of so many millennia."[80]

Colostrum—what a wonderful adjunct to our sexual enhancement regimen!

Time for a
QUICKIE

In colostrum-fed animals, plasma IGF-I was higher than that in the animals of a control group, despite equal nutrient intake and lower circulating growth hormone.

PALM OIL TOCOTRIENOLS
Vitamin E for the New Millennium

Because vitamin E is essential for the release of estrogen from our cells—a most important aspect of sexual function—I feel fortunate to be aware of a source of vitamin E that is *not* an extraction and is also highly absorbable and safe. Like the other supplements described, palm oil tocotrienols make a strong contribution to our sexuality and do a great deal more.

About twelve years ago, after lecturing in Malaysia, I was invited to visit and confer with a group of scientists involved in palm oil research in Kuala Lumpur. I knew that Americans used very little palm oil, so you can imagine my surprise when I learned that palm oil is the second most common vegetable oil produced in the world because of its extraordinary health benefits.

Armed with medical data, I wrote the first article about this subject for American audiences on my return home. Eventually, the importance of tocotrienols derived from palm oil began to surface here, and now it is not uncommon to see palm oil tocotrienols incorporated as a main ingredient in many supplements.

The information that follows is based on the newest research and developments, and, consequently, the availability of the best palm oil tocotrienol supplements—an addition that will surely be in your best health interest. You will see that it's also in your best sex interest, too.

The term vitamin E is now considered to be a generic name describing the activity of both tocopherol (the vitamin E you are more familiar with) and tocotrienol derivatives. There are, however, distinguishing differences in the chemical structure of these two classes of vitamin E, and the variance is dramatic. (Just one quick example: Tocotrienols have the power to inhibit or destroy tumors; not so with tocopherols.) Some manufacturers have improved the tocopherol product by offering the mixed bag, rather than the isolated and very popular alpha-tocopherol alone. (The alpha faction is just one part of the vitamin E complex; the mixed tocopherols offer a more natural supplement.) But even the mixed tocopherols fall short when compared with tocotrienols.

> **Time for a QUICKIE**
>
> Palm tocotrienols are removed from crude palm oil without toxic solvents and without adverse environmental impact.

The average diet today contains significantly less natural vitamin E than it did fifty years ago, and fifty years ago it was much less available than at the turn of the last century. Vitamin E deficiency has been associated with acne, anemia, infections, some cancers, periodontal disease, cholesterol, gallstones, and dementias such as Alzheimer's disease. This is no surprise to anyone who understands vitamin E as it relates to our changing food habits and our unchanging biochemistry.

<u>Why we are vitamin-E depleted</u>

~ All vitamin Es are somewhat unstable and readily used up when in contact with polyunsaturated or rancid fats and oils. So there's a pretty good chance you deplete vitamin E when you eat foods like salad dressings.

~ The processing and milling of food, bleaching of flours, and even ordinary cooking remove most of the vitamin E content of whole foods.

~ Fried foods contain oxidized fat byproducts, thereby increasing your requirement for vitamin E whenever you eat these foods (which are usually devoid of any vitamin E to begin with!).

~ Chlorine, a component of tap water, reduces the absorption of vitamin E.

~ Synthetic estrogen also depletes vitamin E, increasing your body's demand for this nutrient.

We consume 90 percent less vitamin E than we did one hundred years ago.

<u>Why palm oil tocotrienols are superior to tocopherol</u>

~ Palm tocotrienols have the ability to reverse blockage of the carotid artery (as in arteriosclerosis) and platelet aggregation (the clumping together of blood cells), thereby reducing the risk of stroke, arteriosclerosis, and other heart disease problems.

Tocopherol may prevent further plaque formation, but only tocotrienol can successfully reverse the problem.

~ Tocotrienols can help to prevent skin aging and damage from free radicals generated by ultraviolet rays from the sun and from environmental pollutants. Melanoma, on the increase, can be inhibited with the use of tocotrienols. (Melanoma is a serious disease of tumors of the skin and other organs, too often malignant.) When applied topically, vitamin E tocotrienols are quickly absorbed into the deep layers of the skin.

~ The tocotrienol-rich fraction of palm oil is capable of protecting the brain against oxidative damage and thereby from the adverse alterations that accompany aging.

~ Vitamin E appears to be a stronger factor in lung function than other antioxidant vitamins.[81]

~ In progestin-only contraceptive users, higher lipid peroxide and lower vitamin E concentration may cause endometrial cell damage. Tocotrienols may counteract these unwanted side effects.[82]

~ Vitamin E enhances the use of estrogen stores in adrenal and fat tissues, so its deficiency explains, in part, why so many women are placed on estrogen therapy. Estrogen may be in your cells, but will not be released without vitamin E. Since estrogen depletes vitamin E, a vicious cycle is started with the widely prescribed synthetic estrogens.

Most vitamin E used in the dietary supplement market is in the alpha-tocopherol form, extracted from soy oil distillate.While tocopherols are generally present in common vegetable oils, tocotrienols are concentrated in cereal grains (oat, barley, rye, rice bran), with the highest level found in crude palm oil. Tocotrienols have been found to be forty to sixty times stronger as an antioxicant than its tocopherol cousin.

Constituents in tocotrienols can inhibit certain types of cancer, including human breast cancer. The fact that this form of vitamin E protects against both hormone-sensitive and -insensitive breast cancer cells has caught the attention of many research groups.[83] This means tocotrienols can prevent the growth of unwanted cells in the presence as well as in the absence of estradiol, thereby protecting against both hormone-related and other kinds of breast cancer!

Six different scientific centers worldwide have demonstrated that these particular tocotrienols prevent the growth of both kinds of cancer. Among these centers are: University of Reading, UK; University of Louisiana, US; University of Western Ontario, Canada; University of North Carolina, US; and the Palm Oil Research Institute, Malaysia.

With the increase in breast cancer, the prevention of breast-cancer cell growth by palm tocotrienols could have extraordinarily important clinical implications for women's health.

Breast tissue cells more readily take up tocotrienols than tocopherols. So at least part of the reason tocotrienols display greater potency is because a greater amount can accumulate in cells. The highly beneficial tocotrienols play a physiological role in modulating normal mammary gland growth, function, and remodeling.[84]

The inhibitory effect on cancer cell growth is most pronounced with the delta faction of the tocotrienols, totally missing in a tocopherol preparation.

I have joined the group of medical research reporters who predict that palm oil tocotrienols are destined to be the "new and improved" vitamin E supplement. It is a natural and more potent vitamin E, with many additional biological benefits over the more customary tocopherol. It has superior antioxidant effects and fewer contraindications than the tocopherol-based vitamin E that has been the supplement standard.

I cannot emphasize enough that consuming the whole product, rather than isolates, is the best approach. No doubt, as we continue the research, other advantages will surface for the various, perhaps as yet unidentified, constituents in palm tocotrienols. Greater power is always achieved from whole, more natural substances than from their parts.

With its help in normalizing estrogen metabolism and its anti-breast cancer propensities, tocotrienols are also an important part of our sexuality program.

TEA FOR TWO

Sipping a cup of herbal tea with your partner can be whatever you would like it to be: a relaxing experience, a sharing experience, a healthful experience, and even a sexual experience.

A marvelous group of herbal teas has just been introduced from Switzerland. We are privileged to have ten of their dozens of varieties now available here in the United States—just enough to fulfill many of our needs.

For example, the *Anti-Stress Tea* promotes a feeling of calmness. A lack of sexual energy could be caused by something as simple as stress. This tea is a great defense against the pressures of the day, with its St John's wort, balm leaves, Valerian root, and a touch of lavender flowers. (You might even find you can give up your libido-robbing antidepressant when you start drinking this tea regularly.)

If you're not feeling quite up to par because that wisdom tooth is aching or your back problem has flared up, but your partner has that "let's-do-it-now" look, try the *Pain Formula Tea*. The herb here is real willow bark, not ersatz aspirin that wreaks havoc on your stomach.

If elimination problems plague you, give the *Bladder and Kidney Tea* a try. This tea aids in the improvement of passing of water and induces the elimination of metabolic waste products via the kidneys. It contains birch and nettle leaves, plus the herb horsetail—all having long histories as remedies for bladder and kidney problems.

You're feeling hungry, but watching your weight? Try the *Slim Line Tea* for a quick feeling of hunger reduction. Yerba matte has long been known to do just that.

If your indigestion is overtaking your libido, go for the *Spice Tea*. Its fennel, anise, and caraway herbs will quickly reverse that equation. The incredible aroma will also help to put you in the mood, but even better, fennel has long been known as an aphrodisiac.

Are the kids overly restless? Will they come knocking on your door at the wrong moment? Try giving them a cup of *Sleep Tight Tea for Children* with their dinner. With the right amounts of the right herbs, mild yet effective, this tea can alter troubling night habits for the hyperactive child and the bed wetter. It's so mild (yet effective), it can even be given to infants.

If the children are prone to tummy aches, a cup of *Fennel Tea for Children* helps their digestive processes. Between the digestive and the sleep-tight teas, you won't need a Do-Not-Disturb sign on your door.

You want a little stimulation without being up all night? *Green Tea with Spearmint* has half the caffeine of a cup of coffee, but unlike regular tea, it contains the wonderful phytochemicals that are so conducive to health.

Everything under control? You just want to sip a cup of tea as you look into each other's eyes? Try the delicious

Fruit Tea for a refreshing beverage. It contains an array of herbal delights, including black currants, lime blossom, orange zest, rose petals, and cherry stalks. It's good for the body *and* it's delicious!

If you've had the ideal experience, you probably won't need the last tea on our list. Save it for nights when you and your partner are not romantic. It's the *Good Night Sleep Tea for Adults*. You'll find that you'll fall asleep quickly and awake invigorated. It has a perfect and safe combination of Hop cones, balm leaves, orange blossoms, and Valerian root.

The Swiss company that has made these wonderful teas available considers the production of herbal teas an art, reflected in the pleasant palatability and effectiveness of each variety. The teas are available at your local health store.

Why am I recommending these particular teas? The herbs used are pharmaceutical grade (that's a step *above* organic!), and this company operates under the strictest quality control methods. They import their herbs from more than one hundred countries, and then "fine-cut" them, helping to maintain peak flavors. Even the filter bags allow for more surface area than the usual, and each is wrapped in a flavor-preserving foil sachet. If that's not enough, the teas are date-stamped on both the box and the double-wrapped tea bags. No wonder it's the number one brand in Europe!

Why use tea as a delivery system for a food-type supplement? Doesn't heat destroy the fragile phytochemicals that give natural remedies their effectiveness? Doesn't the long shelf life of a tea bag work against the potency of these trace substances?

Good questions with good answers. Virtually all nutraceuticals undergo some level of processing to get from plant to capsule or tablet. They are extracted, tinctured, decocted, infused, or pressed to extract the material out of the plant and into the supplement delivery system. In the case of tea, that processing—generally a hot-water infusion or a boiling water decoction process—takes place right in your own teacup, just minutes before use. Prior to that, the phytochemicals have been stored in the best possible packaging—the intact plant leaf, stem, or root itself. Conclusion: tea, despite its mundane familiarity, is actually one of the best delivery systems going. Enjoy!

Time for a
QUICKIE

According to Chinese legend, the first tea came about quite by accident five thousand years ago. An Emperor was making his supper when leaves of a tea plant fell into water he was boiling. He spread the word that it was better to drink such a beverage than to drink wine, which loosens the tongue, or unboiled water, which is infectious.

ORGANIC GERMANIUM (GE-132)

(not to be confused with germanium dioxide or the geranium flower)

If arthritis interferes with your sex life, a most interesting characteristic of organic germanium is its ability to relieve pain. It does this by inhibiting the enzyme that, in turn, inhibits the production of your body's endorphins—your self-produced feel-good "morphine." (Endorphins are produced in your brain, and have the effect of diminishing pain.)

And that's only the beginning of how organic germanium can help sexuality. As stated in a primary medical textbook used by medical students in their first year, lack of cellular oxygen supply is probably the most common cause of cell injury and may also be the ultimate mechanism of damage.[85] Examples of causes of diminished oxygen supplies are atherosclerotic plaques or thrombi, which *restrict the flow of blood*—an obvious disadvantage for optimal sex. Organic germanium to the rescue!

In true adaptogenic style, organic germanium helps to alleviate minor or major health imbalances, and to help keep you free of health problems. It appears to play a role as an oxygen catalyst, an antioxidant, an electro-stimulant, and an immune enhancer. Organic germanium is found in significant quantities in garlic, aloe, comfrey, chlorella, ginseng, shelf fungus (a variety of Reishi mushroom), and watercress.

No nutrient—whether it is protein, fatty acid, vitamin, or mineral—fulfills its functions in its original form.

Nutrients are mechanical substances necessary for converting the dormant or potential energy in your foods into usable energy for you to get out of bed, get the kids off to school, put in a full day at work, or to have sex. In other words, nutrients supply energy for your everyday living activities.

For the conversion to take place from food to energy, oxygen is utilized. This process is called oxidation: the combining of a food substance with oxygen to release the stored chemical energy.

Note these reports:

~ A physician in San Diego uses organic germanium both orally and intramuscularly to relieve problems of impotency.

~ A doctor in New York considers it an obligation to offer germanium to most of her patients.

~ A scientist in San Francisco takes a few 50-milligram capsules when he wants to stay up late and work with a clear mind. (Think about this at times when your partner is interested in sex and you feel just too tired.)

~ Children in China with Kashin-Beck disease, a serious degenerative osteoarticular disorder, had much lower levels of organic germanium than their healthy peers.[86]

~ Common yeast infections (*Candida albicans*) occur more frequently in an oxygen-poor body.

~ Use of drugs, whether recreational or prescribed, depletes cellular oxygen because oxygen is required to metabolize most toxic chemicals.

~ Organic germanium can help to delay the progression of cataracts.[87]

~ When administered to test animals with normal blood pressure, the use of organic germanium shows no change. When given to test animals with high blood pressure, the animals return to normal within seven to ten days. (This demonstrates the adaptogenic quality of germanium.)

~ Organic germanium provides relief from the debilitating symptoms of the chronic Epstein-Barr Virus Syndrome, an affliction that may be affecting millions of Americans.[88]

~ Organic germanium has lasting effects for a considerably long period after it is discontinued. Again, this is typical of adaptogenic substances.

~ Organic germanium may possess antimutagenic potential.[89]

Not unlike some of the other supplements described, organic germanium detoxifies heavy metals. It can do this rapidly because its cubic structure contains negatively charged oxygen atoms capable of trapping heavy metals (which are positively charged), and discharging them safely out of the body.

Organic germanium improves glutathione metabolism, helps to relieve depression, and has been reported to increase bone mass. Some of its effects are analogous to that of thyroid hormones. It improves overall metabolism of the cell, thus the organ, the system, and therefore sexual enjoyment.[90]

In Summary

These products are not meant to be the only prescribed list for supplementation. Needless to say, other food-type supplements of interest are available. I defined these products as a backdrop for you to appreciate the concepts involved. When making your selections, look for those that deliver their special attributes in somewhat the same way. Hopefully, the number of whole-food-type supplement will both increase and become more readily available.

When it comes to sexuality, the blueprint for normal function is usually still intact. In other words, libido loss is not necessarily the result of genetic fate or irreparable damage. Sexual function can can almost always be resurrected and retained, and I believe that this kind of supplementation can help to make that happen. These supplements will be of great value long-term, and their use may take time for effectiveness. For more immediate help (tonight?) see chapter nine.

"Is your husband
good at foreplay?"

"Are you kidding? He
gets through it with
three words."

"Three words?
What are they?"

"He says:
'Brace yourself, Barbara.'"

Chapter Eight

SHE'S <u>ALWAYS</u> HAD TO HAVE IT: SEXUAL WISDOM FROM DAY ONE

Married women are heavier than single women because single women come home, see what's in the refrigerator and go to bed; married women come home, see what's in the bed and go to the refrigerator.

Yogis Bare: The Art of Tantric Sex

Tantra (a Sanskrit word meaning "woven together") can be loosely defined as a system of Hindu yoga which worships the sexual union of men and women, encouraging us to be in tune with our own sexual energy. Historically the movement has its roots in the physical and spiritual union of man and woman, which leads to a form of sexual ritual where slow, non-orgasmic sex is believed to be "a path to experience the divine."[1]

The Tantric traditions of ancient India and other cultures viewed sexual energy as the source of life itself and as one of the most powerful forces available to human beings. In the Tantric view, all life and every aspect of creation including sexuality is celebrated and held as sacred. Through the sacred act of love, Tantric sex seeks the merging of the dual nature of sexuality into an ecstatic union.

Through Tantric sex one learns to prolong the act of making love and to channel orgasmic energies moving through the body, thereby raising your level of consciousness. (A far cry from the "Quickie"!) It embraces the concept that sex is good for your health, and regards men and women as distinctly different—each possessing qualities which are of value to the other.

Tantra expresses the fact that lovemaking between a man and woman, when entered into with awareness, is a gateway to both sexual and spiritual ecstasy, and is both playful and joyful. In India, traditional Tantrikas spent many years under the guidance of a spiritual teacher and engaged in elaborate yogic rituals to purify and master body and mind. These practices were intended to awaken the powerful psychic energies through which the adept could enter into higher states of consciousness.

In such a sex-positive culture, sophisticated lovemaking skills were developed and taught as a science and art.

The suggestions in the final chapters offer another way to achieve some of these goals. The development of particular love- making skills is one of the most appropriate areas for human exploration.

Qigong: Both Sides Now

When I read the following section, offered specifically for this book by Qigong masters Francesco and Daisy Lee Garripoli, I found myself enveloped in a sense of calm and peace. Among the many concepts that I found extraordinary was the reference to the overlap of Yin and Yang—so contrary to what I had learned about men and women as I grew up. For example, my high school biology teacher would have been shocked to know that both men and women manufacture the same hormones; that men require estrogen for *maleness*; that women need testosterone for *desire*. A literal translation, to be sure— but the Chinese masters somehow grasped the concept 2,500 or more years ago!

A Quigong Perspective
by Francesco and Daisy Lee Garripoli

Qigong (Chi Kung), the ancient Chinese healthcare system similar to Yoga and the "mother" of Tai Chi, is a product of the philosophical systems of Taoism and Buddhism. Taoism is attributed to a wise old Chinese sage named Lao Tzu who lived some 2,500 years ago and wrote the famous "Tao Te Ching," a treatise that has influenced the thinking of millions, if not billions, of people.

We don't know if Lao Tzu was a man or a woman, or for that matter whether the writing was about men or women. This creates a joyful dilemma for modern trans-lators of Lao Tzu's work. Adding to the dilemma is the fact that the Chinese language is genderless. There are no words such as "his" or "hers" and "she" or "he."

This presents a situation that forces us to look at how deep our "separation of the sexes" goes. How is it that we always gravitate toward "separation" and not "inte-gration?"

One of the basic tenets of Taoism, and hence, Qigong, is the concept of Yin and Yang. We all know that this concept is depicted by a round symbol with a wave of black embracing a wave of white and vice versa. Many are quick to interpret this as depicting a bipolar di-chotomy that is, well, black and white. Upon this misin-terpretation, we wrongly map sexuality, seeing only clear-cut separation between the sexes.

Qigong, through the lexicon of Taoism, helps us to see that in the Yin-Yang symbol, Yin—the feminine, nur-turing, dark, physical energy of the Universe—is in a constant, interactive dance with Yang—the masculine, active, light, formless energy of the Universe. They are not "opposed" as we may think, and in fact, one con-tains the other. When you look at the symbol drawn in its traditional style, there is always a dot of Yin within the Yang, and a dot of Yang within the Yin. This was Lao Tzu's way of reminding us that we are a dynamic melding of energies.

Whether we are Taoists or not, it seems to be human nature to see things as extremes, as definable in a linear way. Maybe this is the work of the "ego," that part of us that requires an identity in relationship to the world around us. The ego judges others—and itself—in an attempt to see where it fits in, where it "ranks." The ego, from this perspective, can be equated with fear. It is diametrically opposed to the nature of our soul or "higher self." In a world and in a society that supports the importance of the ego in everything from television ads to popular magazines, how do we migrate to the realm of the "higher self"? How do we seek that spiritual layer we so desire in our lives and in our relationships? This is what the practice of systems such as Qigong can do for us and for our intimate relationships.

We know on our "soul" level that these dynamic forces of Yin and Yang cannot survive at their extremes. The key to life is in the pursuit of balance, and herein lies the path of true healing and intimacy. Both Taoism and Buddhism seek to offer us some insight into this pursuit of balance. And Qigong is the toolkit from which we can draw practical exercises that help secure the essence of these gentle, commonsense philosophies.

Breathing and movement, stretching and visualizing— these are the outward actions of Qigong practice that instigate and stimulate the spirit. It is through conscious breathing and joyful visualization, linked with gentle movement of the body, that Qigong becomes the tool to discover our true nature.

The Traditional Chinese Medicine perspective is that all pain and disease is the result of blocked or stagnant Qi. Whether this manifests in weakened sex drive, an emotional roller-coaster, or endometriosis, it's all related to blocked Qi, the energy that vitalizes us, keeps us alive, and must flow smoothly throughout our body and spirit. What we eat, drink, think, and whom and what we interact with affects the state and fluidity of our Qi. This is why it is critical to our health to do everything we can to promote smooth and balanced Qi flow. Practices like Qigong have been proven to enhance the effects of a good diet and nutritional supplementation. Qigong has even been shown to reduce the need for medication. This is the gift of balance.

Even simple, daily Qigong exercises such as gently tapping the lower back (kidneys and adrenals) can do wonders for improving the state of our Jing—the energy that ultimately drives our sexual center, controlling everything from our kidney function to our reproductive organs. It is believed that Jing comes to us in a finite amount and that we cannot easily collect more over our lifetime. As Jing is depleted, our hair becomes gray and thin, and our sex drive lessens. Qigong has been shown to be very effective in keeping the Jing Qi strong and slowing the depletion process.

Part of our pursuit of balance is getting in touch on the deepest levels with the richness of who we are. We must be willing to "do the work" to draw upon the infinite resource within us and move toward a centered approach to life. Women are in a better position than men to achieve this and find acceptance of the Yang within their Yin. Men have to deal with many cultural barriers that often keep them from acceptance. Just because one is a women doesn't make one more Yin, however. Yin is just a propensity. Each of us is an amalgam of Yin and Yang, which are present in infinite proportions within us and around us.

Understanding and practicing Qigong can help us bring our actions "to the surface" and become more conscious in our lives. To live in this way is to be truly awake, what the psychologist Carl Jung called the "individuated person," someone who is not living in two worlds, one of which is suppressed and asleep most of the time.

When we awaken to our full potential, we can feel without fear, we can breathe deeply and smell the fragrances, savor the essential nature of life, and see all things, all people as participants in a beautiful dance. The feminine then becomes the true expression of Yin and Yang: hard, yet soft; powerful, yet yielding; flexible in action and thought, yet firm in conviction . . . compassionate to the core.

Daisy Lee, Qigong practitioner and martial artist, says:

"During my Qigong 'movement meditations,' I visualize the Yin and Yang nature of my Qi, my life force energy. Through my breath, I accept all that the world has to offer me in a Yin-embracing in-breath. As I exhale, I accept my Yang nature and build confidence through decisive action.

"When I do my daily Qigong workout, it's really a prayer seeking balance. I don't specifically think about balancing my emotions, thinking, or energy. I simply open myself to balancing the smooth and natural flow of Qi throughout my body and spirit."

Note about learning the exercises associated with the practice of Qigong: You will find basic exercises and movements from Wuji Qigong, Bagua Xun Dao Gong, and Shaolin Qigong in the book *Qigong: Essence of the Healing Dance* by Garri Garripoli and friends (Deerfield Beach, FL: Health Communications, Inc., 1999).

For information about this book and programs in Qigong, visit the website www.WujiProductions.com.

Oy, Yay! Judaism's Surprising Stand on Female Sexuality

Rabbi Rita Leonard (the only female rabbi in Hawaii) supplied the following information:

Under ancient Jewish law, men were "legally bound" to be intimate with their wives! The Jewish marriage contract, the ketubah, was an early voice for women's sexual rights. Husbands were required to uphold certain provisions for their wives and put this decree down in witnessed and signed legal documents.

Along with food and shelter, husbands were required to engage in regular sexual activity. A wife denied sex could request from a Jewish court of law (the "Bet Din") a divorce based on the grounds that her husband was not keeping up his end…of the bargain, that is!

The Jewish way in law and practice is clearly and ultimately designed to imbue holiness within every human action, including sexual intercourse. Simply understood in Jewish terms, sex is both sacred *and* divinely intended.

The Torah also contains some interesting mandates of the subject of a man's obligation to his wife's "cheer":

"When a man taketh a new wife, he shall not go out in the host, neither shall he be charged with any business, he shall be free for his house one year, and shall cheer his wife with whom he has taken."[2]

Leave the "Spanish Fly" At Home: The Truth About Aphrodisiacs

Sexual drive (the feeling of being "turned on") is the result of an extremely complicated process. It begins with hormonal signals sent to your brain, where they are amplified by responses to visual and other sensory patterns.

These responses can be influenced by your individual experiences and histories, or hard-wired by your genetics, but the end result is more hormonal signals reflected back to your endocrine system. This leads to a chain of hormone production, but the action site ultimately comes back to your brain, which then directs your body to do very complicated and unlikely things (which you may or may not regret in the morning!).

It's not hard to see how easy it would be for some of this process to go awry. At the same time, it's clear that there is more Darwinian "survival value" to libido than anything else, short of eating and breathing. So our psyches are a tangle of landmines and safeguards. But if it didn't work, at least most of the time, we wouldn't be here.

Finding the right aphrodisiac is an exercise in using the built-in capabilities of your mind and body to work around the problem spots that often develop in this most complex of all human behaviors.

Men *and* women have long dreamed about the possibility of increasing sexual capacity or of stimulating sexual desires, including food and pharmaceuticals.

Can food really be an aphrodisiac? Here's what the *Encyclopedia Britannica* has to say on this subject:

> The combination of various sensuous reactions—the visual satisfaction of the sight of appetizing food, the olfactory stimulation of their pleasing smells and the tactile gratification afforded the oral mechanism by rich, savory dishes—tend to bring on a state of general euphoria conducive to sexual expression.

Some of you may remember the movie, *Tom Jones*, which clearly demonstrated this phenomenon. A shared meal between two people, totally devoid of any nudity or X-rated paraphernalia, was one of the sexiest scenes in cinema history.

The following foods are among the very many that have long histories as aphrodisiacs:

~ Fennel. Used during Pharaonic time, fennel was well known for its medical properties, including its use as an aphrodisiac as well as a laxative.

~ Pine nuts. Roasting does not destroy the aphrodisiac qualities of pine nut and can enhance the taste. Keep in mind, though, that pine nuts roast quickly in comparison to other nuts and also burn easily.

~ Shrimp. Since shrimp and pine nuts are well known for their aphrodisiac qualities, imagine what would happen if you combine these ingredients!

~ Oysters. No doubt oysters are effective because of their high zinc content.

~ Onions. Onions have been used as an aphrodisiac for endless centuries. Egyptian priests were not allowed to eat onions in case the temptation became too great.

~ Spicy foods, especially chilies and curries. Because of their ability to raise heart rate and even cause sweating (reactions experienced during sex), spicy foods are thought to be aphrodisiacs.

~ Garlic. The aphrodisiac effects of garlic are discussed in chapter seven.

~ Commonly used herbs. Among the herbs touted today are: Yohimbe, avena sativa, ginseng, catuaba, Mucuna pruriens, Shilajit, and Ashwagandha.[3]

~ Chocolate. Theorized to be an aphrodisiac because of its content of phenylethylamine, which is also present in the brain, and produced in greater quantity when people are in love (although never proven to be so). Chocolate is everywoman's favorite aphrodisiac.

Less familiar aphrodisiacs run the gamut. One includes components derived from fertilized, partly incubated chickens' eggs, used successfully in Norway to treat diminished sexual desire in men.[4]

Our knowledge of pheromones, well known to attract potential mates and to act in concert with other stimuli to promote mating, are, in a sense, *airborne aphrodisiacs*. One study shows that receptive female rats apparently broadcast a volatile pheromone that promotes an erection in males, provided the males are downwind of the females. In this case, the volatile pheromone acts alone to evoke a sexual response.[5]

Finding a sexually receptive partner of the opposite sex is a challenge, and one solution is to advertise—as in personal ads. The South African clawed frog does the same thing! Constraints on reproduction have led to fertility advertisement by these female frogs. When their time for fertility is imminent, they swim to an advertising male and produce an aphrodisiac call, *rapping*, that stimulates both male vocalization and approach. Males respond to rapping with a distinctive answer call. The rapping-answer interaction thus forms a duet between partners of a receptive pair.[6]

Time for a
QUICKIE

Although men seem to have sought aphrodisiacs more than women, the concept is named after Aphrodite, the Greek goddess of love.

Time for a
QUICKIE

Viagra is good not only for treating male impotence, but small concentrations of the drug dissolved in a vase of water can also double the shelf life of cut flowers, making them stand up straight for as long as a week beyond their natural life span. Viagra has been tested on strawberries, legumes, roses, carnations, broccoli and other perishables. One milligram of Viagra (compared with 50 mg in one pill taken by men) in a solution appears to be enough for the beneficial effect.

Viagra has a similar effect on plant ripening as it does on men's sexual organs. Viagra increases the vase life of flowers by retarding the breakdown of cyclic guanosine monophosphate. If the flower industry uses this preservation method, edible flowers may become more popular than ever before.

Source: *British Medical Journal* 1999 July;319-274.

Here's how some of the aphrodisiacs work:[7]

Substances Containing Chemicals Resembling Sex Hormones

Angelica sinensis (Chinese variety only; also known as Dang Gui, and more commonly known as Dong Quai) is one of the best examples of this category, and a potent source of phytoestrogens. It is strongly adaptogenic, and practitioners claim to have used it with success both in cases where estrogen levels are too low or too high.

How can one substance do both? The phytoestrogens in Chinese Angelica are close, but not exact, matches to human estrogen. They can bind with human estrogen receptor sites to produce similar but less potent effects. If estrogen levels in the body are too high, the presence of the phytoestrogens in the receptors blocks the human estrogens from working.

So especially in cases where human estrogen is unstable or fluctuating quickly (resulting in "hot flashes"), or where supply is chronically too high or too low, Angelica seems to provide a stable and milder replacement.

This is what makes it so good as a moderator of menstrual difficulties and menopausal symptoms—and along the way it's also thought to correct a deficient sex drive. Perhaps it's merely a side effect of pain reduction, but it seems at least equally likely that the estrogen-mimicking capabilities have a wide range of effects.

Substances That Stimulate the Production Of Testosterone Or Other Hormones

In both men and women, testosterone is the primary hormone responsible for libido. It is not really a "male" hormone, although it is found in much greater concentration in men than in women. Stimulation of the pituitary gland is one possible mode of action.

Velvet antler is my favorite functional food supplement in this category, although the exact mechanism is still not fully understood. It might stimulate testosterone production directly, or its effectiveness might have more to do with growth hormone stimulants and their precursors. I discuss velvet antler in more detail in chapters nine and ten.

Antidepressants

Although many popular antidepressants are known to *suppress* libido, the ones that do not have this effect are almost certain to enhance it. No surprise here; people are more interested in sex when they're feeling good. That is, feeling good without some physiological monkey wrench in the works that suppresses the sex drive.

Ginkgo biloba is a good example of a natural antidepressant, and is also discussed in detail later.

Garum armoricum has the distinction of being among the oldest surviving health foods in this category. We're not just talking centuries, but rather, millennia! The Greeks knew and used salted fish products as early as the fifth century BC. Garum has been to the West what ginseng has been to the East. Those who are currently familiar with garum tout it with as much enthusiasm as in those ancient times. Today we suggest the standardized pure supplement, prepared under highly controlled conditions, available in capsule form.

Energy Enhancers

Not quite the same as antidepressants, these are substances that help restore physical energy, rather than emotional well being. The result is similar: People with more energy tend to be more interested in sex.

The "Yang Kidney tonics" of Chinese herbal medicine fall into this category.

Another good example is *Epimedium grandiflorum*, also known as licentious goat wort.

"One of my favorite herbs and one that should be as popular as ginseng," says herbalist Stuart FitzSimmons in his excellent website about Chinese herbal remedies.[8] Epimedium has been shown to cause significant increases in serotonin and dopamine in test animals, and the dopamine particularly is thought to account for the aphrodisiac effects. Dopamine stimulates the pituitary gland to produce more leutinizing hormone, which in turn stimulates testosterone production.

Epimedium is also thought to enhance skin sensitivity, a possible indirect contributor to sexual enjoyment, if not to libido.

Chinese researchers have observed Epimedium extracts to have a testosterone-like effect in men, improving the performance of the muscles that participate in erection and ejaculation.

Like most adaptogenic herbal remedies, Epimedium offers a broad range of positive effects. Dialysis patients, for example, show improved immune response along with improved sexual function with its use.[9,10,11]

Topical Stimulants and Transdermal Delivery

Topical stimulants are not strictly a category of aphrodisiacs, but they are among the most effective means of improving the ability to reach orgasm. Topical creams are applied directly to the vaginal tissue and clitoris, to stimulate, to increase sensitivity, and to increase the permeability of the skin.

This last effect is important in products that combine topical stimulants with other aphrodisiac or orgasm-enhancing substances. Menthol is typically used as a stimulant and vasodilator, and certain amino acids added with the menthol to a cream base provide a critical supply of nitrogen to help with clitoral erection. Nutraceuticals with aphrodisiac properties are also readily absorbed via the transdermal route.

Natural products sometimes don't feel as potent as engineered drugs. Most of them work, but they often work slowly and indecisively, frequently demanding full cooperation with diet and lifestyle changes. But occasionally we find one that is remarkable.

A topical stimulant combined with an array of transdermal nutraceuticals is one such "natural product" that is well worth it.

Get Ready For Chapter Nine

My favorite orgasm-enhancing products are gel-creams that combine a very mild menthol stimulant with the amino acids arginine and ornithine. velvet antler, ginkgo biloba, Siberian ginseng, palm tocotrienols, and other trace nutrients. The addition of these special ingredients can be a very important part of the mix.

Read on to see how and why these ingredients all work together.

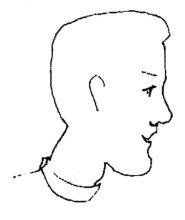

"Baby, you're
my first!"

"Do you mean
this weekend?"

Chapter Nine

TAKING CONTROL OF
YOUR SEXUAL RESPONSE

Rodney Dangerfield has been quoted as saying: "My first sexual experience was terrifying. It was a dark, dreary night, and I was so very scared. I was all alone."

How To Have It!

More than half a century ago, when my close friends and I got together to talk about our new lives as young married women, it was inevitable that the topic of sex would surface. Why, we kept asking, were the men so *gung ho* for sex *all the time*? Was their experience different from ours? And if so, was there anything we could do to change things?

It took each of us awhile to overcome the sexual repression that pervaded our society at that time, and, eventually, to learn how to reach the orgasmic state—a seemingly natural and "built-in" process for our men. Although science hasn't provided all the answers yet, recent research can help women of all ages to understand the process with far greater clarity than explained in *The Joy of Sex,* the only mainstream reference for decades.

The exciting news is that for those women who do not have adequate arousal, there is a new category of products that offers safe, quick, and reliable results. And these are not drugs with side effects that can compromise your overall health. Quite the opposite: when the quality is good and the formulation is correct, these products can enhance your health while facilitating sexual euphoria as you've never experienced before.

The products that make this possible are topical creams or gels (or sometimes "gel-creams") based on amino acids, local stimulants, and other natural ingredients known for aphrodisiac and adaptogenic effects. Topical means that the product is applied directly to the area of action—to the vagina and clitoris.

The combination of stimulation, lubrication, and transdermal absorption of the natural nutrients required for sexual response can produce amazing results. (Transdermal absorption refers to absorption through the skin.)

A well-formulated topical cream can stimulate vaginal lubrication and intensify sexual orgasm almost immediately for almost all women—regardless of age.

These products have been heralded as the first effective "orgasm enhancing substances" for a very good reason: **they work!**

What I find especially intriguing about them is that they allow you to take control of your sexual response. Not only do they help women reach orgasm more often and more quickly, but they can also increase sexual desire and sensation. The resulting tingling feeling, in combination with the physical stimulation of the clitoris during intercourse, leads to heightened pleasure.

The two most important ingredients in the best topical orgasm-enhancers are arginine and menthol. Arginine is an amino acid that helps with the physiology of erection and orgasm, as will be explained in detail. Menthol is a local stimulant, and also helps with the transdermal absorption of all the other ingredients, which appear to work synergistically: the best formulations may also include *ginseng* (adaptogenic aphrodisiac), *Gingko biloba* (energy and alertness), *tocotrienols* (powerful antioxidants), and *ornithine* (another amino acid that works with arginine). Some products even include more exotic sexual nutraceuticals like *velvet antler* or *epimedium*.

Chapter ten describes the mechanism of orgasm, graphically demonstrating what happens before, during, and immediately after the orgasmic experience. Sexual physiology is complex, and so are my attempts to explain it, so don't worry if you need to skip over some of the biochemistry. **You don't need to know the science to enjoy the result.** But before you get to the science, here's a brief overview of how a well-formulated product works.

Chapter two touched on a few factors involved in orgasm. Specifically, the following was emphasized:

~ the endocrine pathways involved

~ the need for an oxygen supply for vaginal muscle contraction

~ the influence of local vasodilatation (or blood flow)

...all of which are required to experience the clitoral sensation, culminating in orgasm.

These important points should be kept in mind:

~ Female response to arousal relates mainly to the vagina—thickening of the vaginal wall due to vasodilation, lubrication, and widening of the vaginal cavity.

~ Vasodilation increases the diameter of blood vessels, causing greater blood flow, necessary for orgasm.

~ Orgasm is brought about by stimulation of the skin of the clitoris.

~ Sexual intercourse itself does not produce the degree of intense physical stimulation for women as does direct clitoral manipulation.

Oral preparations of L-arginine have been shown to enhance male erectile response in animal studies.[1] In this context the female biochemical pathways are similar. Very simply, an enzyme converts L-arginine to nitric oxide, which brings blood to the vaginal area, causing clitoral arousal. When the clitoris is stimulated, orgasm occurs.

Ornithine shares arginine's capability to supply bioavailable nitrogen for nitric oxide production—needed for the orgasmic process. Evidence supports the fact that arginine and ornithine work together to stimulate important hormones that play a role in achieving orgasm.[2] Ornithine is more expensive, so most vaginal formulations emphasize arginine. Personally I think it's better to use a product that contains both, to cover all the bases.

Menthol, a compound obtained from peppermint and other mint oils, is a vasodilator, causing blood vessels to relax and increase in diameter. It enhances the sensitivity of nerve endings, making the clitoris more responsive to external stimulation. Vasodilation also stimulates the vagina's own ability to produce lubricants. The bonus value of vasodilation is that it improves the absorption of all the other ingredients present in a topical application.[3,4] For example, if arginine is present, a small amount of menthol will help to ensure that the arginine is absorbed in effective concentrations.

Other than aiding orgasm, nothing in menthol is sex- or health-enhancing. While menthol is commonly used in nasal inhalers, chest rubs, and cough drops, it can be a mild irritant to sensitive clitoral and vaginal tissue. So I'm an advocate of using menthol in very small amounts—only in combination with other components that activate the natural pathways to sexual euphoria.

Figure 10

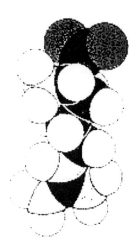

The white cells are hydrogen.
The black cells are carbon.
The light gray cells are nitrogen.
The dark gray cells are oxygen.

How the chemical configuration of arginine helps to produce orgasm is explained in detail in chapter ten.

Arginine Molecule

A vaginal gel-cream works by increasing the production of nitric oxide in clitoral tissue with the use of arginine (as opposed to preventing the breakdown of nitric oxide, which is how Viagra works in men). Nitric oxice is a powerful blood vessel dilator and is responsible for the blood engorgement of the clitoris and vaginal tissue.

Supplemental arginine has also been shown to enhance wound healing. Deficiency of this amino acid can result in hair loss, constipation, a delay in wound healing, and liver disease. Arginine has a positive effect on the immune system. It may increase male fertility by increasing sperm production and motility. When used in supplemental form with ornithine, it has muscle-building effects.

"Honey, I've been seeing other supplements."

Because of the complexity of sexual physiology, for best results it's important to combine several different substances, with varying modes of sexually enhancing actions. Here's a brief overview of why I recommend these specific valuable additions to a topical sexual stimulant.

Ginseng

Ginseng has long been touted as a sex aid. An active constituent in ginseng encourages arousal by contributing to vasodilation. But ginseng does so much more! For example, it keeps the level of prolactin normalized.[5] (Recall that too much prolactin reduces desire.) Studies have been done at the University of Nap- els, University College of Medicine in Korea, Yale University School of Medicine, New Haven, and at Semmelweis University Medical School, Budapest, Hungary—among other research centers—to validate the significance of ginseng in the sexual response.[6,7,8,9]

Time for a
QUICKIE

A substance in ginseng acts as a nitric oxide donor, working through the L-arginine/nitric oxide pathway.

Ginkgo biloba

As stated in chapter one, Ginkgo biloba extract is noted for causing cerebral enhancement. This natural herb helps to maintain and restore cognitive function,[10] and to improve mental sharpness by increasing blood flow to the brain.[11] Women are more responsive to its sexual enhancement. Recall that Ginkgo biloba generally has a positive effect on all four phases of the sexual response cycle: *desire, excitement* (lubrication), *orgasm*, and *resolution* (afterglow).[12]

Ginkgo, too, is a vasodilator, and this effect appears to be particularly important around nerve tissue.

Velvet antler

Velvet antler, the biologically active tissue of antlers shed annually by deer and elk, has a millennia-long history of success as a health supplement. One of its most attractive roles is its positive attributes for sexual function (for both men *and* women). Numerous animal studies confirm these effects on sexual activity.[13] As for anecdotes, members of my family, my friends, and I can offer testimonials for its libido-enhancing abilities. (We have been using velvet antler for several years, long enough to overrule any placebo effects.) Velvet antler naturally contains particular amino acids responsible for stimulating testosterone release from the cells that produce this hormone (leydig cells), which may explain how it works to contribute to sexual arousal.

Tocotrienols

You already know that vitamin E is essential for the release of estrogen from your cells, and that one faction of tocotrienols (the delta faction), may prevent and reverse breast cancer—both hormone- and nonhormone-initiated (that is, estrogen-receptor positive *and* negative cells).[14]

Applying this food-based natural product vaginally has additional benefits, especially for vaginal dryness. For those with serious vaginal dryness, I recommend (in addition to a vaginal enhancement cream) the vaginal insertion of a tocotrienol capsule as well. After using a transdermal vaginal gel-cream for a while, however, the problem of vaginal dryness usually disappears.

Recent studies show that vitamin E can improve the activity of nitric oxide, an effect that is independent of its antioxidant protection. And it appears to be a two-way street: the presence of nitric oxide spares the use of vitamin E in protecting your delicate cell membranes against oxidation. It performs its duties as an antioxidant for good lung function, demonstrating to be superior to both vitamin C and retinol for this purpose. It also helps in the regulation of your steroid profile, and even offers to protect against Alzheimer's disease. All of these factors can only improve sexual function!

The substances listed above are explained in more detail in chapter ten.

Why transdermal?

Transdermal vaginal gel-cream is available two ways:
1. In a jar, which allows you to apply as much or as little as you ultimately find effective.

2. In a very small packet, where the amount is controlled, usually called a "pillow" pack. Most women find this a-mount adequate; others find the packet effective for two or three applications. Instructions are usually included with your purchase of a gel-cream.

Recall that hormones work in almost unbelievably small concentrations. Think of that single salt crystal dissolved in the swimming pool referred to in chapter two, and the effects of stomach acids, digestive enzymes, and fi-nally, first-pass removal by the liver, explained in chap-ter five. The latter takes out most of the foreign hor-mones that have made it through your intestinal walls into your bloodstream, to insure that your body's own endocrine system remains in charge.

This is fine, but what happens when you want to take a drug? The real problem with oral drugs in general is that it's very difficult to get a complicated molecule past these important defense systems intact. One strategy is enteric coatings that protect small particles of the sub-stance from outside attack until they're well into the intestines. Progress is still being made in this area, with new technologies like micro-encapsulation showing promise. But only certain substances can be absorbed through intestinal walls, even if they survive the upper digestive system. And they still have to make it beyond that first pass through the liver. That's why so many therapies involving large molecules require direct injection of a drug or hormone.

Transdermal application offers an alternative. Skin is surprisingly penetrable, even to relatively large molecules. This is especially true for sensitive and tender areas of skin, where the layers of protective dead cells are thinnest and these substances can most easily diffuse down into capillaries just below the surface. From there they are carried into the surrounding tissue and via blood circulation to the rest of your body.

Sexual stimulation lends itself very well to transdermal application. The skin of the genital area is thin and sensitive, the substances need to do their work close to the site of application, and the neurological effect requires topical stimulation. It's a perfect fit, and makes oral delivery of sexual enhancement (such as with Viagra) look positively primitive by comparison.

If a transdermal vaginal cream is applied properly to the underside of the clitoris, the chances of stimulating a clitoral erection are dramatically improved. Recall that while men do not have to have an erection for orgasm and ejaculation, a clitoral erection is a requirement for a complete female orgasm.

You can see why a well-formulated topical application can make a big difference, and why they are becoming so popular.

Jane decided it was finally time to have sex with her boyfriend. The boyfriend, being prepared, produced a box of six condoms and they used one of them.

Next week he was over at Jane's place again, but this time, when he took out the box of condoms, Jane noticed that there were only four left in the box. Jane asked about the missing condom, and the boyfriend explained that he had used it for masturbation.

Jane wasn't too sure about this, but let it slide. However, a few days later she double-checked with a male friend: "Have you ever done that?" she asked.

"Sure," he answered, "several times."

"You've masturbated with a condom?" Jane responded in surprise.

"Oh no," answered her friend. "I've lied to my girlfriend."

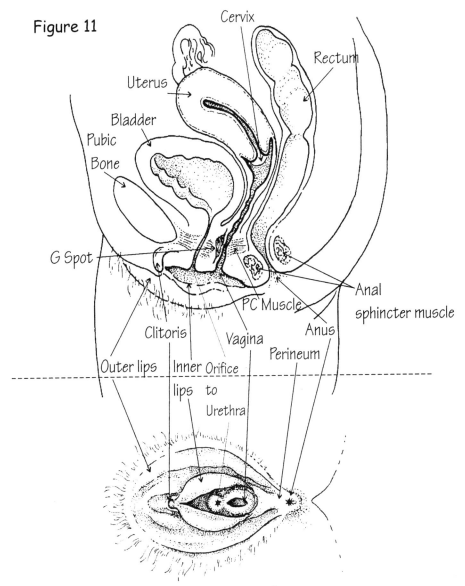

Female Genital Area

During increased arousal, both the outer and innr lips become swollen with blood, much as a man's penis becomes engorged during sexual arousal.

What to Expect When Using a Vaginal Stimulant

For those women who are not very familiar with the "geography" of the genital area, you may want to study the illustration on page 249 (figure 11).

Since the application of a topical vaginal cream may be a new experience for most women, I would like to share information about what you can expect with its use.

~ The immediate sensation after application is one of a mild "cool burning," an awareness that usually disappears quickly—within minutes. In fact, with repeated use, the feeling itself disappears.

~ The optimum arousal effect may occur within ten to thirty minutes after application, but for some women, it may take longer to reach that pinnacle. The more you use a gel-cream, however, the less time it should take for peak results, and the more potent the reactions.

~ Depending on your own individual differences, plus the frequency of use, a pleasant tingling sensation can remain in place from a short while or as long as all day, and sometimes even into the next day.

~ Some women report tremendous improvement after the first use; many report major benefit after three applications, and for some it could take a bit longer.

~ Gel-cream ingredients should work to keep the integrity of your genital area healthy—forevermore!

~ Surveys reveal about an 87 percent success rate with the use of such a cream. Women who do not respond favorably do not necessarily have adverse results. For this small minority, sometimes digital vaginal "touching" is not always comfortable.

~ Should any irritation occur, discontinue use. Do not use if you are pregnant or breastfeeding, unless your physician suggests otherwise.

~ If you experience discomfort, try applying a mild progesterone cream (with herbs!) vaginally for a few weeks to "build up" the sensitive vaginal tissue. Or, try a gel-cream with a lower dose of menthol.

~ For most women, the best part of a topical transdermal application is how easy it is to use, and how little it disrupts your favorite sexual routines.

Female genital tissue is fragile, so a well-formulated product includes ingredients in dilute amounts. You don't require a lot for effectiveness.

A good gel-cream formulation is safe, effective, and not expensive. With easy availability, there's no excuse to ever again find yourself lying awake, unsatisfied and frustrated, while your partner rolls over and starts to snore.

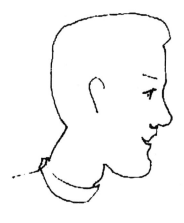

"You never tell me when you're having an orgasm."

"You're never around!"

Chapter Ten

UNDERSTANDING THE MECHANICS OF ORGASM

A woman went to her family doctor to complain about her husband screaming every time he had an orgasm. "What's wrong with that?" asked the doctor. She replied: "He wakes me up!"

The Nuts and Bolts

To have satisfying orgasms, it isn't really necessary to know the differences between atoms, molecules, and amino acids. But to really understand the nuts and bolts of sexual arousal, that's the language we must use.

Let's start with amino acids—especially the amino acid *arginine* (pronounced ar jin een). Amino acids are often described as the alphabet or building blocks of protein. Proteins, in turn, are the very large and specialized molecules that are responsible for most of the biochemical "intelligence" of our bodies.

Enzymes, antibodies, growth factors, even muscle tissue, and collagen are all proteins, and all are made of long chains of amino acids, strung together like long strings of beads.

There are actually only twenty kinds of amino acids, but arranged in the correct order, like letters in the words of a novel, they create billions of different proteins. All proteins in all living species—from bacteria to elephants—are made of the same set of twenty amino acids.

Proteins made of these amino acids have been on earth for at least three billion years!

Time for a
QUICKIE

Arginine, like most amino acids, can have two different mirror-image arrangements of the same group of atoms: L-arginine and D-arginine. L stands for levo-rotary and D for dextro-rotary. The two forms are different "isomers" of the same substance, having the same atoms bonded to each other in the same pattern, except for this right-handed or left-handed difference.

The L-arginine is the isomer of arginine from which proteins are made, and is the more natural form of this amino acid. Most of the research has been conducted with L-arginine, although D-arginine may also have a role to play. All the discussion in this book is based on L-arginine, and I will usually leave out the L for simplicity.

Arginine, one of the longer amino acids, is a string of atoms that ends with a side-chain array of three nitrogen atoms around one carbon. It's the nitrogen on the end of the arginine molecule side-chain that provides bioavailable nitrogen. (See figure 10, page 242.)

To nutritionists, arginine is probably best known as the amino acid that can stimulate the production of growth hormone. This is the large and complicated protein made in the pituitary gland controlling a wide range of growth, healing, and immune functions. Production of growth hormone begins to decrease a few years after puberty.

Supplementation of dietary arginine was first promoted in the early 1980s by advocates of various nutritional "life-extension" regimens. It still shows promise as part of a rejuvenation strategy, although there are problems associated with self-directed oral ingestion.

Arginine seems to be a necessary ingredient for the production of nitric oxide, an extremely simple molecule made of just one nitrogen atom and one oxygen atom.

Nitric oxide plays a critical role in sexual function.

How this works is a surprisingly recent discovery; it resulted in a Nobel Prize for Medicine in 1998 for the discovery of the L-arginine-nitric oxide pathway, the discovery that produced Viagra for men.

What was discovered is that nitric oxide can act as a signal molecule.

This means that it causes some other action to take place in a location other than where it was produced, and is not itself consumed in the process. This is very much like the action of a hormone, except that the nitric oxide molecule is amazingly simple and short-lived compared to even a modest hormone.

Identifying nitric oxide as a signal molecule was revolutionary because there is no other known example of such a small molecule having this kind of biological signaling function. Nitric oxide can very easily penetrate cell membranes, gaining easy access to the "controls" of other cells.

However, nitric oxide is extremely short-lived and unstable, converting to more stable molecules by combining with additional oxygen atoms. This conversion takes less than ten seconds—so it must be produced very close to the site of action.

Endothelial cells are cells that line the insides of blood vessel walls. They can function as nitric oxide generator cells. Whenever an arginine molecule comes within range, an enzyme called *NO synthase* (NO stands for nitric oxide, and "synthase" simply means it's the enzyme that makes nitric oxide) strips a nitrogen atom from the end of the amino acid and combines it with an oxygen atom. This forms the small nitric oxide molecule.

In the next couple of seconds, the nitric oxide diffuses to adjacent smooth muscle tissue in the blood vessel, causing muscles to relax and allowing the blood vessel to enlarge slightly. The result is that blood pressure goes down, in much the same way that a bicycle inner tube taken out of the tire expands and depressurizes.

"Smooth" muscles are the involuntary muscles, the ones that work without conscious control. Distinct from skeletal and heart muscles, they surround arteries and organs of your digestive and reproductive systems.

The action of smooth muscles is critical to digestion and childbirth—and to orgasm.

The link between arginine, nitric oxide, and blood pressure had been detected as early as 1988, but it was nitric oxide's role as a messenger molecule that was demonstrated. And the importance of arginine is still coming into focus.

"The discovery that L-arginine is the substrate from which the ubiquitous mediator nitric oxide is synthesized provides a possible explanation for many hitherto seemingly unrelated actions of arginine observed over the past thirty years," according to clinical pharmacologists writing in the British medical journal, *Lancet,* in 1997.[1]

There is an intriguing connection between arginine and cardiovascular health: Impaired availability of nitric oxide has recently been found to be strongly associated with high cholesterol and other risk factors for cardiovascular disease.[2,3]

Ongoing use of oral arginine supplementation has been shown to improve endothelial function by enhancing its ability to release nitric oxide as required.[4]

This is important because the endothelium is where arterial damage begins, and high cholesterol is more properly thought of as a *symptom* of arterial damage, not the *cause*. This was enough to send me running to my food composition tables to check for foods high in arginine. These include meats, nuts, cheese, grains, eggs (the usual high protein foods) and, to everyone's delight, chocolate! (Could *this* be the reason chocolate is considered an aphrodisiac?)

The effect of arginine and nitric oxide on blood pressure is what led to the development of the Viagra predecessors. Remember that this drug was originally used for blood pressure control, and not as a sex aid.

But why does low blood pressure help with female orgasm?

The clitoris, like the penis, becomes engorged with blood and is hypersensitive during arousal. Normally, the arteries that supply blood to the clitoris and other vaginal tissue are somewhat constricted, while the veins are wide open. When the exit door is wider than the entrance, there's unlikely to be a crowd in the hallway. So the clitoris and other tissue remain flaccid.

Erection and engorgement occur when the artery wall muscles relax, effectively opening the inlet valve.

In other words, the expansion of the blood vessels, which reduces the pressure, causes the blood to rush in to fill the vessels, resulting in engorgement—which, in turn, causes the clitoral erection. The engorgement with blood results in increased sensitivity of the clitoris and vagina.

Time for a
QUICKIE

Dr Ann de Wees Allen, a long-time advocate of growth hormone stimulation using carefully designed arginine supplementation strategies, offers this warning against indiscriminate oral ingestion of arginine: "Do not rush out and buy plain L-arginine, because L-arginine without the correct synergists and cofactors or an improperly prepared L-arginine formula can cause reactivation of the herpes virus as well as the stimulation of peroxynitrate. Formulas containing free forms of both L-arginine and lysine are to be avoided."[5]

Since free L-arginine is highly unstable, you can be assured that the L-arginine in a properly formulated vaginal cream does not use free forms, but rather a complex to help stabilize the L-arginine, so that the final product is in your best health interest.

Joe complained to his doctor that he hadn't made love to his wife for a very long time.

The doctor suggested that he walk ten miles a day, and call back to report his progress in a week.

Joe called his doctor a week later. "Hey, doc," he said, "I've done just as you said. I've been walking ten miles a day."

Well," asked the doctor, "do you think it has helped?"

"How would I know, doc," answered Joe, "I'm seventy miles from home."

Arginine and Ornithine Pathways

The hypothalamus is the link between the brain and the endocrine system. It functions as part of the brain, but has several links to the pituitary gland immediately below it. The pituitary, however, is part of the endocrine system, and works by introducing hormones into the bloodstream. Signal hormones that direct other organs to produce sex hormones are made by the pituitary.

Arginine and nitric oxide have been shown to have important roles to play in sexual hormonal pathways that begin in the hypothalamus.

"It is becoming increasingly clear," concludes one research team, "that nitric oxide…is a critical neurotransmitter and biological mediator of the neuroendocrine axis. Current evidence suggests that nitric oxide modulates the activity of both the hypothalamic-pituitary-gonadal axis and the hypothalamic-pituitary-adrenal axis."[6]

This means that nitric oxide, probably produced with the help of arginine,[7] is essential to your brain's ability to control hormones made in your ovaries (the hypothalamic-pituitary-gonadal axis) and in your adrenals (hypothalamic-pituitary-adrenal axis).

By helping to provide nitric oxide to the hypothalamus, it appears that arginine strengthens the signals to the pituitary, which in turn signals the ovaries and adrenal glands, and they in turn produce more sex hormones.

It's like having the output of one amplifier fed right into the input of another amplifier. A very small signal can result in a very big response.

In laboratory animals, nitric oxide release initiates the chain of events that eventually leads to ovulation: The nitric oxide first stimulates release pulses of LHRH (luteinizing hormone releasing hormone), from the hypothalamus, followed by luteinizing hormone itself from the pituitary, followed by ovulation.

Keep in mind that luteinizing hormone also stimulates testosterone production, which controls libido in both men and women.

Animal studies verify these pathways. Rats given a drug that blocked nitric oxide synthase failed to reproduce.[8] And when test animals are deprived of arginine, their sexual development is halted.[9]

Ornithine is another amino acid that plays a role in sexual arousal.

Although it's not one of the twenty building blocks of protein, it's readily made from arginine. As indicated earlier, ornithine appears to share arginine's capability to supply the vascular system's short term second-to-second requirements for bioavailable nitrogen as it is needed for nitric oxide production.

This need for bioavailable nitrogen is like the spot market for electricity during a power shortage. When you need it now, it doesn't matter how much capacity you have off-line. The spot market drives the price. When instantaneous supply does not meet demand, the price can skyrocket. But when supply is plentiful, the price stays low. And "cheap" nitrogen means better sex. Arginine and ornithine keep the supply up and the price down.

Extra Help From Menthol

Menthol, a terpenoid alcohol found in peppermint, causes a cooling sensation when applied to the skin, and is commonly used to reduce pain and suppress itching.

Menthol, as a vasodilator, causes blood vessels to relax and increase in diameter.

Arginine is most effective in situations where there is a nitric oxide deficiency, and where the processes involving nitric oxide synthase are still intact. If there is plenty of arginine but some other part of the process is malfunctioning, arginine will not be effective. But menthol acts directly on the blood vessel muscles, and will always work as a vasodilator.

Even in very small quantities, menthol alone has a sufficient vasodilating effect to improve the likelihood of orgasm. A typical effective dose for direct application of menthol might be one or two grams of a good cream containing only a fraction of a percent of menthol. This is far less than the amount of menthol in a cough drop.

The following five illustrations graphically demonstrate the pathways to orgasm.

Pathways to Pleasure

NATURAL EXTERNAL STIMULANTS

Physical stimulation of the vulva produces natural lubricants which enhance the response by the vaginal and vulval tissue and the clitoris.

Pheromones, which can act like a natural but subconscious aphrodisiac perfume, may also be produced. When the "chemistry" is right, there may be a partner involved who produces more pheromones.

The brain is stimulated by romantic emotion or fantasy, and possibly by pheromones from the partner. Pheromones have been referred to as "airborne aphrodisiacs."

Figure 12

Natural External Stimulants

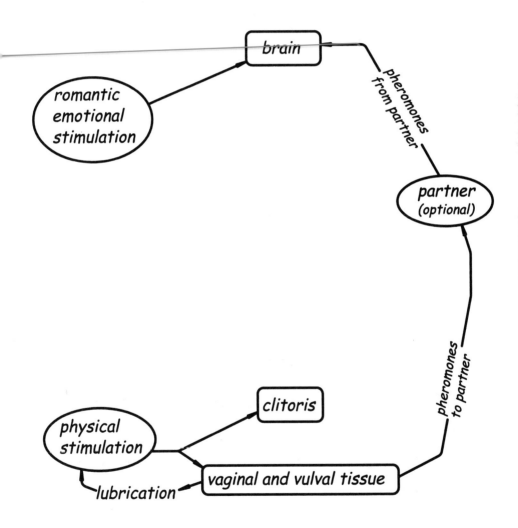

Figure 13

THE HYPOTHALAMUS-
PITUITARY-ADRENAL AXIS

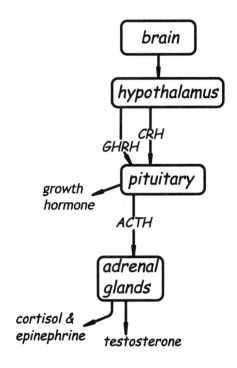

The brain sends neurological signals that instruct the hypothalamus to make two hormones (CRH or corticotropin-releasing hormone and GHRH, or growth-hormone-releasing hormone). The pituitary responds to these chemical signals from the hypothalamus by making a hormone that is used all over your body (growth hormone), and another hormone that acts on your adrenal glands (ACTH, or adrenocorticotropic hormone). The adrenal glands, located on top of each kidney, produce energizing hormones (cortisol and epinephrine), and the libido-enhancing hormone (testosterone).

Figure 14

THE HYPOTHALAMUS-
PITUITARY-GONADAL AXIS

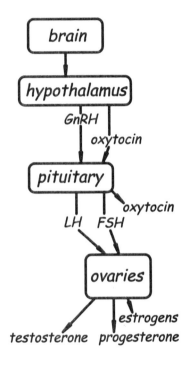

The brain sends neurological signals that instruct the hypothalamus to make two more hormones (GnRH. or gonadotropin-releasing hormone, and oxytocin). One of these hormones (oxytocin) passes through the pituitary and is released into the blood-stream, then acts on breast tissue and other selected smooth muscle sites. The other hormone (GnRH) signals the pituitary to make two more hormones (LH, or luteinizing hormone and FSH, or follicle stimulating hormone). These in turn control production of the sex hormones estrogen, progester- one, and testosterone by the ovaries.

HOW A TOPICAL CREAM STIMULANT WORKS

A very small amount of menthol stimulates the skin sensors on the clitoris and vulva directly.

Natural lubricants produced in response to the stimulation enhance the effect. Menthol causes vasodilation of these tissues, which improves transdermal absorption of arginine, ornithine, herbal aphrodisiacs, and other substances in the cream.

Arginine facilitates the production of nitric oxide as needed by the clitoris and the hypothalamus.

Figure 15

HOW A TOPICAL CREAM
STIMULANT WORKS

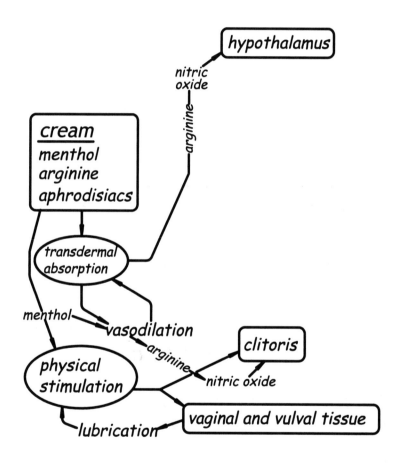

AHHH!

The brain, under the influence of emotional stimulation and possible response to pheromones from a partner, signals the hypothalamus-pituitary-adrenal axis and the hypothalamus-pituitary-gonadal axis into action.

The brain is also influenced by testosterone and other hormone levels. Nitric oxide from arginine or ornithine enhances the production of hypothalamic control hormones.

The clitoris, also using arginine to make nitric oxide, becomes erect. Surrounding tissue becomes engorged.

Oxytocin from the pituitary causes nipple erection, and, along with cortisol and epinephrine from the adrenals, produces the orgasm response.

Figure 16

AHHH!

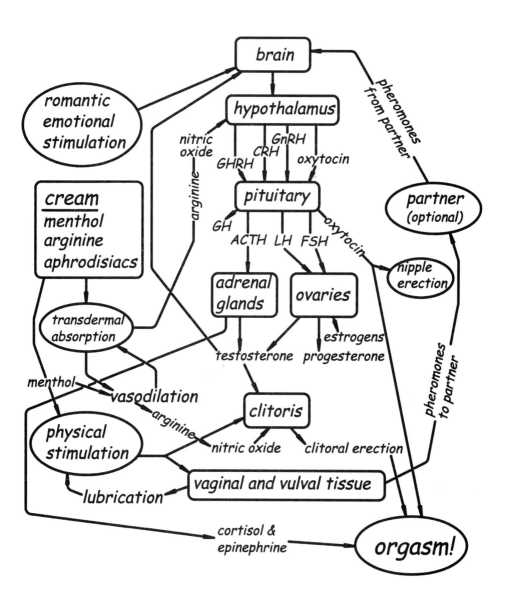

Playing the field:
Cofactors and Coconspirators

In conventional pharmacology there is a strong tendency to reduce things to their "active ingredient." But the best adaptogens, functional foods, and nutraceuticals usually consist of dozens of cofactors that all work together to varying degrees—not a single chemical, but a balanced "complex" of related substances.

We've only just begun to understand the role of these nutrient complexes in relation to isolated nutrients. As demonstrated in chapter seven, epidemiologists have known for a long time that populations eating foods containing certain nutrients show much better results than similar populations taking supposedly equivalent nutrient supplements.

Time for a
QUICKIE

Ginkgo biloba can protect brain tissue against oxidative damage.

Life Sciences;15;39(24):2327-34.

Following is the more in-depth detail of the other ingredients outlined in chapter nine that could and should be included in any transdermal vaginal cream—providing valuable additions as a topical sexual stimulant.

Ginseng

Ginseng has been described as the most frequently recommended herbal treatment in the last 2,000 years of Chinese medicine, with velvet antler (despite its zoological rather than botanical nature) taking the number two position.

This root has been used traditionally to promote qi (vital energy), to "normalize body function," stimulate appetite, and to treat fluid retention, rheumatoid arthritis, insomnia, and even lower back pain.[10] It has been scientifically demonstrated to increase sexual performance and resistance to stress and aging.

More recently, ginseng has been shown to be a potent immune function enhancer, dramatically increasing T cell and helper cell count.[11] Extensive research from the former Soviet Union in the 1980s validates ginseng's ability to enhance alertness, athletic endurance, and performance under stress.[12] This helps to account for its effectiveness for women as a sex aid, and we are just beginning to understand the complex mechanisms involved.

Ginseng is one of the best examples of an adaptogen, described earlier. Recall that adaptogens are non-specific normalizing agents that seem to work in whatever direction is necessary to resstore health. In sharp contrast to drugs, which have much more predictable and unidirectional biochemical effects, adaptogens are responsive to natural feedback loops and built-in physiological control systems. The same adaptogen might have a completely opposite effect in different individuals, or even in the same individual at different times. (Angelica sinensis, discussed in chapter eight, provides another good example of adaptogenic action: This herbal aphrodisiac appears to help in cases of both too much and too little estrogen.)

The adaptogenic properties of ginseng are believed to be due to its effects on the hypothalamic-pituitary-adrenal axis. The ginseng strengthens the signals to the pituitary, which in turn signals the ovaries and adrenal glands, and they in turn produce more sex hormones (corticotropin and corticosteroids).

Studies suggest that an active constituent in ginseng is a nitric oxide donor, and works through the arginine/nitric oxide pathway.[13] It helps to relax the smooth muscle.

When used appropriately, ginseng is safe.

Time for a
QUICKIE

Several recent studies, reported at Yale University School of Medicine, have suggested that the antioxidant and organ-protective actions of ginseng are linked to enhanced nitric oxide synthesis in the endothelium of lung, heart, and kidney, and in the corpus cavernosum. Enhanced nitric oxide synthesis thus could contribute to ginseng-associated vasodilatation and also to an aphrodisiac action of the root.

Ginkgo biloba

Many varieties of Ginkgo have been growing wild in China for at least two hundred million years, but only one species, Ginkgo biloba, survived the ice age that ended ten thousand years ago. Ginkgo biloba has been used effectively against short-term memory loss, depression, cognitive problems, arterial diseases, and tinnitus. One of its modes of action is vasodilation.

Several studies have validated Ginkgo as an effective treatment for male erectile dysfunction, especially after long-term use: At the conclusion of an eighteen-month trial, half of sixty men suffering from this disorder had regained the ability to have erections.[14] And as we noted earlier, Ginkgo is considered to be even more effective for women.

In 1973, injected Ginkgo biloba extract was shown to increase cerebral blood flow by as much as 70 percent.[15] More direct results were demonstrated in 1985, when a year of Ginkgo supplementation improved short-term memory loss, headache, vertigo, tinnitus, mood disturbance, and "loss of vigilance" among 112 people averaging seventy years old.[16]

These and other research studies, along with a long history of positive user response, have given Ginkgo a deserving reputation as a "smart" supplement. It is popular among college students cramming for exams, and used in a wide range of other situations in which a non-drug energy, mood, and concentration booster is desired.

Current research shows that Ginkgo can reduce certain kinds of allergic response.[17,18] So adding Ginkgo to any cream might be a useful strategy for mitigating the effects of a potential allergen in the product.

We have no way of knowing if the full effectiveness of Ginkgo as an aid to female orgasm is only realized after six months of use, as appears to be the case for men, or if there is some advantage for a first-time user. A human trial would not be difficult to design, but who would want to be in the control group?

Time for a
QUICKIE

Ginkgo biloba can protect brain tissue against oxidative damage.

~ Life Sciences;15;39(24):2327-34

Velvet Antler

Antlers are nothing like rhinoceros horns or tiger's teeth. Elk and deer antlers regenerate every year, and are among the fastest growing animal tissue known. In fact, antler is the *only* mammalian bone structure that regenerates annually. "Velvet" antler, the form used for nutritional purposes, is harvested about halfway through the annual growth cycle. Unlike the fully calcified horn or tooth, velvet antler is loaded with growth and immune factors, leutinizing hormone (the hormone that stimulates testosterone), prostaglandins, cartilage, glucosamine sulfate, chondroitin sulfate and collagen. These last two substances are in favor by those seeking a natural remedy for arthritis.

Even the FDA recognizes their effectiveness, allowing structure and function claims for joint health. But when naturally packaged in velvet antler, these cofactors result in a significant performance edge over the isolated chemicals.

Velvet antler is one of a very few natural sources for IGF-I and II, the secondary hormones that do the work for growth hormone. The only other *natural* sources of growth hormone that I am familiar with are found in colostrum and in the algae nucleus, chlorella being one of the best and most available. But the most intriguing role of velvet antler is its effect on sexual function and libido. Numerous animal studies have confirmed antler's positive effects on growth and sexual activity.[19]

Much of this is old news (more than two thousand years old to Chinese and Korean herbalists. Anecdotal evidence for velvet antler remains compelling, with reports along the lines of "it turned my sexual clock back ten years" being common.

For the full velvet antler story, may I recommend my book, *The Remarkable Healing Power of Velvet Antler*, available through my website at www.bettykamen.com.

Tocotrienols

You already know that tocotrienols offer a potent form of vitamin E, and act as a powerful antioxidant.

Catalase is an enzyme that protects cells from oxidative stress, but sometimes it can overextend its power. It was found that Vitamin E supplementation decreases adverse catalase activity and improves the state of oxidative stress in those suffering from anemia, inflammatory problems, tumors, diabetes, cardiovascular diseases, and Wilson's disease.

New research on tocotrienols supports its use in a vaginal stimulant cream: It turns out that tocotrienols have greater bioavailability *through the skin*, penetrating rapidly and efficiently.

Tocotrienols have important neuroprotective effects that are independent of its antioxidant activity. This supplement plays an important role in the signaling aspects of smooth muscle cells, which you now know is essential in the orgasm-initiating process. And because of the breast-cancer suppression capability (discussed earlier), it is suggested that tocotrienols be used with any anti-estrogen therapy.

For more in-depth information on tocotrienols, please refer to chapter seven, and to Newsletter #6 at my website at www.bettykamen.com.

Exercise

Why is it so difficult to get people excited about exercise as a strategy for better sexual health? Probably for the same reasons that it's hard to get people excited about exercise for any other aspect of health. Exercise is hard work and it takes time. (And it doesn't usually require buying a product, so the commercial push is missing.) But the benefits of exercise on sexuality are clear and powerful.

This is intuitive—you already know that exercise is good for you. But, as indicated earlier, there's clinical evidence that a relatively small amount of exercise will also improve your orgasms. The study we described in the first chapter demonstrated that "only twenty minutes of vigorous exercise significantly increased vaginal pulse amplitude responses to an erotic stimulus," while the response to a non-erotic stimulus (erotic or non-erotic films were used) showed a significant reduction of vaginal pulse amplitude. The effect was measured in both sexually functional women and in women described as having "low sexual desire."[20]

There is a significant association with physical activity and erectile dysfuntion. The highest dysfunction risk was seen "among men who remained sedentary and the lowest among those who remained active or initiated physical activity." Although women often get left out of these studies, we know that a program of even moderate exercise will help women, too.

Growth Hormone:
Why Orgasms are Good for You

One beneficial consequences of arginine and ornithine nitric oxide production is the release of growth hormone.

Growth hormone has a deceptively simple name, but it's an enormously complex molecule. Human growth hormone is made of 191 amino acids strung together in an intricate pattern of loops and folds, connected back to itself in just the right places to make a very specific spatial arrangement. It's this complex interaction of geometry and chemistry that makes a hormone "fit" into one—and only one—kind of receptor site on the cells that it's intended to activate.

Growth hormone, unique in its ability to stimulate skeletal growth before and during puberty, has quite a different effect in adults. One of its functions is to reduce stored fat and increase muscle and tissue mass. And it has an important role in immunity. The point is that the daily production of growth hormone is enormously important as we age.

Unfortunately, growth hormone production falls off very quickly as we leave our teen years. At age 22 to 23, daytime growth hormone levels begin to drop. And by age thirty, even the growth hormone released in response to vigorous exercise is substantially reduced; in fact, it's considered to be nonexistent, according to some researchers. In older adults, the nighttime growth hormone released during sleep is the primary supply.

Growth hormone is produced in your pituitary gland, an organ about the size of a pea hanging in a cavity at the base of your brain. It gets its signals from your hypothalamus, which can be thought of as a part of the brain that forms the bridge between your brain and your endocrine system.

The hypothalamus can be driven by emotion and sensation. When your brain wants a hormone made, it flips the appropriate switch in the hypothalamus. The hypothalamus in turn sends out a chemical signal, in this case *GHRH*, or *"growth-hormone-releasing hormone."* Your pituitary then reacts to the GHRH and makes growth hormone, among others.

The hormones from the pituitary then make their way to the adrenal cortex, located on top of each kidney. These glands, along with the testes or ovaries, are also responsible for most of your sex hormone production.

Insulin, the hormone sent out by your pancreas to help metabolize sugar, is *anabolic*, as is growth hormone. The term anabolic refers to any biological process that builds complex compounds from simple ones, promoting tissue growth. (Those hormones that tend to have the opposite effect, promoting breakdown of tissues, are known as *catabolic* hormones.) The term "anabolic steroids" is known to body-builders and athletes who experiment with performance-enhancing drugs.

Some of the effects of growth hormone are similar to insulin, and some are in conflict. Growth hormone can impair glucose uptake in cells by suppressing insulin receptors, while at the same time causing fatty acids to be released from fatty tissue.[21] The net effect is to burn up fat rather than sugar (or other carbohydrates).

How does this relate to orgasm? Orgasm appears to stimulate growth hormone production through the neurological pathway.

Every orgasm is a potentially health-enhancing experience because of all the beneficial effects that naturally produced growth hormone has on almost every part of your body. That's just one reason why it feels so good!

The same amino acids that promote orgasm also seem to directly promote growth hormone production.

Time for a
QUICKIE

The most important growth hormone release occurs in adults about an hour after falling asleep. But note that growth hormone is suppressed by high blood sugar. Bad news for late evening and midnight snackers! Avoid sweets after dinner and at bedtime!

Oxytocin, And More Good News

As explained earlier, oxytocin is the hormone responsible for the "let down" reflex during breast feeding. It causes milk produced in the breast to become accessible by moving it from the cells that manufacture it to the "storage tanks" from which it can flow to the nipple. It also has a role in childbirth, and seems to act by causing contractions in smooth (involuntary) muscles.

There is now evidence to suggest that even in non-lactating women, oxytocin can have a detoxifying effect that is protective against breast cancer.[22] This is consistent with the lower risk of breast cancer among women who have had children and breastfed, compared to those who haven't.

Oxytocin is a neurohormone. It's made by nerve cells in the hypothalamus, which can be thought of as part of the brain. From there it flows down to the pituitary gland, and from there into the blood stream. Oxytocin production is strongly influenced by emotions: In one recent study, "relaxation massage" was shown to produce higher levels of oxytocin, whereas unhappy images resulted in lower levels.[23]

Even more significant, there is a close correlation between orgasm and short-term peaks in oxytocin output.[24]

These findings associated biochemical specifics to the role of emotion in achieving orgasm. They also explain nipple erection and breast enlargement during orgasm.

There's very little that happens in human physiology without a good reason. So, we have to ask, "Why would we need oxytocin during sex?"

The mode of action appears to be similar to that in other functions involving muscle contractions. Oxytocin is probably one factor that assists the rhythmic contractions of the lower reproductive system during orgasm.

And, if the research indicating the link to reduced breast cancer risk is borne out, we now have a very good reason to seek the most powerful orgasms possible. This could be especially important for women who do not plan to ever become mothers. **Good orgasms cleanse the breasts.**

Heavy Breathing

No discussion of the physiology of orgasm would be complete without mentioning adrenalin, or, more properly, the adrenal hormones *cortisol* and *epinephrine*. (Those of my vintage will remember saying, when we were under stress or excited about something: "My adrenalin is flowing.")

Cortisol and epinephrine are hormones made by the adrenal glands, and they produce the "fight or flight" response to danger and stress, modes of action with which we are all familiar. But we now know we can add passion to the list! This is what cranks up the pulse rate and starts the perspiration flowing.

The pathway begins in the brain-regulated hypothalamus. When our neurological programming forecasts the physical demands of passionate sex in the immediate future, the hypothalamus sends a control hormone called CRH (corticotropin-releasing hormone) to the pituitary gland.

The pituitary in turn releases ACTH (adrenocorticotropic hormone) into the bloodstream, and that causes the adrenal glands, located on top of each kidney, to release cortisol. Epinephrine release is regulated more directly by the hypothalamus, bypassing the pituitary control system. But there's more to it than heavy breathing. ACTH is actually synthesized as part of a much larger precursor protein that contains endogenous opioid compounds, among other important substances.

These natural opioids are the source of the emotional high associated with heavy exercise, and an important component of the euphoria of sex.

It's also interesting to note that one of the long-term effects of ACTH is to cause beneficial growth and increased capacity of the adrenal glands.

 It all points in the same direction: exercise and sex, sex and exercise, to keep your endocrine system working and your mood up.

In Summary

Orgasm happens...

Let's put the science aside, and follow the yellow brick road.

So much of the orgasmic response is involuntary—it just happens. Good thing! Chances are we'd never get it right if we had to be the dispatcher for all these goings-on!

Physical and emotional hangups notwithstanding, there are many roads to Rome. But in this case, **we take all or most of the roads at the very same time.** And despite the complexities of the parallel pathways, it's really easier than it looks.

The process can start in your brain, initiated by physical stimulation (with or without a partner, with or without romantic emotion, or with or without the chemical stimulation of testosterone). Once your brain gets the message, it starts the hormonal rush by way of your hypothalamus, pituitary gland, adrenal cortex, and your clitoris—and on to orgasm.

Another route is physical stimulation directly to the vaginal tissue and clitoris. This causes the vaginal lubrication and clitoral erection—and on to orgasm.

Then there is the vaginal gel-cream process that works two ways. When applied to the vaginal tissue and the clitoris, transdermal absorption of the cream's constituents stimulates blood flow, causing engorgement, clitoral erection, and, with the assistance of a loving partner—on to orgasm.

The second route of the vaginal cream process, because of the transdermal absorption "down there," stimulates your hypothalamus, and then on to your pituitary, your adrenal cortex, your ovaries, and your clitoris—and on to orgasm.

And all these simultaneous roads to Rome may be accompanied by other pleasures.

Imagine that you are on a sailboat with your lover. The winds are perfect, the seas are calm, and you just had the best lobster dinner of your life. The sunset is the most beautiful you have ever seen, and all the above happens at the same time—WOW!

AFTERWORD

I am seventy-five years old and enjoy a vigorous love life. I do not say that to boast, but I do say it with appreciation—appreciation not just at the pleasure it gives me (and my partner), but how this is just a reflection of my general vitality and overall good health. Good sex depends on good health.

I am pleased that I am an example of how following the same principles Betty Kamen lays out in this book (but translated into male terms) has kept me energetic, virile, and full of the joy of life. And I have seen many, many women of all ages helped by following the dos and don[1]ts that Betty so masterfully lays out in this much-needed guide.

There are thousands of books on sexuality, dating back to ancient times. Dr Kamen's book is unique in that it addresses the problems that women face today in a profound way by addressing the cellular basis that underlies issues of lack of desire, physical attractiveness, emotional openness, and mutually satisfying relationships.

Almost seventy years ago the psychiatrist Wilhelm Reich pioneered the notion that the unobstructed expression of sexuality was key to both the physical and psychic health of the individual and, by extension, the health of our society. One needs only to observe animals in nature to see that the impetus of life from a species perspective is to reproduce. Sexuality is not a non-essential aspect of life—it is the basis of life. Human beings have evolved even further, by engaging in sex not just to reproduce but also to express love.

It is an absolute tragedy that in the vast majority of cases in which people cannot express this love, the causes are manmade. The pollution of our planet, our toxic and nutrient-deprived diet, our poisonous modern "medicines," and our stressful contemporary culture—all these take a terrible toll on our health in general and sexuality in particular. Betty Kamen's book shows how individual women can take control of their internal environment and, in so doing, enrich their own lives and the lives of their loved ones.

~ Burton Goldberg

Publisher, Alternative Medicine: The Definitive Guide , The Definitive Guide to Women's Health, and Alternative Medicine Magazine

GLOSSARY

Adaptogen – A food substance or trace nutrient that tends to normalize a physiological process or condition. Unlike drugs, which always tend to influence a process or condition in the same predictable direction, adaptogens may have reverse effects depending on the individual and the physiological environment.

Adrenal glands – Small glands located on the top of each kidney. They secrete cortisol, epinephrine, and other related "stress" hormones. In women the adrenal glands are a major source of testosterone.

Androgen – The "male" sex hormones, one of which is testosterone. Androgens have an important role in maintaining libido in both men and women.

Androstenedione – An androgen secreted by the ovaries and adrenal glands; the major precursor of estrogen after menopause.

Anorgasmia – An involuntary inhibition of the orgasmic reflex.
  Primary anorgasmia: orgasm has never been achieved
  Secondary anorgasmia: orgasm has been achieved in the past
  Absolute anorgasmia: orgasm impossible in all situations
  Situational anorgasmia: orgasm impossible only in certain situations

Antiandrogens – Drugs that block the effects of testosterone. They prevent testosterone from binding to the androgen receptor.

Argininine – An amino acid that appears to be critical for the production of nitric oxide when and where it is needed.

Bioflavonoids – A group of chemicals found in fruits and plants that are essential for health and helpful in many processes of cell structure and function, including the absorption of vitamin C.

Cervix – The lower and narrow end of the uterus. It's the portion of the uterus or womb that forms its lower end and projects into the upper portion of the vagina. Although not visible from the outside, it can be felt by inserting a finger or two deeply into the vagina and bearing down.

Climacteric – The several years preceding menopause when certain physical and hormonal changes may occur.

Climax – Period of greatest intensity during orgasm.

Clitoral Hood – Tissue surrounding the clitoris (see below for definition of clitoris). When the clitoris enlarges, it becomes more sensitive during the arousal phase. When fully enlarged, continuous stimulation allows multiple orgasms to occur. As the clitoris enlarges and becomes more erect during the arousal phase, the clitoral hood is elevated and this places the labia minora in tension.

Clitoris – The small organ in the female genitalia which corresponds to the male penis, located between the upper folds of the labia minora. It possesses the ability to enlarge. Its function is to serve as a base of sexual stimulation. It differs principally in size and in having the urethra empty below it instead of passing through it, as in the male penis.

Coitus – Sexual intercourse or copulation.

Contraceptive – Anything used to prevent conception.

Cortisol – Hormone released by adrenal glands in response to chemical signals from pituitary. Along with epinephrine, cortisol helps produce the "fight or flight" response to high stress.

Cunnilingus – The application of the mouth or tongue to the vulva.

DES (diethylstilbestrol) – Refers both to a group of synthetic estrogen-containing drugs and to one of those drugs called diethylstilbestrol.

Detumescence – The process of the sexual organs being drained of the excess blood supply and returning to their normal size.

Dose-dependent – Having an effect in proportion to the dose given or the amount applied or ingested. A "dose-dependent response" is often considered to be strong evidence of a cause-effect relationship between a treatment and a physiological response.

Dyspareunia – Coitus that is difficult or painful for a woman.
　　　Primary: pain always occurs during sexual activity
　　　Secondary: pain occurs after period of pain-free coitus

Endocrine system – The body's system of glands that secretes hormones.

Endometrium – The inner lining of the uterus. The endometrium grows during each menstrual cycle and is then shed during menstruation.

Ejaculation – The discharge of semen from the penis at the climax of the male orgasm.

Emission – The discharge of semen from the penis, especially when involuntary, as nocturnal emission or "wet dreams" (during sleep).

Endogenous – An internal cause or source.

Erection – In males, the condition of the penis becoming rigid and elevated, usually a result of sexual stimulation. In females, the hardening or stiffening of erectile tissue of the clitoris, the breast, or elsewhere.

Erogenos areas (or zones) – Parts of the body that produce an erotic response or arousal when stimulated.

Erotic – Arousal or stimulation of sexual thoughts or desire.

Erotophilic – Having love of eroticism or sexuality.

Erotophobic – Having fear of eroticism or sexuality.

ERT – Estrogen replacement therapy. Commonly recommended for postmenopausal women as a means of replacing sex hormones no longer being produced in significant quantities by the ovaries. HRT often consists of synthetic estrogen and synthetic progesterone (called progestins).

Estrogen – The "female" sex hormones. The estrogens are a group of hormones needed for the development of female sexual characteristics and reproduction. Estrogens are produced by the ovaries, adrenal glands, placenta, and fat cells. Estradiol, estrone, and estriol are the three major forms found in women. Men also produce estrogen, but not in the same quantity. Estrogens can block a signal transmitted by the pituitary gland called luteinizing hormone (LH), which stimulates testosterone.

Exogenous – An external cause or source.

Fellation – The act of taking the penis into the mouth. (This is not considered a perversion by modern medical authorities.)

Free radicals – Molecules lacking an unbalanced electrostatic charge due to one or more missing or extra electrons. Free radicals easily react with many other molecules in the body, and can create more free radicals in a chain reaction leading to significant damage if not checked by antioxidants.

FSH – Follicle-stimulating hormone, made with LH by pituitary in response to signals from hypothalamus. Key hormone in menstrual cycle; stimulates growth of ovum-containing follicles.

Fibroids – Muscle tumors of the uterus. Fibroids are almost always benign, but may interfere with fertilization.

Foreplay – Sexual play or stimulation by a partner prior to intercourse.

Genitals – The external organs of reproduction.

GHRH – Growth hormone releasing hormone. Made in the hypothalamus, it signals the pituitary to produce growth hormone.

Glans clitoridis – The head or sensitive visible portion of the clitoris seen in the upper part of the vulvar cleft.

GnRH – Gonadotropin-releasing hormone. Made in the hypothalamus, it stimulates LH and FSH release by the pituitary.

GH – Growth hormone; made by the pituitary gland; controls wide range of growth, healing, and immune functions. Abundant in children and teenagers, but production begins to decrease a few years after puberty. It's almost undetectable in people older than age thirty

Gonads – Glands that produce germ cells (spermatozoa and ova). These are the testicles in males and and the ovaries in females.

Gynecologist – Specialist in the diseases of women's reproductive systems.

Heterosexuality – Sexual interest in or sexual activity between members of the opposite sex.

Homosexuality – Sexual interest in or sexual activity between members of the same sex.

Hormone – A chemical produced in small quantities by an endocrine gland, then carried to another part of the body by the blood where it causes specific physiological effects.

HRT – Hormone replacement therapy. (See ERT.)

Hypothalamus – Part of the brain that connects to the endocrinesystem, and serves as a link between emotional or neurological signals and a number of physiological processes regulated by hormones. The hypothalamus is responsible for regulating temperature, water balance, sleep, and hormone production by the pituitary gland. Most of its work is done by signaling the pituitary gland below it to make hormones. It also produces neurohormones such as oxytocin that can act directly.

Hypothyroidsm – Underactive thyroid, a condition with various causes in which abnormally low amounts of thyroid hormone are produced. Symptoms include dry skin, weight gain, and sluggishness.

Hysterectomy – (total, partial, or radical) – Surgical removal of the uterus including the cervix. A total hysterectomy includes removal of the uterus, cervix, ovaries, and fallopian tubes.

Impotence – In males, the inability to have an erection.

Intercourse – Sexual copulation. The act of inserting the erect penis into the vagina accompanied by coital movements.

Ischemia – Local reduction of the blood supply due to obstruction of inflow or arterial blood.

Labia majora – Thicker outer lips of the vagina, covered with hair on the outside.

Labia minora – Smaller, inner lips of the vagina, which have no hair. The labia minora outline the vaginal entrance on either side and physically connect the vaginal entrance to the clitoris via the clitoral hood. Penile penetration sometimes causes movement and stretching of the labia minora that pulls down on the clitoral hood to stimulate the clitoris.

Lactation – The production of breast milk, usually beginning a few days after childbirth.

LH – Luteinizing hormone, made along with FSH by the pituitary gland in response to signals from the hypothalamus. LH is a key hormone in the menstrual cycle, causing the follicle on the ovary to enter the luteal phase after ovulation. LH signals the testes to make testosterone in males, and signals the ovaries to make smaller but equally important amounts of testosterone and other "male" sex hormones in females.

Libido – Sexual motivation, desire, or energy.

Lubrication – Sexual secretion of vaginal fluids which enhance sensitivity of the clitoris and surrounding tissue, and facilitate easier insertion of the penis. Lubrication can also be applied manually from external sources such as creams. Both the amount of lubrication produced and the speed of production decrease with age and with a lower level of estrogen.

Masters & Johnson Institute—Part of Washington University Medical Center; opened in 1964 to provide sex therapy and counseling based on the extensive human sex research of William H Masters and Virginia Johnson.

Masturbation – The act of producing sexual orgasm without sexual intercourse with a partner. Self-stimulation by hand or by means of mechanical aids is usually involved.

Menarche – The beginning of menstruation.

Menopause – The period of cessation of menstruation in the female, occurring usually between the ages of 45 and 51. The ovaries produce decreasing levels of hormones and menstrual periods end.

Menstruation – The bloody discharge from the uterus that occurs about every lunar month (28 days) in women between the ages of puberty and menopause, usually beginning from 12 to 14 and ending from 45 to 51.

Neurotransmitters – Signals sent from a transmitter in one nerve cell to a receptor in another.

Nitric oxide – A molecule consisting of one hydrogen and one oxygen atom. When produced by endothelial cells in blood vessels, nitric oxide causes the muscle lining to relax and the blood vessel to enlarge, causing vasodilation, engorgement, and erection in the clitoris or penis.

Oopherectomy – An operation to remove one or both ovaries.

Orgasm – The climax of the sexual act and culmination of sexual excitement, accompanied by rapid involuntary contractions of the muscles surrounding the vagina.

Orgasmic platform – Term coined by Masters and Johnson to describe the swelling that occurs as a result of vasocongestion in the vagina.

Ovary – The female sexual gland of reproduction or gonad that produces the egg cells or ova. The ovaries also produce estrogens, androgens, and other hormones regulating the reproductive process.

Oxytocin – A neurohormone made in the hypothalamus, distributed by the pituitary, and acting primarily on tissue in the breast and lower reproductive tract.

Pheromones – Scent-like but undetectable chemical signals believed to enhance sexual attraction and response between individuals.

Perimenopausal – The period of time before menopause, generally within 5 to 10 years.

Perineum – The area between the thighs, between the vulva and rectum, or below the vagina, and the inner lips that join together in a very muscular area covered with normal skin and sometimes hair. An episiotomy (a cut which may be made to widen the birth canal during childbirth) involves a small incision in the perineum.

Penis – The male sex organ that is inserted into the vagina during sexual intercourse.

Phytoestrogens – Also called plant estrogens; found in plants that have an estrogen-enhancing or estrogen-like effect.

Phytosterols – Specialized hormones found in plants.

Pituitary Gland – A small gland at the bottom of the brain that makes certain key control hormones that in turn regulate other glands. Along with the hypothalamus, the pituitary forms the interface between neural signals from the brain and hormonal signals that flow to the rest of the body.

Placebo – A pill with no active ingredients, given for its suggestive effects. The effects of a placebo are due entirely to the expectations of the person taking it.

PMS – Premenstrual syndrome: mood disturbances that occur after ovulation and normally end with the onset of the menstrual flow.

Postpartum – The six-week time period following childbirth.

Progesterone – A hormone produced by the ovaries during the second half of the menstrual cycle; promotes the growth of the uterine lining prior to menstruation.

Progestins – Synthetic progesterones, which do not have similar effects on the body as the naturally occurring hormone.

Prolapse (of the uterus) – A condition in which the uterus has dropped down slightly, compared to its usual position, as a result of weakening of the surrounding muscles.

Promiscuous – Frequent sexual activity with many different partners.

Prostate – A gland about the size of a hickory nut or table-tennis ball that is situated at the base of the bladder and close to the bulb of the penis, only in the male. Its main function is to make part of the fluid for semen.

Puberty – The period at which the sex organs become capable of exercising the functions of reproduction: pubic hair appears on the genital regions in both sexes. The average ages are 12 to 15, but the range may be from 10 to 17 or even 18. Signaled in boys by a change of voice and discharge of semen; in girls by the beginning of periodic menstruation.

Pubococcygeal – Also referred to as PC; the pelvic floor muscle that you "squeeze" when you try to hold back urine. Tightening or squeezing the pubococcygeal muscle should feel like 'pulling everything up inside of your pelvis, rather than pushing down.

Receptors – Highly specific "locks" in cells that are opened, or activated, only by certain hormones or chemical signals, which act as "keys." Receptors are part of the system by which very small quantities of hormone can produce significant physiological results.

Semen – The fluid that transports sperm, and is ejaculated during the male orgasm.

Sexual dysfunction – Disorders of the sexual process in women categorized by pain associated with intercourse or by a disturbance in the processes that form the sexual response cycle.

Sexual response cycle – Desire, arousal or excitement, orgasmic or plateau, and resolution.

Sperm – The male germ cells carried by semen, capable of fertilizing the ovum and causing impregnation.

STD – Sexually transmitted diseases, including the venereal diseases syphilis and gonorrhea, some types of herpes, and AIDS.

Subjective – Perceived only by the person affected, and often not perceptible or measurable by another.

Testicle – The male gonad or reproductive organ that produces germ cells, or spermatozoa; it also secretes certain hormones related to the sexual activity.

Testosterone – One of the "male" hormones, or androgens. Androgens in women are essential for sex drive and fertility, and play an important role in controlling the menstrual cycle.

Transdermal The application of a trace nutrient, drug, or other substance by application directly to the skin. The substance is absorbed into the blood by diffusing through the skin, bypassing digestive damage and avoiding first-pass removal by the liver.

Transsexual – One who desires or has achieved a sex change, usually by means of surgery and hormone therapy.

Transvestite – One who is sexually excited by dressing in the clothing of the opposite sex (cross-dressing).

Tumescence – The process of swelling or enlarging.

Urethra – The small canal, located below the clitoris, which carries off the urine from the bladder. In the male, the urethra also serves as the genital duct through which semen is expelled.

Uterus – The womb, a pear-shaped organ about three inches long, two inches wide, and one inch thick, hollow with a flat cavity, connecting with the upper end of the vagina below and with the two fallopian or uterine tubes above. The Uterus is the organ which contains and nourishes the fetus previous to birth.

Vagina – The female copulative organ, about three and a half inches in length, which lengthens during sexual excitement. It extends from the vulva to the cervix, and is distensible transversely and longitudinally so that its functional length in sexual intercourse is considerably greater. The vagina is the female sex organ that receives the penis.

Vaginal dryness—The inability to produce lubrication (see lubrication) during the arousal phase of sexual involvement.

Vaginal lubrication – (see lubrication)

Vaginal orgasm – A term of uncertain meaning used by some psychiatrists. Presumably it means that the orgasm is felt in the vagina and that stimulation of the clitoris by the penis or by other means is not necessary.

Vaginismus – Painful contraction or spasm of the vagina due to exaggerated sensitivity or fear, or other contraction of the vaginal openings which prevent intercourse.

Varicosity – A condition in which a vein is irregularly swollen.

Vascular – Having to do with blood vessels. The human vascular system includes arteries, veins, and capillaries.

Vasoconstriction – The constriction or narrowing of blood vessels.

Vasodilation – Relaxation, widening of blood vessel walls, allowing blood pressure to drop and blood engorgement to occur.

Vulva – The female sex organ consisting principally of the labia majora, labia minora (major and minor lips), clitoris, and the vaginal opening.

Womb – (See uterus)

APPENDIX A
Abraham Maslow

Early in his career, when Abraham Maslow (the "father" of American humanism), taught full time at Brooklyn College, he came in contact with many European intellectuals who had immigrated to the US, and Brooklyn in particular—people like Adler, Fromm, Horney, as well as several Gestalt and Freudian psychologists.

Maslow began to develop his now famous hierarchy of needs theory (some needs take precedence over others) when working with baby rhesus monkeys. For example, if you are hungry and thirsty, you will tend to try to take care of the thirst first. After all, you can do without food for weeks, but you can only do without water for a couple of days, and so on.

Beyond the details of air, water, food, and sex, he laid out five broader layers: the physiological needs, the needs for safety and security, the needs for love and belonging, the needs for esteem, and the need to actualize the self, in that order.

Physiological needs include the needs we have for oxygen, water, protein, salt, sugar, calcium, and other minerals and vitamins. They also include the need to maintain a pH balance (getting too acidic or base will kill you) and temperature (98.6 or near to it). Also, there are the needs to be active, to rest, to sleep, to get rid of wastes (CO_2, sweat, urine, and feces), to avoid pain, and to have sex. Quite a collection! Maslow believed, and research supports him, that these are, in fact, individual needs

Maslow saw all needs as essentially survival needs. Even love and esteem are needed for the maintenance of health. He said we all have these needs built in to us genetically, like instincts. In fact, he called them instinctoid (instinct-like) needs.

At the end of his long list of the hierarchy of needs, Maslow discussed the matter of becoming the most complete, the fullest "you"—hence the term, self-actualization. When lower needs are unmet, you can't fully devote yourself to fulfilling your potentials. (Note that sex is included in his first set of needs.)

Among the attributes of those who are self-actualized, Maslow described people who have an unhostile sense of humor—preferring to joke at their own expense, or at the human condition, and never directing their humor at others. They have a quality he called acceptance of self and others. And these people have a certain freshness of appreciation, an ability to see things, even ordinary things, with wonder.

Self-actualized people are also problem-centered, meaning they treat life's difficulties as problems demanding solutions, not as personal troubles to be railed at or surrendered to.

His messages are, first and foremost, about people, real people in real lives, and not about computer models, statistical analyses, rat behavior, test scores, and laboratories.

What do you think Abraham Maslow would have had to say about vaginal gel-cream to help women meet one of the early basic needs in his order of hieracrchy ?

APPENDIX B
Margaret Sanger

When Margaret Sanger's mother died from tuberculosis at the age of fifty, she, the sixth of eleven children, pointed to her mother's frequent pregnancy as the underlying cause of her premature death. Margaret sought to escape what she viewed as a grim class and family heritage.

Later, Sanger's work as a visiting nurse focused her interest in sex education and women's health. In 1912 she began writing a column on sex education for the New York Call entitled "What Every Girl Should Know." This experience led to her first battle with censors, who suppressed her column on venereal disease, deeming it obscene.

Increasingly, it was the issue of family limitation that attracted Sanger's attention as she worked in New York's Lower East Side with poor women suffering the pain of frequent childbirth, miscarriage and abortion. Influenced by the ideas of anarchist Emma Goldman, Sanger began to argue for the need for family limitation as a tool by which working-class women would liberate themselves from the economic burden of unwanted pregnancy.

Shocked by the inability of most women to obtain accurate and effective birth control, which she believed was fundamental to securing freedom and independence for working women, Sanger began challenging the 1873 federal Comstock law and the various "little Comstock" state laws that banned the dissemination of contraceptive information.

In 1914, Sanger embarked on a nationwide tour to promote birth control. Arrested in several cities, her confrontational style attracted even greater publicity for herself and the cause of birth control.

Sanger did eventually succeed in the courts. In 1936, the US Court of Appeals ruled that physicians were exempt from the Comstock Law's ban on the importation of birth control materials. This decision gave doctors the right to prescribe or distribute contraceptives (though the ban on importing contraceptive devices for personal use was not lifted until 1971!).

Through all her work for birth control, Sanger was consistent in her search for simpler, less costly, and more effective contraceptives. Not only did she help arrange for the American manufacture of the Dutch-based spring-form diaphragms she had been smuggling in from Europe, but also in subsequent years she fostered a variety of research efforts to develop spermicidal jellies, foam powders, and hormonal contraceptives.

Finally in the 1950s, her role in helping to find critical research funding made possible the development of the first effective anovulant contraceptive—the birth control pill.

The 1965 Supreme Court decision, Griswold v. Connecticut made birth control legal for married couples. Only a few months later, on September 6, 1966, Margaret Sanger, the founder of the birth control movement, died in a Tucson nursing home at the age of 87.

What do you think Margaret Sanger would have thought of the use of a vaginal gel-cream stimulant?

APPENDIX C
Kathi Kamen Goldmark

When my daughter Kathi was about ten or eleven, someone had given us an excellent 16 mm film developed by
Walt Disney Studios, describing the process of menstruation. The film was educational, humorous, and extremely well done—especially since the subject was a
sensitive issue for discussion in the late 1950s.

Kathi asked if we could share the film with her Scout
troop. As leader, I contacted each mother asking for
permission to show the film. All the mothers consented,
and a few moms even came to join us.

When one woman of the local "upper echelon" of the
Scout organization learned that I had shown the film, I
was excommunicated. My dismissal letter did not mention the film, but, believe it or not, stated that I had
used Sterno at a camp outing instead of starting a cooking fire with more natural means.

This is a true story! I was told I could no longer be a
troop leader for this group of girls. It was my daughter's
first awareness that an absolutely normal physiological
process, experienced by every female in the world, was
considered taboo for discussion and was a subject not
to be talked about openly, even when parents had agreed
it would be beneficial for their daughters. (And Kathi
learned a little bit about the ways of the world— including how people can use "power" inappropriately.)

In the early 1970s, Kathi taught both drama and sex
education at an alternative private school.

In the late 1970s, Kathi implemented and directed an innovative radio campaign for the Population Institute, designed to reach teenagers—with "non-preachy" messages—about responsible sexuality and parenthood. (The basic premise of the message was focused on why teenagers should not have children.) Working within the music industry, Kathi produced public service announcements in which popular music stars expressed their feelings about parenthood and sexuality. The spots, distributed nationwide as free public service programming, won critical acclaim as BillBoard Magazine's Public Service Announcement of the Year, and as finalists in the Clio Awards.

Kathi has been a guest speaker at Planned Parenthood workshops, and was a workshop leader at Planned Parenthood Annual Meetings.

She co-sponsored National Condom Week (1978-1980).

Like her grandmother and greatgrandmother before her, Kathi has been ahead of her time when it comes to getting the message out about important social issues.

Kathi has just sold her first novel, a charming page-turner about a young singer-songwriter and her loving family and friends, dealing with sex and relationship issues that are both contemporary and timeless.

APPENDIX D
Comstock Laws

Birth rates declined in the United States between 1800 and 1900, the most rapid decades of decline being the 1840s and 50s. Most of this decline was due to extensive practice within marriage of traditional birth control techniques—sexual abstinence and male withdrawal before ejaculation. The latter practice was called "male continence."

In 1873, Congress passed the "Comstock Laws," prohibiting sending information and devices for the prevention of conception through the mails, on the grounds that such are "obscene, lewd, lascivious, filthy, indecent and disgusting."

Books banned from the US mails under the Comstock Law included many of the greatest classics: Aristophanes Lysistrata, Rabelais's Gargantua, Chaucer's Canterbury Tales, Boccaccio's Decameron, and even The Arabian Nights.

Modern authors censored included Honore de Balzac, Victor Hugo, Oscar Wilde, Ernest Hemingway, Eugene O'Neil, James Joyce, DH Lawrence, John Steinbeck, F Scott Fitzgerald, among others. A special agent for the US Post Office was appointed, carrying a gun to attack "pornographers."

The fact that birth control was practiced to enable women to have more control over their lives and afforded them the time to pursue endeavors outside of childrearing inspired a new movement.

During the early years of the twentieth century, feminists, suffragists, and other civil libertarians argued that women's freedom to control their own bodies was fundamental to women's fight for social, economic, and political equality. In violation of the Comstock Laws, Margaret Sanger published pamphlets on the use of contraception, which she called "birth control."

In 1918, the New York Court of Appeals empowered legally practicing physicians to prescribe contraceptives for married couples if necessary "to cure or prevent disease." But in 1929, Sanger's clinic was raided, physicians and nurses were arrested, and supplies and records were seized.

In 1936, Sanger challenged the Comstock Laws by importing a package of diaphragms.

North Carolina became the first state to recognize birth control as a public health measure to provide contraceptive services to low income mothers through its public health programs in 1937.

In 1940, Connecticut upheld a state statute that made use of contraceptives illegal. It wasn't until 1962 that the US Supreme Court found the Connecticut law prohibiting birth control for married couples unconstitutional.

The Birth Control Federation of America, Inc., changed its name to Planned Parenthood Federation of America, Inc. in 1942. In 1960, the Food and Drug Administration approved the use of oral contraceptives.

Finally, in 1971, Congress repealed most of the provisions of the federal Comstock Laws. Two years later, the US Supreme Court struck down a Massachusetts statute barring distribution of contraceptives to unmarried people.

We can only guess what Comstock Law proponents would have thought of a vaginal-stimulant cream!

REFERENCES

Chapter One

1 Nusbaum MR et al. The high prevalence of sexual concerns among women seeking routine gynecological care. *Journal of Family Practice* 2000; 49(3):229-32.

2 Berman JR et al. Female sexual dysfunction: anatomy, physiology, evaluation and treatment options. *Current Opinions in Urology* 1999;9:563A.

3 Op cit, Nusbaum.

4 Shokrollahi P et al. Prevalence of sexual dysfunction in women seeking services at family planning centers in Tehran. *Journal of Sex and Marital Therapy* 1999;25(3):211-5.

5 Dunn KM et al. Sexual problems: a study of the prevalence and need for health care in the general population. *Family Practice* 1998 Dec;15:519.

6 Berman JR et al. Clinical evaluation of female sexual function: effects of age and estrogen status on subjective and physiologic sexual responses. *International Journal of Impotence Research Archives* 1999;11 Suppl 1:S31-8.

7 Avery-Clark C. Sexual dysfunction and disorder patterns of working and nonworking wives. *Journal of Sex and Marital Therapy* 1986 Summer;12(2):93-107.

8 Fisher WA et al. Students' sexual knowledge, attitudes toward sex, and willingness to treat sexual concerns. *Academic Medicine* 1988;63: 379 .

9 Koutroulis G. The orifice revisited: women in gynecological texts. *Community Health Study* 1990;14(1):73-84.

10 Halvorsen JG, Metz ME. Sexual dysfunction, Part II: Diagnosis, management, and prognosis. *Journal of the American Board of Family Practice* 1992 Mar-Apr;5(2):177-92.

11 Butcher J. *ABC of sexual health:* Female sexual problems I: Loss of desire: what about the fun? *British Medical Journal* 1999;318:41-43.

12 Leiblum SR. Definition and classification of female sexual disorders. *International Journal of Impotence Research* 1998 May;10 Suppl 2:S104-6; discussion S124-5.

13 Heiser K et al. *Zentralbl Gynakol* 2000;122(11):566-70.

14 Gozzo T de O. Female sexuality: understanding its significance. *Review of Latin American Enfermagem* 2000 Jul;8(3):84-90.

15 Hoon PW. Physiologic assessment of sexual response in women: the unfulfilled promise. *Clinical Obstetrician Gynecology* 1984;27(3):767-80.

16 Ackard DM et al. Effect of body image and self-image on women's sexual behaviors. *International Journal of Eating Disorders* 2000;28(4):422.

17 Pfaus JG. Neurobiology of sexual behavior. *Current Opinion in Neurobiology* 1999;9(6):751-8.

18 Barton D, Joubert L. Psychosocial aspects of sexual disorders. *Aust Family Physician* 2000 Jun;29(6):527-31.

19 Ryding EL. Sexuality during and after pregnancy. *Acta Obstetrician Gynecology Scandinavia* 1984;63(8):679-82.

20 Tolor A, DiGrazia PV. Sexual attitudes and behavior patterns during and following pregnancy. *Archives of Sex Behavior* 1976 Nov;5(6):539-51.

21 Gjerdingen DK et al. Changes in women's physical health during the first postpartum year. *Archives Family Medicine* 1993 Mar;2(3):277-83.

22 Barrett G et al. Women's sexual health after childbirth. *British Journal of Gynecology* 2000 Feb;107(2):186-95.

23 Sayle AE et al. Sexual activity during late pregnancy and risk of preterm delivery. *Obstetrics and Gynecology* 2001 Feb;97(2):283-9.

24 von Sydow K. Sexuality of older women. The effect of menopause, other physical and social and partner related factors. *Z Arztl Fortbild Qualitatssich* 2000;94(3):223-9.

25 Avis NE et al. Is there an association between menopause status and sexual functioning? *Menopause* 2000;7(5):297-309.

26 Sarrel PM. Psychosexual effects of menopause: role of androgens. *American Journal Obstetrics and Gynecology* 1999 Mar;180(3 Pt 2):S319.

27 Roselli CE, Chambers K. Sex differences in male-typical copulatory behaviors in response to androgen and estrogen treatment in rats. *Neuroendocrinology* 1999 Apr;69(4):290-8.

28 Kamen B. *Hormone Replacement Therapy—Yes or No: How to Make an Informed Decision* (Novato, CA: Nutrition Encounter, 6th ed, 1997).

29 Coope J. Hormonal and non-hormonal interventions for menopausal symptoms. *Maturitas* 1996;23(2):159-68.

30 Schmid-Mast M et al. Sexuality in the second half of the life span. *Gynakol Geburtshilfliche Rundsch* 2000;40(1):13-9.

31 Kaplan HS. Injection Treatment for Older Patients. In: Wagner G, Kaplan HS, eds. *The New Injection Treatment for Impotence* (New York: Brunner/Mazel, 1993), p142.

32 Gelfand MM. Sexuality among older women. *Journal of Womens Health: Gender Based Medicine* 2000;9 Suppl 1:S15-20.

33 Hawton K et al. Sexual function in a community sample of middle-aged women with partners: effects of age, marital, socioeconomic, psychiatric, gynecological, and menopausal factors. *Archives Sexual Behavior* 1994 Aug;23(4):375-95.

34 Kaplan HS. Sex, intimacy, and the aging process. *Journal of the American Academy of Psychoanalysis* 1990 Summer;18(2):185-205.

35 Brecher EM. *Love, sex and aging. Consumer's Union Report.* Boston, MA: Little, Brown, 1984.

36 Butt DS. The sexual response as exercise. A brief review and theoretical proposal. *Sports Medicine* 1990 Jun;9(6):330-43.

37 Lauritzen C. Biology of female sexuality in old age. *Z Gerontol* 1983 May-Jun;16(3):134-8.

38 Rhodes JC et al. Hysterectomy and sexual functioning. *Journal of the American Medical Association* 1999 Nov 24;282(20):1934-41.

39 Eicher W. Sexual function and sexual disorders after hysterectomy. *Geburtshilfe Frauenheilkd* 1993 Aug;53(8):519-24.

40 Pinion SB et al. Randomized trial of hysterectomy, endometrial laser ablation, and transcervical endometrial resection for dysfunctional uterine bleeding. *British Medical Journal* 1994;309:891-892;979-983.

41 Helstrom L et al. Sexuality after hysterectomy: a factor analysis of women's sexual lives before and after subtotal hysterectomy. *Obstetrician Gynecology* 1993 Mar;81(3):357-62.

42 Shifren JL et al. Transdermal testosterone treatment in women with impaired sexual function after oophorectomy. *New England Journal of Medicine* 2000 Sep 7;343(10):682-8.

43 Coope J. Hormonal and non-hormonal interventions for menopausal symptoms. *Maturitas* 1996;23(2):159-68.

44 Goldberg DC et al. The Grafenberg spot and female ejaculation: a review of initial hypotheses. *Journal of Sex and Marital Therapy* 1983 Spring, 9:27-37

45 Syed R. Knowledge of the "Grafenberg zone" and female ejaculation in ancient Indian sexual science. A medical history contribution. *Sudhoffs Archives Z Wissenschaftsgesch* 1999;83(2):171-90.

46 Darling CA et al. Female ejaculation: perceived origins, the Grafenberg spot/area, and sexual responsiveness. *Archives of Sexual Behavior* 1990 Feb;19(1):29-47.

47 Alzate H, Hoch Z. The "G spot" and "female ejaculation": a current appraisal. *Journal of Sex and Marital Therapy* 1986 Fall;12(3):211-20.

48 Davis AR. Recent Advances in Female Sexual Dysfunction. *Current Psychiatry Report* 2000 Jun;2(3):211-214.

49 Ellison JM. Antidepressant-induced sexual dysfunction: review, classification, and suggestions for treatment. *Harvard Review of Psychiatry* 1998 Nov-Dec;6(4):177-89.

50 Rosen RC et al. Effects of SSRIs on sexual function: a critical review. *Journal of Clinical Psychopharmacology* 1999 Feb;19(1):67-85.

51 Labbate LA et al. Serotonin reuptake antidepressant effects on sexual function in patients with anxiety disorders. *Biological Psychiatry* 1998;43:904-7.

52 Lane RM. A critical review of selective serotonin reuptake inhibitor-related sexual dysfunction; incidence, possible etiology and implications for management. *Journal of Psychopharmacology* 1997;11(1):72-82.

53 Rothschild AJ. New directions in the treatment of antidepressant-induced sexual dysfunction. *Clinical Therapy* 2000;22 Suppl A:A42-57..

54 Breggin PR, Cohen, D. *Your Drug May Be Your Problem: How and Why to Stop Taking Psychiatric Medication.* (Reading, MA: Perseus Books, 1999).

55 Cohen AJ, Bartlik B. Ginkgo biloba for antidepressant-induced sexual dysfunction. *Joural of Sex and Marital Therapy* 1998;24(2):139-43.

56 Dimeo F et al. Benefits from aerobic exercise in patients with major depression: a pilot study. *British Journal of Sports Medicine* 2001;35:114.

57 Duncan LE et al. Does hypertension and its pharmacotherapy affect the quality of sexual function in women? *American Journal of Hypertension* 2000;13(6 Pt 1):640-7.

58 Webster L. Management of sexual problems in diabetic patients. *British Journal of Hospital Medicine* 1994;51(9):465-8.

59 LeMone P. The physical effects of diabetes on sexuality in women. *Diabetes Education* 1996;22(4):361-6.

60 Sexual dysfunction. *International Journal of Gynecology and Obstetrics* 1995;51(3):265-77.

61 Ciacci C et al. Sexual behavior in untreated and treated celiac patients. *European Journal of Gastroenterology and Hepatology* 1998;10(8):649.

62 Sjogren K, Fugl-Meyer AR. Chronic back pain and sexuality. *International Rehabilitaiton Medicine* 1981;3(1):19-25.

63 Op cit, Butcher.

64 Abbey A et al. Alcohol's effects on sexual perception. *Journal Study of Alcoholism* 2000;61(5):688-97.

65 Nirenberg TD et al. The sexual relationship of male alcoholics and their female partners during periods of drinking and abstinence. *Journal Study of Alcoholism* 1990 Nov;51(6):565-8.

66 Harvey SM, Beckman LJ. Alcohol consumption, female sexual behavior and contraceptive use. *Journal Study of Alcoholism* 1986 Jul;47(4):327.

67 Miller NS, Gold MS. The human sexual response and alcohol and drugs. *Journal of Substance Abuse and Treatment* 1988;5(3):171-7.

68 Gavaler JS et al. Sexuality of alcoholic women with menstrual cycle function: effects of duration of alcohol abstinence. *Alcohol Clinical ExperimentalResearch* 1993 Aug;17(4):778-8.

69 Op cit, Butt.

70 McKey PL, Dougherty MC. The circumvaginal musculature: correlation between pressure and physical assessment. *Nursing Research* 1986;35 (5):307-9.

71 Meston CM, Gorzalka BB. Differential effects of sympathetic activation on sexual arousal in sexually dysfunctional and functional women. *Journal of Abnormal Psychology* 1996 Nov;105(4):582-91.

72 Bartlik BD et al. Psychostimulants apparently reverse sexual dysfunction secondary to selective serotonin re-uptake inhibitors. *Journal of Sex and Marital Therapy* 1995 Winter;21(4):264-71.

73 Meston CM, Heiman JR. Ephedrine-activated physiological sexual arousal in women. *Archives of General Psychiatry* 1998 Jul;55(7):652-6.

74 Kaplan SA et al. Safety and efficacy of sildenafil in postmenopausal women with sexual dysfunction. *Urology* 1999;53(3):481-6.

75 Tuckerman EM et al. Do androgens have a direct effect on endometrial function? An in vitro study. *Fertility and Sterility* 2000 Oct;74(4):771.

76 *Our Bodies, Ourselves: For the New Century.* The Boston Women's Health
   Book Collective (NY: Touchstone Press, 1998), p 229.

Chapter Two

1 Hoon PW. Physiologic assessment of sexual response in women: the unfulfilled promise. *Clinical Obstetrics and Gynecology* 1984;27(3):767-80.
2 Cutler WB et al. Sexual response in women. *Obstetrics and Gynecology*
   2000;95(4 Suppl 1):S19.
3 Kratochvil S. Vaginal contractions in female orgasm. *Cesk Psychiatry*
   1994;90(1):28-33.
4 Butler CA. New data about female sexual response. *Journal of Sex and
   Marital Therapy* 1976 Spring;2(1):40-6.
5 Sholty MJ. et al. Female orgasmic experience: a subjective study. *Archives
   of Sexual Behavior* 1984 Apr;13(2):155-64.
6 Shokrollahi P et al. Prevalence of sexual dysfunction in women seeking
   services at family planning centers in Tehran. *Journal of Sex and Marital Therapy* 1999;25(3):211-5.
7 Hurlbert DF. The role of assertiveness in female sexuality: a comparative
   study between sexually assertive and sexually nonassertive women. *Journal of Sex & Marital Therapy* 1991 Fall;17(3):183-90.
8 Ibid.
9 Whipple B et al. Physiological correlates of imagery-induced orgasm in
   women. *Archives of Sexual Behavior* 1992 Apr;21(2):121-33.
10 Van Goozen SH et al. Psychoendocrinological assessment of the menstrual cycle: the relationship between hormones, sexuality, and mood.
   Archives of Sexual Behavior 1997 Aug;26(4):359-82.
11 Clayton AH et al. Assessment of sexual functioning during the menstrual
   cycle. *Journal of Sex and Marital Therapy* 1999 Oct-Dec;25(4):281-9.
12 Clifford R. Development of masturbation in college women. *Archives of
   Sexual Behavior* 1978 Nov;7(6):559-73.
13 Ibid.
14 Hoch Z. Vaginal erotic sensitivity by sexological examination. *Acta Obstetrics Gynecology Scandinavia* 1986;65(7):767-73.
15 Kelly MP et al. Attitudinal and experiential correlates of anorgasmia. *Archives of Sexual Behavior* 1990 Apr;19(2):165-77.
16 Raboch J, Bartak V. Coital and orgastic capacity. *Archives of Sex Behavior*
   1983 Oct;12(5):409-13.
17 Sjoberg RL. Child testimonies during an outbreak of witch hysteria: Swe-
   den 1670-1671. *Journal of Child Psychological Psychiatry* 1995 Sep;
   36(6):1039-51.
18 Duncan LE et al. Does hypertension and its pharmacotherapy affect the
   quality of sexual function in women? *American Journal of Hypertension* 2000;13(6 Pt 1):640-7.

19 Exton MS et al. Cardiovascular and endocrine alterations after masturbation-induced orgasm in women. *Psychosomatic Medicine* 1999 May-Jun;61(3):280-9.

20 Fox CA. Some aspects and implications of coital physiology. *Journal of Sex and Marital Therapy* 1976 Fall;2(3):205-13.

21 Davey-Smith G et al. Sex and death: are they related? Findings from the Caerphilly Cohort Study. *British Medical Journal* 1997;315(7123):1641.

22 Exton NG et al. Neuroendocrine response to film-induced sexual arousal in men and women. *Psychoneuroendocrinology* 2000;25(2):187-99.

23 Sarlin CN. The role of breast-feeding in psychosexual development and the achievement of the genital phase. *Journal of the American Psychoanalytical Association* 1981;29(3):631-41.

24 Turner RA et al. Preliminary research archives on plasma oxytocin in normal women: investigating emotion and interpersonal distress. *Psychiatry* 1999 Summer;62(2):97-113.

25 Blaicher W et al. The role of oxytocin in relation to female sexual arousal. *Gynecology and Obstetrics Investigation* 1999;47(2):125-6.

26 Carmichael MS et al. Relationships among cardiovascular, muscular, and oxytocin responses during human sexual activity. *Archives of Sexual Behavior* 1994 Feb;23(1):59-79.

27 Carter CS. Oxytocin and sexual behavior. *Neuroscience of Biological Behavior Review* 1992 Summer;16(2):131-44.

28 <http://www.incontinet.com/articles/art_urin/kegelbib.htm>

29 Kaplan HS. The New Sex Therapy. In: Wagner G, Kaplan HS, eds. *The New Injection Treatment for Impotence.* (New York: Brunner/Mazel, 1974).

30 Bump RC et al. Assessment of Kegel pelvic muscle exercise performance after brief verbal instruction. *American Journal of Obstetrics and Gynecology* 1991 Aug;165(2):322-7; discussion 327-9.

31 Graber B, Kline-Graber G. Female orgasm: role of pubococcygeus muscle. *Journal of Clinical Psychiatry* 1979 Aug;40(8):348-51.

32 Chambless DL et al. The pubococcygens and female orgasm: a correlational study with normal subjects. *Archives Sex Behavior* 1982;11:479.

33 Roughan PA, Kunst L. Do pelvic floor exercises really improve orgasmic potential? *Journal of Sex and Marital Therapy* 1981 Fall;7(3):223-9.

34 Ishiko O et al. Hormone replacement therapy plus pelvic floor muscle exercise for postmenopausal stress incontinence. A randomized, controlled trial. *Journal of Reproductive Medicine* 2001;46:213-220.

35 Raboch JJ et al. First sexual intercourse in women. *Zentralbl Gynakol* 1995;117(1):29-31.

36 Raboch JJ. Coital anorgasmia in marriage. *Zentralbl Gynakol* 1994;116(2):102-6.

37 Darling CA. Female sexual response and the timing of partner orgasm. *Journal of Sex and Marital Therapy* 1991 Spring;17(1):3-21.

38 Singh D et al. Frequency and timing of coital orgasm in women desirous of becoming pregnant. *Archives of Sexual Behavior* 1998;27(1):15-29.
39 Levin RJ, Wagner G. Orgasm in women in the laboratory—quantitative studies on duration, intensity, latency, and vaginal blood flow. *Archives of Sexual Behavior* 1985 Oct;14(5):439-49.
40 Wiederman MW. Pretending orgasm during sexual intercourse: correlates in a sample of young adult women. *Journal of Sexual & Marital Therapy* 1997;23(2):131-9.
41 Darling CA, Davidson JK. Enhancing relationships: understanding the feminine mystique of pretending orgasm. *Journal of Sex and Marital Therapy* 1986 Fall;12(3):182-96.
42 Dove NL, Wiederman MW. Cognitive distraction and women's sexual functioning. *Journal of Sex & Marital Therapy* 2000;26(1):67-78.
43 Raboch JJ. Anorgasmic women. *Cesk Gynekol* 1991;56(7-8):397-401.
44 Op cit, Hoon.

Chapter Three
1 Vance EB, Wagner NN. Written descriptions of orgasm: a study of sex differences. *Archives of Sexual Behavior* 1976 Jan;5(1):87-98.
2 Baldwin JD, Baldwin JI. Gender differences in sexual interest. *Archives of Sexual Behavior* 1997 Apr;26(2):181-210.
3 Exton NG et al. Neuroendocrine response to film-induced sexual arousal in men and women. *Psychoneuroendocrinology* 2000;25(2):187-99.
4 Swartz LH. Absorbed states play different roles in female and male sexual response: hypotheses for testing. *Journal of Sexual and Marital Therapy* 1994 Fall;20(3):244-53.
5 Dove NL, Wiederman MW. Cognitive distraction and women's sexual functioning. *Journal of Sexual and Marital Therapy* 2000 Jan-Mar;26(1):67.
6 Dunn KM et al. Sexual problems: a study of the prevalence and need for health care in the general population. *Family Practice* 1998 Dec;15:519..
7 Wiley D, Bortz WM. Sexuality and aging—usual and successful. *Journal of Gerontology: A Biological Science and Medical Science* 1996 ;51:M142.
8 Haavio-Mannila E, Kontula O. Correlates of increased sexual satisfaction. *Archives of Sexual Behavior* 1997;26(4):399-419.
9 Snyder DK, Berg P. Determinants of sexual dissatisfaction in sexually distressed couples. *Archives of Sexual Behavior* 1983 Jun;12(3):237-46.
10 Spector IP, Carey MP. Incidence and prevalence of the sexual dysfunctions: a critical review of the empirical literature. *Archives of Sex Behavior* 1990 Aug;19(4):389-408.
11 Hoch Z et al. An evaluation of sexual performance—comparison between sexually dysfunctional and functional couples. *Journal of Sex & Marital Therapy* 1981 Fall;7(3):195-206.
12 Abbey A et al. Alcohol's effects on sexual perception. *Journal of Studies of Alcoholism* 2000;61(5):688-97.

13 Op cit, Haavio-Mannila.

14 Nigel-Dickson N et al. First sexual intercourse: age, coercion, and later regrets reported by a birth cohort. *British Medical Journal* 1998;316:29.

15 Darling CA, Davidson JK. Coitally active university students: sexual behaviors, concerns, and challenges. *Adolescence* 1986 Summer;21:403.

16 Op cit, Nigel-Dickson.

17 Hutchinson KA. Androgens and sexuality. *American Journal of Medicine* 1995 Jan 16;98(1A):111S-115S.

18 Neto F, Ruiz F. Sex differences in perceptions of romantic acts in Portuguese adolescents. *Psychology Report* 2000 Apr;86(2):541-5.

19 Hyde JS, Durik AM. Gender differences in erotic plasticity—evolutionary or sociocultural forces? Comment on Baumeister (2000). *Psychology Bulletin* 2000 May;126(3):375-9; discussion 385-9.

20 Baumeister RF. Gender differences in erotic plasticity: the female sex drive as socially flexible and responsive. *Psychology Bulletin* 2000;126:347.

21 Cox BJ. *Sexual Techniques During Prescribed Continence.* (NY: Medical Press, 1968), p 49.

22 Rako S. *The Hormone of Desire* (NY: Harmony Books, 1996), p 78.

23 Cohen AJ, Bartlik B. Ginkgo biloba for antidepressant-induced sexual dysfunction. *Journal of Sex and Marital Therapy* 1998;24(2):139-43.

24 Raboch J et al. Menarche, orgasmic capacity and coitarche. *Zentralbl Gynakology* 1993;115(8):374-7.

25 Harvey SM. Female sexual behavior: fluctuations during the menstrual cycle. *Journal of Psychosomatic Research* 1987;31(1):101-10.

26 Op cit, Baumeister.

27 Masters WH et al. *Human Sexuality,* 5th ed. (NY: Harper Collins, 1995), p 376.

28 Heiby E, Becker JD. Effect of filmed modeling on the self-reported frequency of masturbation. *Archives of Sexual Behavior* 1980 Apr;9(2):115.

Chapter Four

1 Gray LE Jr. Xenoendocrine disrupters: laboratory studies on male reproductive effects. *Toxicology Letter* 1998 Dec 28;102-103:331-5.

2 Sone H. Endocrine disrupter and reproductive disorders in women. *Nippon Rinsho* 2000 Dec;58(12):2521-6.

3 Sumpter JP. Xenoendorine disrupters—environmental impacts. *Toxicology Letter* 1998;102-103:337-42.

4 Sugimura K et al. Endocrine-disrupting chemicals in CAPD dialysate and effluent. *Blood Purifier* 2001;19(1):21-3.

5 McLachlan JA et al. Gene imprinting in developmental toxicology: a possible interface between physiology and pathology. *Toxicology Letter* 2001 Mar 31;120(1-3):161-164.

6 Bogh IB et al. Endocrine disrupting compounds: effect of octylphenol on reproduction over three generations. *Theriogenology* 2001 Jan 1;55(1):131-50.

7 Toppari J, Skakkebaek NE. Sexual differentiation and environmental endocrine disrupters. *Baillieres Clinical Endocrinology Metabolism* 1998;12:143-56.

8 Op cit, Sumpter.

9 Facemire CF et al. Reproductive impairment in the Florida panther: nature or nurture? *Environmental Health Perspective* 1995;103 Suppl 4:79.

10 Dold C. Hell. *Discover* Sep 1996 p 53.

11 Guillette LJ, Jr. Endocrine-disrupting environmental contaminants and reproduction: lessons from the study of wildlife, in *Women's Health Today: Perspectives on Current Research and Clinical Practice* 1994. Popkin DR and Peddle LJ, eds. (NY: Parthenon Publ Group, 1994), pp 201-207.

12 Ansar Ahmed S. The immune system as a potential target for environmental estrogens (endocrine disrupters): a new emerging field. *Toxicology* 2000 Sep 7;150(1-3):191-206.

13 Elsby R et al. Obstacles to the prediction of estrogenicity from chemical structure: assay-mediated metabolic transformation and the apparent promiscuous nature of the estrogen receptor. *Biochemical Pharmacology*. 2000 Nov 15;60(10):1519-30.

14 Bhatt RV. Environmental influence on reproductive health. *International Journal of Gynacology and Obstetrics* 2000;70(1):69-75.

15 Sharpe RM; Slakkebbaek NE. Are oestrogens involved in falling sperm counts and disorders of the male reproductive tract? *Lancet*. 1993 May 29;341(8857):1392-5.

16 Kitajewski J, Sassoon D. The emergence of molecular gynecology: homeobox and wnt genes in the female reproductive tract. BioEssays 22:902-910, 2000.

17 Parker L. Causes of testicular cancer. *Lancet* 1997;350(9081):827-8.

18 Reinisch JM et al. Effects of prenatal exposure to DES. *Hormones and Behavior* 1992;26(1):62-65.

19 Reinish JM et al. Hormonal contributions. *Psychoneuroendocrinology* 1991;16(1-3):213-78.

20 Walsh PC, Worthington JF. *Prostate: A Guide for Men and the Women Who Love Them* (Baltimore: John Hoppkins University Press, 1995), p 147.

21 Foster W et al. Detection of endocrine disrupting chemicals in samples of second trimester human amniotic fluid. *Journal of Clinical Endocrinology Metabolism* 2000 Aug;85(8):2954-7.

22 *Our Bodies, Ourselves: For the New Century.* (NY: Simon & Schuster, 1998), p 562.

23 Bohannon AD et al. Exposure to 1,1-dichloro-2,2-bis(p-chlorophenyl) ethylene (DDT) in relation to bone mineral density and rate of bone loss in menopausal women. *Archives of Environmental Health* 2000;55(6):386.

24 Brien SE et al. Effects of an environmental anti-androgen on erectile function in an animal penile erection model. *Journal of Urology* 2000 Apr;163(4):1315-21.

25 Gray LE Jr. Xenoendocrine disrupters: laboratory studies on male reproductive effects. *Toxicology Letter* 1998 Dec 28;102-103:331-5.

26 Gregoraszczuk EL et al. Dose-and-time dependent effect of 2,3,7,8-tetrachlorodibenzo-P-dioxin (TCDD) on progesterone secretion by porcine luteal cells cultured in vitro. *Journal of Physiology Pharmacology* 2000;51:127-35.

27 Kurokawa Y, Inoue T. Risk assessment of dioxins and the effect as the endocrine disrupters. *Kokuritsu Iyakuhin Shokuhin Eisei Kenkyusho Hokoku* 1998;(116):1-12.

28 <http://www.epa.gov/ncea/pdfs/dioxin/dioxin %20questions%20and %20 answers.pdf>

29 Tilson HA, Kavlock RJ. The workshop on endocrine disrupter research needs: a report. *Neurotoxicology* 1997;18(2):389-92.

30 Juberg DR. An evaluation of endocrine modulators: implications for human health. *Ecotoxicology & Environmental Safety* 2000 Feb;45(2):93.

31 Kato Y et al. Reduction of thyroid hormone levels by methylsulfonyl metabolites of tetra- and pentachlorinated biphenyls in male Sprague-Dawley rats. *Toxicology Science* 1999 Mar;48(1):51-4.

32 Kato Y et al. Reduction of thyroid hormone levels by methylsulfonyl metabolites of polychlorinated biphenyl congeners in rats. *Archives of Toxicology* 1998 Jul-Aug;72(8):541-4.

33 Vinggaard AM et al. Identification and quantification of estrogenic compounds in recycled and virgin paper for household use as determined by an in vitro yeast estrogen screen and chemical analysis. *Chemical Research Toxicology* 2000 Dec;13(12):1214-22.

34 Song YS et al. Analytical procedure for quantifying five compounds suspected as possible contaminants in recycled Paper/Paperboard for food packaging. *Journal of Agriculture and Food Chemistry* 2000 Dec;48(12):5856-9.

35 Multigner L et al. Secular sperm trends in stallions between 1981 and 1996. *Journal of Andrology* 1999 Nov-Dec;20(6):763-8.

36 Diel P et al. In vitro test systems for the evaluation of the estrogenic activity of natural roducts. *Planta Med* 1999;65(3):197-203.

37 Parks LG et al. The plasticizer diethylhexyl phthalate induces malformations by decreasing fetal testosterone synthesis during sexual differentiation in the male rat. *Toxicology Science* 2000 Dec;58(2):339-49.

38 Api AM. Toxicological profile of diethyl phthalate: a vehicle for fragrance and cosmetic ingredients. *Food Chemistry and Toxicology* 2001;39:97.

39 Hill SS et al. The clinical effects of plasticizers, antioxidants, and other contaminants in medical polyvinylchloride tubing during respiratory and non-respiratory exposure. *Clinical Chim Acta* 2001 Feb;304(1-2):1-8.

40 Ulrich EM et al. Environmentally relevant xenoestrogen tissue concentrations correlated to biological responses in mice. *Environmental Health Perspective* 2000 Oct;108(10):973-7.
41 Pavan B et al. Phthalic acid mimics 17beta-estradiol actions in WISH cells. *Toxicology Letter* 2001 Jan 3;118(3):157-64.
42 Op cit, Gray.
43 Ohtani H et al. Effects of dibutyl phthalate as an environmental endocrine disruptor on gonadal sex differentiation of genetic males of the frog Rana rugosa. *Environmental Health Perspective* 2000 Dec;108(12):1189.
44 Manabe A et al. Detection of bisphenol-A in dental materials by gas. chromatography-mass spectrometry. *Dental Maternity Journal* 2000: 19:75.
45 Exposure to estrogen-based plastics speeds onset of puberty. *Nature* 1999;401:763-765.
46 Elsby R et al. Comparison of the modulatory effects of human and rat liver microsomal metabolism on the estrogenicity of bisphenol a: implications for extrapolation to humans. *Journal of Pharmacology & Experimental Therapy* 2001 Apr 1;297(1):103-113.
47 Toppari J, Skakkebaek NE. Sexual differentiation and environmental endocrine disrupters. *Baillieres Clinical Endocrinology Metabolism* 1998;12(1):143-56.
48 Colburn T et al. Developmental Effects of Endocrine-Disrupting Chemcials in Wildlife and Humans. *Environmental Health Perspectives* 1993;10:378-381.
49 Symposium, Environmental Estrogens: Pathway to Extinction?, May 13, 1995, Sonoma, CA.
50 David Feldman M.D. Editorial: Estrogens from Plastic—Are We Being Exposed? *Endocrinology* 1007;138:1777-1779.
51 Berman JR, Adhikari SP. Anatomy and physiology of female sexual function and dysfunction: classification, evaluation and treatment options. *European Urology* 2000;38(1):20-9.

Chapter Five

1 Graziottin A. The biological basis of female sexuality. *Internal Clinical Psychopharmacoogy* 1998;13 Suppl 6:S15-22.
2 Rajapakse R et al. Defining the impact of weakly estrogenic chemicals on the action of steroidal estrogens. *Toxicological Sciences* 2001;60:296.
3 Walsh PC, Worthington, JF. *The Prostate: A Guide for Men and the Women Who Love Them.* (Baltimore: Johns Hopkins University Press, 1995), p 170.
4 von Sydow K. Sexuality of older women. The effect of menopause, other physical and social and partner related factors. *Z Arztl Fortbild Qualitatssich* 2000;94(3):223-9.

5 Gower BA, Nyman L. Associations among oral estrogen use, free testosterone concentration, and lean body mass among postmenopausal women.
   Journal of Clinical Endocrinology and Metabolism 2000;85:4476.
6 Mulnard RN et al. Estrogen replacement therapy for treatment of mild to
   moderate Alzheimer disease: A randomized controlled trial. *Journal of
   the American Medical Association* 2000;283:1007-1015,1055-1056.
7 Seshadri s et al. Postmenopausal estrogen replacement therapy and the risk
   of Alzheimer disease. *Archives of Neurolology.* 2001;58:435-440.
8 Erb A et al. Hormone replacement therapy and patterns of osteoarthritis:
   baseline data from the Ulm Osteoarthritis Study. *Annals of Rheumatoid
   Diseases* 2000;59:105-109.
9 van Baal WM et al. Cardiovascular disease risk and hormone replacement
   therapy (HRT): a review based on randomised, controlled studies in postmenopausal women. Current Medical Chemistry 2000 May;7(5):499.
10 Kavanagh AM et al. Hormone replacement therapy and accuracy of mammographic screening. *Lancet* 2000;355:270-274.
11 Ibid.
12 Sarrel PM. Effects of hormone replacement therapy on sexual psycho-
   physiology and behavior in postmenopause. *Journal of Women's Health
   and Gender-Based Medicine* 2000;9 Suppl 1():S25-32.
13 Weiderpass E et al. Low-potency estrogen and risk of endometrial cancer:
   a case-ontrol study. *Lancet* 1999; 353.
14 Heald A et al. Progestins abrogate estrogen-induced changes in the insulin-like growth factor axis. *American Journal of Obstetrics and
   Gyncecology* 2000;183:593-600.
15 Ninety-first Annual Meeting of the American Association for Cancer Research, April 2000.
16 Sopwers MF et al. Association of bone mineral density and sex hormone
   levels with osteoarthritis of the hand and knee in premenopausal women.
   American Journal of Epidemiology 1996;143(1);38-47.
17 Buist DSM. Low bone mineral density associated with decreased risk of
   breast cancer. *Journal of Clinical Epidemiology* 2001;54:417-422.
18 Canaris GJ et al. The Colorado Thyroid Disease Prevalence Study *Ar
   chives of Internal Medicine* 2000;160:526-534.
19. Kraemer RR et al. Effect of estrogen on serum DHEA in younger and
   older women and the relationship of DHEA to adiposity and gender.
   Metabolism 2001 Apr;50(4):488-493.
20 Ronald K, Ross RK et al. Effect of hormone replacement therapy on breast
   cancer risk: Estrogen Versus Estrogen Plus Progestin. *Journal of the
   National Cancer Institute* 2000;92:328-332.
21 Natale V et al. Exploration of cyclical changes in memory and mood in
   postmenopausal women taking sequential combined estrogen and
   progestogen preparations. *British Journal of Obstetrics and Gynecology.* 2001 Mar;108(3):286-90.

22 Kamen B. *Hormone Replacement Therapy—Yes or No: How to Make an Informed Decision*. (Novato, CA: Nutrition Encounter, Sixth ed, 1997.)

23 Ibid, p 104.

24 Derby CA et al. Prior and current health characteristics of postmenopausal estrogen replacement therapy users compared with nonusers. *American Journal of Obstetrics and Gynecology* 1995;173:544-50.

25 Grodstein F et al. Postmenopausal Hormone Therapy and Mortality. *New England Journal of Medicine* 1997;336:1769-75.

26 Hemminki E, McPherson K. Impact of postmenopausal hormone therapy on cardiovascular events and cancer: pooled data from clinical trials. *British Medicine Journal*, 1997;315:149-53.

27 Matthews KA. Prior to use of estrogen replacement therapy, are users healthier than nonusers? *American Journal of Epidemiology* 1996;143:971.

28 Coope J. Hormonal and non-hormonal interventions for menopausal symptoms. *Maturitas* 1996;23(2):159-68.

29 Shifren JL et al. Transdermal testosterone treatment in women with impaired sexual function after oophorectomy. *New England Journal of Medicine* 2000 Sep 7;343(10):682-8.

30 Sarrel PM. Psychosexual effects of menopause: Role of androgens. *American Journal of Obstetrics & Gynecology* 1999;180:S319-24.

31 de Jonge FH et al. The influence of estrogen, testosterone and progesterone on partner preference, receptivity and proceptivity. *Physiology Behavior* 1986;37(6):885-91.

32 Davis SR. Androgen replacement in women: a commentary. *Journal of Clinical Endocrinology and Metabolism* 1999;84(6):1886-91.

33 Davis SR. The therapeutic use of androgens in women. *Journal of Steroid Biochemistry and Molecular Biology* 1999;69(1-6):177-84.

34 Dabbs, JM, Jr. Testosterone measurements in clinical and social psychology. *Journal of Social and Clinical Psychology* 1992;11:302-321.

35 Bancroft J et al. Mood, sexuality, hormones, and the menstrual cycle. III. Sexuality and the role of androgens. *Psychosomatic Medicine* 1983Dec;45(6):509-16.

36 DeCherney AH. Hormone receptors and sexuality in the human female. *Journal of Womens Health: Gender Based Medicine* 2000;9 Suppl: S9.

37 Dabbs, J. M et al. Trial lawyers: Blue collar talent in a white collar world. *Journal of Applied Social Psychology* 1998;2: 84-94.

38 Siiteri PK. Adipose tissue as a source of hormones. *American Journal of Clinical Nutrition* 1987;45: 277-282.

39 Ibid.

40 Dabbs, JM, Jr, Mohammed, S. Male and female salivary testosterone concentrations before and after sexual activity. *Physiology and Behavior* 1992;52:195-197.

41 Van Goozen SH et al. Psychoendocrinological assessment of the menstrual cycle: the relationship between hormones, sexuality, and mood.
Archives of Sexual Behavior 1997 Aug;26(4):359-82.
42 Lindman RE et al. Drinking, menstrual cycle, and female sexuality: a diary
study. *Alcohol and Clinical Experimental Research*1999;23(1):169-73.
43 Sherwin BB, Gelfand MM. The role of androgen in the maintenance of
sexual functioning in oophorectomized women. *Psychosomatic Medicine* 1987 Jul-Aug;49(4):397-409.
44 Davis SR, Tran J. Testosterone influences libido and well being in women.
Trends in Endocrinology Metabolism 2001;12(1):33-37.
45 Redmond GP. Hormones and sexual function. *International Journal of
Fertility and Women's Medicine* 1999;44(4):193-7.
46 Gelfand MM. Role of androgens in surgical menopause. *American Journal of Obstetrics and Gynecology* 1999;180:S325-7.
47 Basson R. Androgen replacement for women. *Canadian Family Physician*
1999;45:2100-7.
48 Berrino F et al. Reducing bioavailable sex hormones through a comprehensive change in diet: the diet and androgens (DIANA) Randomized
Trial. *Cancer Epidemiology Biomarkers & Prevention* 2001;(10):25-33.
49 Rako S. *The Hormone of Desire.* (New York: Crown Publishers, Inc., 1996),
p 72.
50 Plouffe L, Jr, Simon JA. Androgen effects on the central nervous system in
the postmenopausal woman. *Seminars in Reproductive Endocrinology*
1998;16(2):135-43.
51 Mouchamps E, Gaspard U. Change in sexual desire in the menopausal
woman: a succinct evaluation. *Journal of Gynecology & Obstetrics: Biological Reproduction* (Paris) 1999;28(3):232-8.
52 Greendal GA et al. The Menopause. *Lancet* 1999; 353: 571-80.
53 Op cit, Sasrrel.
54 Op cit, Redmond.
55 Graziottin A. Libido: the biologic scenario. *Maturitas* 2000 Jan;34 Suppl
1:S9-16.
56 Anderson-Hunt M, Dennerstein L. Oxytocin and female sexuality. *Gynecology & Obstetric Investigation* 1995;40(4):217-21.
57 Exton MS et al. Cardiovascular and endocrine alterations after masturbation-induced orgasm in women. *Psychosomatic Medicine* 1999;
61(3):280-9.
58 Buvat J. Influence of primary hyperprolactinemia on human sexual behavior. *Nouv Presse Medicine* 1982 Nov 27;11(48):3561-3.
59 Strucinski P, et al .Selected aspects of xenoestrogens'mode of action taken
from a group of persistent organochlorine compounds. *Rocz Panstw Zakl
Hig* 2000;51(3):211-28.
60 Ali Kubba A. Contraception. *Lancet* 2000; 356: 1913-19.

61 Glick ID, Bennett SE. Psychiatric complications of progesterone and oral contraceptives. *Journal of Clinical Psychopharmacology* 1981;1:350.

62 Tan JK, Degreef H. Oral contraceptives in the treatment of acne. *Skin Therapy Letters* 2001;6(5):1-3.

63 Sherif K. Benefits and risks of oral contraceptives. *American Journal of Obstetrics & Gynecology* 1999;180:S343-8.

64 Rosing J et al. Oral contraceptives, thrombosis and hemostasis. *American Journal of Obstetrics and Gynecology* 1999;180:S343-8.

65 Cosmi B et al. Family history not predictive of thrombosis risk with oral contraceptive use. *British Medical Journal* 2001;322:1024-1025.

66 Thomas DB et al. Human Papillomaviruses and Cervical Cancer in Bangkok. I. Risk Factors for Invasive Cervical Carcinomas with Human Papillomavirus Types 16 and 18 DNA. *American Journal of Epidemiology* 2001 Apr 15;153(8):723-731.

67 Tessaro S et al. Oral contraceptive and breast cancer: a case-control study. *Rev Saude Publica* 2001 Feb;35(1):32-38.

68 Schwartz JB. Oral contraceptive therapy in women: drug interactions and unwanted outcomes. *Journal of Gender Specific Medicine* 1999 Nov-Dec;2(6):26-9.

69 Ibid.60 Ali Kubba A. Contraception. *Lancet* 2000; 356: 1913-19.

70 Horwitt MK et al. Relationship between levels of blood lipids, vitamins C, A, and E, serum copper compounds, and urinary excretions of tryptophan metabolites in women taking oral contraceptive therapy. *American Journal of Clinical Nutrition*, Vol 28, 403-412.

71 Morley JE, *Endocrinology of Aging*, Lucretia van den Berg, eds. New Jersey: Humana Press, 1999. Pp 280.

72 Yeaworth RC, Friedman JS. Exogenous estrogen in systemic lupus erythematosus. *Lupus* 2001;10(3):222-6.

73 Sexuality in later life. *Nursing Clinicals of North America* 1975 Sep;10(3): 565-86.

74 Soory M. Hormonal factors in periodontal disease. *Dental Update* 2000 Oct;27(8):380-3.

75 Op cit, Morley..

76 Op cit, Yeaworth.

77 Dabbs, JM.,Jr, La Rue, D. Salivary testosterone measurements among women: Relative magnitude of daily and menstrual cycles. *Hormone Research* 1991;35:182-184.

Chapter Six

1 Martorano JT et al. Differentiating between natural progesterone and synthetic progestins: clinical implications for premenstrual syndrome and perimenopause management. *Comprehensive Therapy* 1998;24:336-9.

2 Natale V et al. Exploration of cyclical changes in memory and mood in postmenopausal women taking sequential combined oestrogen and progestogen preparations. *British Journal of Gynecology and Obstetrics* 2001 Mar;108(3):286-90.

3 Ross RK et al. Progestin may have important role in HRT elevation of breast cancer risk. *Journal of the National Cancer Institute* 2000;92:328.

4 Jasienska G, Thune I. Lifestyle, hormones, and risk of breast cancer. *British Medical Journal* 2001 Mar 10;322(7286):586-7.

5 Isaksson E et al. Effects of oral contraceptives on breast epithelial proliferation. *Breast Cancer Research and Treatment* 2001 Jan;65(2):163-9.

6 Gran ECG et al. Breast cancer and hormone exposure. *Lancet* 1996;348:682.

7 Poulter NR et al. Risk of cardiovascular diseases associated with oral progestagen preparations with therapeutic indications. *Lancet* 1999;354.

8 Vasilakis et al. risk of idiopathic venous thromboembolism in users of progestagens alone. *Lancet* 1999;354:1610-11.

9 Dennerstin et al. Progesterone and the premenstrual syndrome: a double blind crossover trial. *British Medical Journal*1985;290:1617-1621.

10 Mahesh VB et al. Diverse modes of action of progesterone and its metabolites. *Journal of Steroid Biochemistry and Molecular Biology* 1996;56(1-6 Spec No):209-19.

11 King-Jen Chang et al. Influences of percutaneous administration of estradiol and progesterone on human breast epithelial cell cycle in vivo. *Fertility and Sterility* 1995;63:785-791.

12 Glick ID, Bennett SE. Psychiatric complications of progesterone and oral contraceptives. *Journal of Clinical Psychopharmacology* 1981;1:350.

13 Li TC et al. Endocrinological and endometrial factors in recurrent miscarriage. Jessop Hospital for Woman, Sheffield, UK.

14 Short RE et al. Endocrine responses in cows fed Ponderosa pine needles and the effects of stress, corpus luteum regression, progestin, and ketoprofen. *Journal of Animcal Science* 1995 Jan;73(1):198-205.

15 Fujimaki T et al. Effects of progesterone on the metabolism of cancellous bone in young oophorectomized rats. *Journal of Obstetrics and Gynecology* 1995 Feb;21:31.

16 Levy T et al. Pharmacokinetics of the progesterone-containing vaginal tablet and its use in assisted reproduction. *Steroids* 2000;65:645-9.

17 Persson I. Estrogens in the causation of breast, endometrial and ovarian cancers—evidence and hypotheses from epidemiological findings. *Journal of Steroid Biochemistry and Molecular Biology* 2000;74: 30.

18 Mani SK et al. Progesterone receptor and dopamine receptors are required in Delta 9-tetrahydrocannabinol modulation of sexual receptivity in female rats. *Proceedings of the National Academy of Sciences* USA. 2001 Jan 30;98(3):793-5.

19 The efficacy of progesterone in achieving successful pregnancy: Prophylactic use during luteal phase in anolulatory women. *Journal of Fertility* 1987;32(2):135-8.

20 Adelusi B, Dada OA. prognosis of pregnancy after threatened abortion. *International Journal of Gynecology and Obstetrics* 1980;18(6):444.

21 Trotter A et al. Follow-up examination at the age of 15 months of extremely preterm infants after postnatal estradiol and progesterone replacement. *Journal of Clinical Endocrinology and Metabolism* 2001; 86:601.

22 Harris B et al. Maternity blues and major endocrine changes: Cardiff puerperal mood and hormone study II. *British Medical Journal* 1994; 308:949-953.

23 Rein MS. Advances in uterine leiomyoma research: the progesterone hypothesis. *Environmental Health Perspective* 2000 Oct;108 Suppl 5:791.

24 Siiteri PK.. Adipose tissue as a source of hormones. *American Journal of Clinical Nutrition*, Vol 45, 277-282.

25 Haber E. Progesterone's role in cardiac prevention. *Nature Medicine* 1997; 3:1005-8..

26 Immune responses to ISCOM((R)) formulations in animal and primate models. Sjolander A et al. *Vaccine* 2001 Mar 21;19(17-19):2661-5.

27 Johnson SR, Tattersfield AE. Decline in lung function in lymphangioleiomyomatosis: relation to menopause and progesterone treatment. *American Journal of Critical Care Medicine* 1999;160(2):628-33.

28 McMurray RW et al. Progesterone inhibits glucocorticoid-induced murine thymocyte apoptosis. *International Journal of Immunopharmacology* 2000 Nov;22(11):955-65.

29 Soderstrom R. Will progesterone save the IUD? *Journal of Reproductive Medicine* 1983;28(5):305-8.

30 Leonetti HB et al. Transdermal progesterone cream for vasomotor symptoms and postmenopausal bone loss. *Obstetrics and Gynecology 1999,* 94(2):225-8.

31 Cipolla L et al. New pharmacological approach to therapy of perimenopausal meno-metrorrhagia. Vaginal use of progesterone. *Minerva Ginecologica* 1994;46(11):619-24.

32 McLucas B et al. Uterine fibroid embolization: nonsurgical treatment for symptomatic fibroids. *Journal of the American College of Surgery* 2001 Jan;192(1):95-105.

33 Stewart EA. Uterine fibroids. *Lancet* 2001; 357: 293-98.

34 William C Bryce, Azusa, MD, California. Personal communication, 1996.

35 Hajek Z, Uhlir M. Micronized progesterone in the treatment of imminent necrosis of a myoma during pregnancy. ultrasound changes during treatment. *Ceska Cynekol* 1999;64(3):189-92.

36 Corsello S. *The Ageless Woman* (Corsello Communitcations, Inc, 1999), pp 156-7.

Chapter Seven

1 Dube L, Cantin I. Promoting health or promoting pleasure? A contingency approach to the effect of informational and emotional appeals on food liking and consumption. *Appetite* 2000 Dec;35(3):251-262.

2 Kant AK. "Consumption of energy-dense, nutrient-poor foods by adult Americans: nutrition and health implications." *American Journal of Clinical Nutrition* 72;2000:929-36.

3 Parker RS et al. "Bioavailability of carotenoids in human subjects." *Proceedings of the Nutrition Society* 1999;58:155-62.

4 Cardona PD. Drug-food interactions. *Nutrition in the Hospital* 1999 May;14 Suppl 2:129S-140S.

5 van het Hof KH et al. "Influence of feeding different vegetables on plasma levels of carotenoids, folate and vitamin C. Effect of disruption of the vegetable matrix." *British Medical Journal* 1999;82(3):203-12.

6 RaoAV, Agarwal S. Role of antioxidant lycopene in cancer and heart disease. *Journal of The American College of Nutrition* 2000 Oct;19(5):563.

7 Stahl W, Sies H. Uptake of lycopene and its geometrical isomers is greater from heat-processed than from unprocessed tomato juice in humans. *Journal of Nutrition* 1992;122:2161-6.

8 Bub A et al. Moderate intervention with carotenoid-rich vegetable products reduces lipid peroxidation in men. *Journal of Nutrition* 2000;130(9):2200-6.

9 Rodriguez-Amaya DB. Changes in carotenoids during processing and storage of foods. *Archives of Latin-American Nutrition* 1999;49(3 Suppl 1):38S-47S.

10 Cheryl L. Rock. Nutrition in the prevention of disease. *American Journal of Preventive Medicine* 2000 May;18(4):351-353.

11 Garber G. An overview of fungal infections. *Drugs* 2001;61 Suppl 1:1-12.

12 Kamen B, Kamen, P. *The Remarkable Healing Power of Velvet Antler* (Novato, CA: Nutrition Encounter, 1999), p 13.

13 Guilbaud JF. the treatment of digestive and mico-cutaneous candidiasis by large doses of Ulta-Levure (in French). *Extrait de la Vie Medicale* No 8, Febvruary 1975.

14 Ducluzeau R, Bensaada M. Comparative effect of a single or continuous administration of Saccharomyces boulardii on the establishment of various strains of Candida in the digestive tract of gnotobiotic mice (in French). *Annals of Microbiology* 1982;133B:491-501.

15 Seeger Pg, Wolz S. *Successful Biological Control of Cancer by Combat Against the Causes* (Germany: Neuwied 1990), p 130.

16 Hawkins RL, Nakamura M. Expression of human growth hormone by the eukaryotic alga, chlorella. *Current Microbiology* 1999;38(6):335-341.

17 Tanaka K et al. A novle glycoprotein obtained from Chlorella vulgaris strain CK22 shows antimetastatic immunopotentiation. *Cancer Immunology and Immunotherpay* 1998;45(6):313-20.

18 Travieso L et al. Heavy metal removal by microalgae. *Bulletin of Environmental Contamination and Toxicology* 1999;62(2):144-51.

19 Hasegawa T et al. Oral administration of hot water extracts of Chlorella vulgaris reduces IgE production against milk casein in mice. *International Journal of Immunopharmacology* 1999;21(5):311-23.

20 Morita K et al. Chlorella accelerates dioxin excretion in rats. *Journal of Nutrition* 1999;129(9):1731-6.

21 Singh A et al. Inhibitory potential of Chlorella vulgaris (E-25) on mouse skin papillomagenesis and xenobiotic detoxication system. *Anticancer Research* 1999;19(3A):1887-91.

22 Rosenbaum ME. *The Amazing Superfood of the Orient* (Torrence, CA: Sun Wellness, 1998), p 65.

23 Singh A et al. Perinatal influence of chlorella vulagaris (E-25) on hepatic drug metabolizing enzymes and lipid peroxidation. *Anticancer Research* 1998;18(3A):1509-14.

24 Tanaka K et al. Oral administration of a unicellular green algae, chlorella vulgaris, prevents stress-induced ulcer [letter]. *Planta Medica* 1997;63:465.

25 Dantas DC, Queiroz ML. Effects of chlorella vulgaris on bone marrow progenitor cells of mice infected with Listeria monocytogenes. *Immunopharmacology* 1997;21(8):499-508. Jan;35(3):273-82.

26 Dantas DC et al. The effects of Chlorella vulgaris in the protection of mice infected with Listeria monocytogenes. Role of natural killer cells. *Immunopharmacology and Immunotoxicology.* 1999 Aug;21(3):609.

27 Michael Rosenbaum, MD. Personal communication. April 2001.

28 Sarma SS et al. Population growth of Euchlanis dilatata (Rotifera): combined effects of methyl parathion and food (Chlorella vulgaris). *Journal of Environmental Science and Health* B 2001 Jan;36(1):43-54.

29 Li HB et al. Preparative isolation and purification of lutein from the microalga chlorella vulgaris by high-speed counter-current chromatography. *Journal of Chromatography* 2001 Jan 5;905(1-2):151-5.

30 Hasegawa T et al. Chlorella vulgaris culture supernatant (CVS) reduces psychological stress-induced apoptosis in thymocytes of mice. *International Journal of Immuno-pharmacology* 2000 Nov;22(11):877-85.

31 Wolf L. Bioregeneration in space. *Advanced Space Biology and Medicine* 1996;5:341-56.

32 Noutoshi Y et al. Molecular anatomy of a small chromosome in the green alga chloreall vulgaris. *Nucleic Acids Research* 1998;26(17):3900-7.

33 Harris LJ. *The Book of Garlic* (Los Angeles: Panjandrum/Aris Books, 1979), p 41-2.

34 <www.urologyassociates.com/food1puz.htm>

35 Amagase H. Intake of garlic and its bioactive components. *Journal of Nutrition* 2001;131(3s): 955S-62S.

36 Qidwai W et al. Effect of dietary garlic (Allium Sativum) on the blood pressure in humans—a pilot study. *Journal of Pakistan Medical Association* 2000 Jun;50(6):204-7.

37 Hoshino T et al. Effects of garlic preparations on the gastrointestinal mucosa. *Journal of Nutrition* 2001;131(3s):1109S-13S.

38 Borek C. Antioxidant health effects of aged garlic extract. *Journal of Nutrition* 2001;131(3s): 1010S-5S.

39 Kyo E et al. Immunomodulatory effects of aged garlic extract. *Journal of Nutrition* 2001;131(3s): 1075S-9S.

40 Horie T et al. Alleviation by garlic of antitumor drug-induced damage to the intestine. *Journal of Nutrition* 2001;131(3s):1071S-4S.

41 Ide N, Lau BH. Garlic compounds minimize intracellular oxidative stress and inhibit nuclear factor-kappa b activation. *Journal of Nutrition* 2001;131(3s): 1020S-6S.

42 Moriguchi T et al. The effects of aged garlic extract on lipid peroxidation and the deformability of erythrocytes. *Journal of Nutrition* 2001;131(3s):1016S-9S.

43 Sumi S et al. Isolation and characterization of the genes up-regulated in isolated neurons by aged garlic extract (AGE). *Journal of Nutrition* 2001;131(3s): 1096S-9S.

44 Nishiyama N et al.Ameliorative effect of S-allylcysteine, a major thioallyl constituent in aged garlic extract, on learning deficits in senescence-accelerated mice. *Journal of Nutrition* 2001;131(3s): 1093S-5S.

45 Rahman K. Historical perspective on garlic and cardiovascular disease. *Journal of Nutrition* 2001;131(3s):977S-9S.

46 Okuhara T. A clinical study of garlic extract on peripheral circulation. *Japanese Pharmacology and Therapeutics* 1994;22(8):3695-3701.

47 Op cit, Amagase H.

48 Nakagawa S et al. Effect of raw and extracted-aged garlic juice on growth of young rats and their organs after peroral administration. *Journal of Toxicology Science* 1980;5:91.

49 Sumiyoshi H. New pharmacological activities of garlic and its constituents. *Nippon Yajurigaku Zasshi* 1997 Oct; 110 Suppl 1:93P-97P.

50 Imai J et al. Antioxidant and radical scavenging effects of aged garlic extract and its constituents. *Planta Medica* 1994;60:417.

51 Ide N et al. Scavenging effect of aged garlic extract and its constituents on active oxygen species. *Phytotherapy Research* 1996.

52 Ghannoum MA. Inhibition of Candida adhesion to buccal epithelial cells by an aqueous extract of allium sativum (garlic). *Journal of Applied Bacteriology* 1990;68:163-169.

53 Lau B. *Garlic and You: The Modern Medicine* (Vancouver, British Columbia, Canada: Apple Publishing, 1997), p 110.

54 Buhler C et al. "Small intestinal morphology in eight-day-old calves fed colostrum for different durations or only milk replacer and treated with long-R3-insulin-like growth factor I and growth hormone." *Journal of Animal Science* 1998 Mar;76(3):758-65.

55 Darby WJ et al. *Food: The Gift of Osiris* (New York: Academic Press, 1976), p 770.

56 Chappell JE et al. Vitamin A and E content of human milk at early stages of lactation. Early Human Development1985 Jul;11(2):157-67.

57 Aumaitre A, Seve B.Nutritional importance of colostrum in the piglet. *Annals of Veterinary Research* 1978;9(2):181-92. Review.

58 Ames BN. DNA damage from micronutrient deficiencies is likely to be a major cause of cancer. *Mutation Research* 2001 Apr 18;475(1-2):7.

59 Wang HX et al. Vitamin B(12) and folate in relation to the development of Alzheimer's disease. *Neurology.* 2001 May 8;56(9):1188.

60 Isaacs et al. "More ways mother's milk fights disease." *Science News* Apr 15, 1995, p 231.

61 Grace N et al. "Concentrations of macro- and micro-elements in the milk of pasture-fed thoroughbred mares." *Australian Veterinary Journal* 1999 Mar,77(3):177-80.

62 Wuh HCKm, Fox MM. *Sexual Fitness* (New York: GP Putnam's Sons, 2001), p 69.

63 Savarino L et al. Serum concentrations of zinc and selenium in elderly people: results in healthy nonagenarians/centenarians. *Experimental Gerontology* 2001 Feb;36(2):327-39.

64 Prasad AS et al. Zinc status and serum testosterone levels of healthy adults. *Nutrition* 1996 May;12(5):344-8.

65 Wapnir RA. Zinc deficiency, malnutrition and the gastrointestinal tract. *Journal of Nutrition* 2000 May;130(5 Suppl):1388S-92S.

66 Kamen B, Kamen S. *Total Nutrition for BreastFeeding Mothers* (Boston: Little, Brown and Company, 1986), p 9.

67 Powell SR. The antioxidant properties of zinc. *Journal of Nutrition.* 2000;130:1447S-1454S.

68 Mulligan T. "Reasons for decline of growth hormone in elderly men clarified." *Journal of the American Geriatric Society* 1999;47:1422-1424,1475-1476. Morley JE. Editorial accompanying article.

69 Medical Tribune News Service, Sept 15, 1998.

70 Wilson J. "Immune system breakthrough colostrum." *Journal of Longevity* 1998;4(2).

71 Ballard et al. "The relationship between the insulin content and inhibitory effects of bovine colostrum on protein breakdown." *Journal of Cellular Physiology* 1982;110:249-254.

72 White ME et al. "Comparison of insulin-like growth factor-I concentration in mammary secretions and serum of small- and giant-breed dogs." *American Journal of Veterinary Research* 1999 Sep;60(9):1088-91.

73 Roberts et al. "Transforming growth factor Type B: Rapid induction of fibrosis and angiogenisis in vivo and stimulation of collagen formation in vitro." *Procedures of the National Academy of Sciences* 1986;83:4167-71.

74 Gil et al. "Acid soluble nucleotides of cow's, etc." *Journal of Dairy Research* 1981;(48):35-44.

75 Ziegler TR et al. "Interactions between nutrients and peptide growth factors in intestinal growth, repair, and function." *JPEN J Parenter Enteral Nutr* 1999 Nov-Dec;23(6 Suppl):S174-83.

76 Hinuma S et al. "The quest for novel bioactive peptides utilizing orphan seven-transmembrane-domain receptors." *Journal of Molecular Medicine* 1999 Jun;77(6):495-504.

77 Habata Y et al. "Apelin, the natural ligand of the orphan receptor APJ, is abundantly secreted in the colostrum." *Biochim Biophys Acta* 1999 Oct 13;1492(1):25-35.

78 Lee DK et al. "Characterization of apelin, the ligand for the APJ receptor." *Journal of Neurochemistry* 2000 Jan;74(1):34-41.

79 Twomey JJ. "An immunologic classification of pernicious anemia." *Birth Defects Original Article Series* 1975;11(1):215-8.

80 Op cit, Kamen, B, Foreword, p xiii.

81 Schunemann HJ et al. The relation of serum levels of antioxidant vitamins C and E, retinol and carotenoids with pulmonary function in the general population. *American Journal of Respiratory and Critical Care Medicine* 2001 Apr 1;163(5):1246-1255.

82 Subakir SB et al. Oxidative stress, vitamin E and progestin breakthrough bleeding. *Human Reproduction* 2000 Aug;15 Suppl 3:18-23.

83 Heisler T et al. Peptide YY and vitamin E inhibit hormone-sensitive and -insensitive breast cancer cells. *Journal of Surgery Research* 2000 Jun 1;91(1):9-14.

84 McIntyre BS et al. Antiproliferative and apoptotic effects of tocopherols and tocotrienols on normal mouse mammary epithelial cells. *Lipids* 2000 Feb;35(2):171-80.

85 Robbin SL, Cotran RS. *Pathologic Basis of disease*, 2nd ed (Philadelphia: WB Saunders Co., 1979.

86 Peng X et al. Selenium, boron, and germanium deficiency in the etiology of Kashin-Beck disease. *Biological Trace Element Research* 2000; 77:193. Dec;77(3):193-7.

87 *Experimental Eye Research* 1995; Dept of Biological Sciences, Oakland University, Rochester, MI.

88 Use of organic germanium in chronic Epstein-Barr virus syndrome. *Journal of Orthomolecular Medicine* 1989.

89 Olson B et al. Modifying role of trace elements on the mutagenicity of benzo[a]pyrene. *Mutation Research* 1995;335(1):21-6.

90 Shon JT, Oh, YH. *Miracle Healing Effects of Bio-Germanium (Immune enhance and Edible Oxygen)*. Dept of Biochemistry, Baylor college of Medicine, Houston, Texas.

Chapter Eight
1 Voigt H. Enriching the sexual experience of couples: the Asian traditions and sexual counseling. *Journal of Sex and Marital Therapy* 1991 Fall; 17(3):214-9.
2 The Torah, parasha Ki Tetze Cap. XXIV,24; text found in the Hertz Chumash.
3 <www.ayurveda-herbs.com/Aphrodisiac-Sex-Impotency.htm>
4 Eskeland B et al. Sexual desire in men: effects of oral ingestion of a product derived from fertilized eggs. *Journal of Internal Medicine Research* 1997 Mar-Apr;25(2):62-70.
5 Sachs BD. Erection evoked in male rats by airborne scent from estrous females. *Physiological Behavior* 1997 Oct;62(4):921-4.
6 Tobias ML et al. Rapping, a female receptive call, initiates male-female duets in the South African clawed frog. *Proceedings of the National Academy of Science* USA 1998 Feb 17;95(4):1870-5.
7 <http://www.advancedherbals.com/feat/herbal_aphrodisiacs/aphrodisiacs.shtml>
8 http://us.f141.mail.yahoo.com/ym/" \l "FNote1"
9 http//us.f141.mail.yahoo.com/ym/".\l "FNote2"
10 Chen X. et al. Effect of Epimedium sagittatum on soluble IL-2 receptor and IL-6 levels in patients undergoing hemodialysis. *Chung Hua Nei Ko Tsa Chih*. 1995 Feb;34:102-4.
11 Liao H.J. et al. Effect of Epimedium sagittatum on quality of life and cellular immunity in patients of haemodialysis maintenance. *Chung Kuo Chung His I Chieh Ho Tsa Chih*. 1995 Apr;1594):202-4.

Chapter Nine
1 Moody JA et al. Effects of long-term oral administration of L-arginine on the rat erectile response. *Journal of Urology* 1997 Sep;158(3 Pt 1):942..
2 di Luigi L et al. Acute amino acids supplementation enhances pituitary responsiveness in athletes. *Medicine and Science In Sports and Exercise* 1999 Dec;31(12):1748-54.
3 Morimoto Y et al. Effect of l-menthol-ethanol-water system on the systemic absorption of flurbiprofen after repeated topical applications in rabbits. *Biology and Pharmacology Bulletin* 2000;23:1254.
4 Shojaei AH et al. Transbuccal permeation of a nucleoside analog, dideoxycytidine: effects of menthol as a permeation enhancer. *International Journal of Pharmacology* 1999 Dec 10;192(2):139-46.
5 Murphy LL et al. Effect of American ginseng (Panax quinquefolium) on male copulatory behavior in the rat. *Physiology of Behavior* 1998 Jun 15;64(4):445-50

6   Nocerino E et al. The aphrodisiac and adaptogenic properties of ginseng. *Fitoterapia* 2000 Aug;71 Suppl 1:S1-5.

7   Kim HJ et al. The relaxation effects of ginseng saponin in rabbit corporal smooth muscle: is it a nitric oxide donor? *British Journal of Urology* 1998 Nov;82(5):744-8.

8   Gillis CN. Panax ginseng pharmacology: a nitric oxide link? *Biochemical Pharmacology* 1997 Jul 1;54(1):1-8.

9   CT, Tran Ty Yen. Stimulation of sexual performance in male rats with the root extract of dinh lang (Policias fruticosum L.). *Acta Physiol Hung* 1990;75(1):61-7.

10 Kidd PM. A review of nutrients and botanicals in the integrative management of cognitive dysfunction. *Alternative Medical Review* 1999 Jun;4(3):144-6

11 Gajewski A, Hensch SA. Ginkgo biloba and memory for a maze. *Psychology Report* 1999 Apr;84(2):481-4.

12 Cohen AJ, Bartlik B. Ginkgo biloba for antidepressant-induced sexual dysfunction. *Journal of Sex and Marital Therapy* 1998;24(2):139-43.

13 Suttie JM, Haines, SR. "Evaluation of New Zealand velvet antler efficacy and diagnostic testing." Agresearc, Invermay Agricultural Center, Private Bag 50034, Mosgiel, New Zealand, VARNZ Document V34.

14 Nesaretnam K et al. tocotrienols inhibit the growth of human breast cancer cells irrespective of estrogen receptor status. *Lipids* 1998;33(5):461-469.

Chapter 10

1   Chowienczyk P, Ritter J, Arginine: NO more than a simple aminoacid? *Lancet*, 1997, 350: 901.

2   Drexler, H et al. Correction of endothelial dysfunction in the coronary microcirculation of hypercholesterolaemic patients by L-arginine. *Lancet* 1991;338:1546-50.

3   Clarkson P et al. Oral L-arginine improves endothelium-dependent dilation in hypercholesterolaemic young adults. *Journal of Clinical Investigation* 1996; 97:1989-94.

4   Brown AA; Hu FB. Dietary modulation of endothelial function: implications for cardiovascular disease. Department of Nutrition, Harvard School of Public Health, Boston.

5   Glycemic Research Institute, 601 Pennsylvania Avenue, N.W. Washington, D.C. 20004, from the Arginine Research Website, http://www.arginineresearch.com/

6   Prevot V et al. Median eminence nitric oxide signaling. *Brain Research Review* 2000 Nov;34(1-2):27-41

7   Funabashi T et al. Gonadotropin-releasing hormone exhibits circadian rhythm in phase with arginine-vasopressin in co-cultures. *Journal of Neuroendocrinology* 2000 Jun;12(6):521-8.

8 Mani SK et al. Nitric oxide mediates sexual behavior in female rats. *Proceedings of the National Academy of Science* 1994;91:6468-72.

9 Pau MY, Milner JA. Dietary arginine and sexual maturation of the female rat. *Journal of Nutrition* 1982;112:1834-42.

10 Leung AY, Foster S, Encyc of Common Natural Ingredients Used in Food, Drugs, and Cosmetics, 2nd ed. (New York: John Wiley & Sons, 1996).

11 Bohn B et al. *Arzneimittel-Forschung* 1987;37:119396.

12 N.R. Farnsworth et al., "Siberian Ginseng (Eleutherococcus senticosus): Current Status as an Adaptogen," in H. Wagner et al., eds., Economic and Medicinal Plant Research, vol. 1 (London: Academic Press, 1985).

13 Kim HJ et al. The relaxation effects of ginseng saponin in rabbit corporal smooth muscle: is it a nitric oxide donor? *British Journal of Urology* 1998 Nov;82(5):744-8.

14 The American Pharmaceutical Association Practical Guide to Natural Medicines, Andrea Pierce, 1999 Stonesong Press, Inc.

15 Agnoli A et al. Preliminary results in the modifications of cerebral blood flow using xenon-133 during administration of ginkgo-biloba. *Minerva Medica* 1973 Nov 7;64(79 Suppl):4166-73.

16 Vorberg G. *Clinical Trials Journal* 1985;22.

17 Pincemail J et al. Ginkgo biloba extract inhibits oxygen species production generated by phorbol myristate acetate stimulated human leukocytes. Experientia 1987 Feb 15;43(2):181-4.

18 C.A. Newall et al., Herbal Medicines: A Guide for Health-Care Professionals (London: The Pharmaceutical Press, 1996).

19 Suttie JM, Haines, SR. "Evaluation of New Zealand velvet antler efficacy and diagnostic testing." Agresearch, Invermay Agricultural Center, Private Bag 50034, Mosgiel, New Zealand, VARNZ Document V34.

20 Meston CM, Gorzalka BB. The effects of sypathetic activation following acute exercise on physiological and subjective sexual arousal in women. *Behavior Research and Therapy*, 1995;33:651.

21 Weltman A et al. Relationship between age, percentage body fat, fitness, and 24-hour GH release in healthy young adults: effects of gender. *Journal of Clinical and Endocrinology Metabolism* 1994;78:543.

22 Murrell TG. The potential for oxytocin (OT) to prevent breast cancer: a hypothesis. *Breast Cancer Research Treatment* 1995 Aug;35(2):225.

23 Turner RA et al. Preliminary research on plasma oxytocin in normal cycling women. *Psychiatry* 1999 Summer;62(2):97-113.

24 Carmichael MS et al. Plasma oxytocin increases in the human sexual response. *Journal of Clinical Endocrinology Metabolism* 1987;64:27.

INDEX

A

Acetaminophen 187
ACTH 285
Adaptogens 148-149
Adrenal stress 33
Adrenaline 57
Adrenals 270, 284
Adrenocorticotropic hormone
    266
Afterword 288
Aged garlic extract 187
  See garlic
Ageless Woman 160
Aging 23, 24
  desire 8
  hormones 140
  sex decline 25
Agnus castus 150
Alcohol 38-39, 56, 128
Algae 177-181
Allen, Dr Ann de Wees 259
Alligators 8
Alzheimer's disease 196, 203
  garlic 38, 187
  tocotrienols 245
Amino acids 253
  proteins 254
Androgens 98, 102, 125
  menstrual cycle 127
  postmenopausal 129
Androstenedione 42, 127
Angelica sinensis 150, 231
Anise 209
Anorgasmia 52, 54

Anti-stress tea 208
Antiandrogens 37, 101
Antibodies 253
Antidepressants 30, 31, 232
Antiestrogens 37
Apelin 201
Aphrodisiac 209, 226
  oxytocin 134
Appendix 302-309
Arginine 240, 254, 268
  blood pressure 259
  cardiovascular health 257
  D-arginine 254
  endothelial function 259
  free form 259
  L-arginine 254
  muscle building 242
  nitric oxide 243, 261, 268
  nitrogen 255
  orgasm 253-255
  side chain 255
  supplementation 258
Arginine molecule 242
Arthritis 35
Atherosclerosis 186

B

Back pain 37
Balm leaves 208, 210
Birch 208
Birth control pills 148
Bisphenol A 103-104

344   SHE'S GOTTA HAVE IT!